THE URBAN POLITICAL ELITE IN TRIBAL INDIA

THE URBAN POLITICAL ELITE IN TRIBAL INDIA

Dr. G. C. NAYAK

KALPAZ PUBLICATIONS
Delhi-110052

THE URBAN POLITICAL ELITE IN TRIBAL INDIA

Rs. 750

ISBN: 81-7835-287-7

Published in 2004 in India by
Kalpaz Publications,
C-30, Satyawati Nagar, Delhi-110052
E-mail : Kalpaz@hotmail.com

Laser Typesetting at : Shiva Infosystem, Delhi
Printed at : Mehra Offset Press, Delhi

Contents

LIST OF TABLES AND FIGURES

Preface

This book *The Urban Political Elite In Tribal India* is the product of a Research Work conducted in the Phulbani district of Orissa during the period from 1 994 to 1997. The study is a novel and typical one. Phulbani being one of the most backward tribal districts of India, the study has become uniquely significant. As a representative case study on the subject, it has been constructed upon the primary data collected in the year 1997 and the Secondary data, most of which are, based on the 1991 Census Reports of India and the latest official information collected from the various offices and agencies of the Government of Orissa and the Government of India till 1997. In order to avoid the phenomena of the missing links between and 'the inductive leap' from the micro unit 'Phulbani' to the macro unit 'India', some vital and relevant references to the state of Orissa have been made in the study.

The study of the political elite in relation to urban local bodies has already been taken up in many different ways by various scholars. But this study of the urban political elite of Phulbani District in relation to the tribal community offers a unique venture of unravelling new horizons of knowledge, facts, figures, and establishing new linkages and findings. The tribal pockets and people in India are generally less Urbanised and less modernised. But in the strong currents of nation-building, modernisation, political change, the galloping waves of national development in the post-independence era have inundated every nook and corner of the segregated and uncared tribal promontory like the Phulbani District. Political consciousness and political participation are, no doubt, gathering momentum in tribal areas of India. The urban leadership in its changing perspectives in such tribal areas will serve as an index to know the growing aspirations and changing orientations of the community concerned.

This study has analysed the socio-cultural and politico-economic background of the urban political elites — the councillors including the chairpersons and vice-chairpersons, both past and present, of the two Notified Area Councils of Phulbani district, i.e., Phulbani N.A.C. and G.Udayagiri N.A C. Besides, the political awareness, ideals and aspirations, the approach to development, the role perception, the leadership process and political efficacy of the elites with special emphasis on tribal elites have been systematically studied. On the backdrop of a dominant tribal society, the political dynamics such as the political orientations and the attitudinal changes of the elites and the people in general and their correlations have been analysed. Phulbani district, the target area of research is predominantly a tribal district and is one of the most backward districts of India. Thus, the study has tried to add new knowledge, facts, figures and open new vistas of the tribal political sub-culture and thus, may attract the attention of all concerned including the planners and the policy-makers. This work intends to contribute a new chapter to the tribal political study and add new dimensions to the field of research.

At the time when this project was undertaken, Phulbani district was officially known as the district of Boudh-Khondmals. But practically nobody used this name. Popularly and even in many Government documents and transactions this was referred to as Phulbani district. Thus, for easy perception of all concerned this project preferred to use the name Phulbani for the district instead of the name 'Boudh-Khondmals'. However, later on during 1993-94 in the process of reorganisation of districts which raised the number of districts of the state from 13 to 30, Boudh-Khondmals was divided into two districts such as Boudh and Phulbani. Thus, Phulbani became the official name of the said district from 22nd December, 1993 vide Government of Orissa in Revenue and Excise Department Notification No. 56408/R., of the even date. However, the ethnic crisis which woke up in the first quarter of 1994 had serious ramifications, and even attracted the attention of the whole nation.

The native tribals—the *Kandhas* gradually had developed a sense of insecurity due to various reasons and rose in rebellion. They demanded, *inter alia,* renaming the district as Kandhamal, meaning the homeland of the Kandhas. Ultimately, the state government conceded to their demand and the district of Phulbani became officially the district of Kandhamal vide Government of Orissa in Revenue and Excise Department Notification No. DRC/136/94. 44250/R, dated 13.10.1994. However, the district is still popularly and, even in some cases, officially known as Phulbani district. This compounded with the reorganisation of other districts of the state raising the total number from 13 to 30 created certain problems, particularly for correlation of data and facts in this project which practically fell in a period of transition. Therefore, this must be made clear here that for this research project, Phulbani district will generally refer to the present Kandhamal district with occasionally referring to the undivided Phulbani or Boudh-Khondmals district, wherever it is necessary.

As many as 54 elite members or councillors, both past and present— 31 from Phulbani N.A.C. and 23 from G. Udayagiri N.A.C. were directly interviewed by this researcher with a planned questionnaire containing both closed questions with limited choices as answers and open questions eliciting free answers. The elite members or the councillors who were interviewed ranged from the candidates who faced 1963 elections to those who faced 1997 elections. It is noteworthy to mention here that all of them showed overwhelming enthusiasm and spoke out their mind in all openness during the interview. Interestingly enough, many of them were very curious to know whether their words would reach the government quarters to solve their myriad problems. I am thankful to them for their co-operation and interest in the project.

I am grateful to Prof. B.C. Rout, Retired Principal and Professor of Political Science for his enthusiastic and sincere guidance in the Project. I am also thankful to the then chief functionaries and their staff members of the Department of Welfare and the Department of Housing and Urban Development, Government of Orissa, Bhubaneswar, the S.C. and S.T. Research and Training Institute, Bhubaneswar, the Directorate of Census Operations, Orissa, Bhubaneswar, the State Election Commission, Orissa, Bhubaneswar, the Notified Area Councils at Phulbani and G. Udayagiri and my well-wishers for their cooperation in Collection of materials and final preparation of this work.

Gouranga Charan Nayak

Introduction

The objectives

The objectives of this Research Project entitled "The Urban Political Elite in Tribal India" as sampled out from Phulbani District are :

1. To analyse the background, nature and orientation of the political leadership at the Urban grass root levels in tribal areas of India.
2. to study their levels of development and hindrances thereto; and
3. to study the nature of political societies in Urbanised tribal areas with a focus on their degree of continuity and change.

The Hypotheses

Towards realisation of these objectives, the project starts with the following hypotheses:- that the urban political elite in tribal India as sampled out from Phulbani district:-

a. is traditionally patriarchal and is mostly composed of native tribals;
b. is primarily consisted of cultivators and labourers who generally hail from large size families with small income and without any status symbol;
c. is moderately educated with knowledge in the local and the state languages and not knowing other languages;
d. does have political awareness of very low order;
e. is traditionally backward and less advanced in its political involvement and leadership process;
f. has traditional, poor, and low political ideals and aspirations;

g. is not conscious, reasonable and progressive in its approach to development; and
h. is, in broad outlines and in its composite perspective, poor in background, traditional in nature, backward and non-progressive in its Orientation.

The Variables

The background, nature and Orientation of the urban political elite of tribal India are not anything which can be called objective, concrete and precise. These are subjective and diverse Phenomena. Besides, the members of the target group under study, after all, are human beings. Human nature is subjective, complex, nebulous and inexact. The study of the nature and orientation of the elite would be fruitful by collection of data on them from various angles of their life, living and behaviour. The first and foremost thing is to have an idea of the eiite profile or information on their Socio-economic background. Therefore, the first major variable used in this study is in the form of 'elite profile' or 'socio-economic information' eliciting data regarding their age, sex, caste, language, education, family size, income, occupational structure, status symbols, etc. All these would help in studying the socio-cultural setting and economic background of the elite. This background has a real and definite impact on their nature and role orientation.

The second major variable used to collect primary data on the subject is 'political awareness' through which information is sought from the elite members on their knowledge about some leading statesmen, political heavyweights and public figures, both past and present, of India as well as Orissa; their awareness about some common political and legal issues and problems. The level of awareness of an elite member being an important factor of his/her political strength and political efficacy, this variable has been used to make an effective study of his/her nature and orientation.

The third major variable employed is 'Political involvement and leadership process' under which the sub-variables like political affiliation political participation, political support base, methods of informing and influencing the voters, role in decision-making process, sources of meeting election expenses, etc. have been used to judge the nature, style, orientation and depth of leadership of the urban political elite of tribal India.

'Political ideas and Aspirations' as the fourth major variable has been used to assess the elite's ideals on and approaches to corruption, liquor, dowry, destruction of public property, free and fair elections, state-funding of elections, compulsory voting, abiding code of conduct, reservation, choice of the best party, opposition for the sake of opposition, etc. This will help studying the role perception and orientation of the elite in a better way.

Through 'Approach to Development' which is the fifth and the last major variable, attempts have been made to assess the approaches and attitudes of the elite towards various aspects of development. Under this major variable queries are there in the form of *(a)* should Octroi tax be abolished? *(b)* Establishment of NAC (Urban Body) helpful or harmful? *(c)* Are the NAC (Urban) taxes reciprocal to the services rendered to the people? *(d)* Are the facilities provided by the urban body such as lighting, water supply, medical aid. sewerage and sanitation, education and library, cultural activities, etc. adequate and satisfactory? *(e)* Are you satisfied with the government programmes for tribal development in your area? *(f)* Status of women in your area with suggestions to curb exploitation and atrocities on them, *(g)* should deforestation and shifting cultivation be banned? *(h)* Suggestions regarding marketing of forest and agricultural products of the tribals, and *(i)* Opinion on the fields where tribals have been developed.

The Methodology

This social research project has employed, in combination, the structural, functional, as well as the inductive methods and has used the techniques of observation, questionnaire, schedule, interview and documentary study. The study includes all the present as well as the previous councillors of Notified Area Councils at Phulbani and G.Udayagiri. However, altogether 54 interviewees - 31 from Phulbani NAC and 23 from G.Udayagiri NAC were available for direct interview by this researcher who interviewed them with a planned questionnaire as given in the Appendix. The questionnaire consists of both open and close-end questions. All the interviewees cooperated well during the process of interview and spoke out their mind in all frankness. The only limitation in this process was that the interviewees feared that the real data regarding their income, status symbols, family background, etc. would pose them some problem by the government. But after due clarification about the purpose of research and secrecy of their personal information, they shook off their reluctance and cooperated in all their natural way. In collection of secondary data, competent authorities, persons and officials gave warm-hearted cooperation.

The Contextual Background

The title of the project "The Urban political Elite in Tribal India" would get just treatment if discussion is made on the Urban issues, political elite and the tribal issues and problems before we take up the main argument based on the primary data collected from the target group in Phulbani district. A thesis prepared without the contextual background and, in the case of a micro study like this, without having references moving from highways to interiors would be just like an edifice constructed in the air without a foundation underneath the earth. For a systematic study of the main thesis based on the arguments over the primary data, the project starts with the first chapter named as "The Tribal Horizon". This chapter deals with the history, demographic features including population, literacy, work participation, occupational holding, etc; society, economy, developmental aspects in general and Phulbani district in particular, besides the constitutional and legal safeguards for the tribals. Beginning with the general nature of the tribals, the chapter ends with a discussion about tribals in Phulbani district. The main study is on the tribal society of a typical nature i.e., in relation to the political elite in Urban areas thereof. Without a general discussion on the tribals, it would be inappropriate to move to a micro study on them. The secondary data given in this chapter would help a comparative study of the data *inter se*. Besides, it would help a comparative analysis on the levels of development or backwardness with the rest of society.

The second chapter entitled "The Urban Panorama" is virtually a discussion on the urban issues including its genesis and evolution, democratic decentralisation, the urban government, political sub-centres in urban Orissa with legal and constitutional provisions relating to urban structures in the state with their functions and a review of 1997 Municipal elections in the state duly supported by statistics. As the main study is on the urban areas of tribal society, a background analysis on the urban problems is necessary for a fruitful and relevant research.

The third chapter i.e. "The political Elite" deals with the conceptual and theoretical perspectives, broad profiles and functional syndrome, trends of reality with the scene from tribal Orissa. As the target group of the main study is the political elite in tribal urban areas, it is pertinent to know 'who is an elite', what are his/her broad profiles and functional syndrome, before we deal with the main analysis.

The fourth chapter named as "The Urban Political Elite in Tribal India – A study of two towns" is the core chapter of the study. An introduction about the two towns of Phulbani and G. Udayagiri under the study has been given in the beginning of this chapter as the study about them will be incomplete without it. This chapter also deals with the primary data on which the main argument of the thesis is based. It includes the critical study of five major variables such as the elite profile in urban Phulbani district, political awareness, political involvement and leadership process, political Ideals and Aspirations and Approach to Development.

1
The Tribal Horizon

History and Demography

The tribals of India generally live in the naturally isolated and segregated regions like forests and hills. They are known differently such as, "*Vanyajati* (Castes of forest), *Vanavasi* (inhabitants of forest), *Pahari* (hill dwellers), *Adimjati* (original communities), *Adivasi* (first settlers), *Janajati* (folk people), *Adimjati* (primitive people), *Anusuchit Janajati* (Scheduled Tribe) and so on. Among all these terms 'Adivasi' is known most extensively, and *Anusuchit Janajati:*/Scheduled Tribe is the constitutional name covering all of them."[1]

A.L. Basham observes, "in the Himalayan foothills and the remoter parts of the *Vindhyas* and the Deccan, wild tribes still exist. Most of them are now partly civilised and Hinduized, but some, though happy folk, knit together by tribal custom into solid, self-supporting and self-sufficient communities, still preserve vestiges of ferocious and barbaric tradition."[2] He further writes, "at one time, of course, practically the whole of India was inhabited by such peoples, and in ancient and medieval times they were more numerous and occupied a wider area than at present. From the earliest invasions, they waged a loosing battle against the advancing culture of the Aryans, and at all times they were a source of danger to the outposts of civilisation in the vicinity of their lands.The brief statement of Ashoka's policy towards the forest tribes throws a flood of light on the ruthless policy of earlier kings towards them. Many primitive peoples were exterminated and many more lost their identity in the

the course of the growth of the Hindu civilisation; but some accepted the suzerainty of their civilised overlords and retained their ancestral lands. The *Arthashastra* mentions such people as useful in time of war. Many of these tribes came more and more under the Aryan ways, and their tribal cults were roughly assimilated to Hinduism by wandering brahmans. Such tribes were undoubtedly the ancestors of many lower Hindu castes of later times. Some primitive tribes may well have learnt enough from the Aryans to become powerful, and it has been reasonably suggested that more than one important medieval dynasty originated in such a way."[3]

The tribals in India are considered as, "autochthonous people having distinctive economic and social life and due to various factors they preferred isolation, which practically kept them away in a comparatively less interacted situation."[4] Referring to the primitiveness or aboriginality of the Indian tribes, Bhupinder Singh writes, "the so called 'tribals' of India are the indigenous autochthonous people of the land in the sense that they had been long settled in different parts of the country before the Aryan speaking people penetrated India to settle down first in the Kabul and Indus Valleys and then within a millennium and a half to spread out over large parts of the country along the plains and river valleys. At much later stage of history, there came to this land wave after wave of other foreigners of Greeks, Romans, Sakas, Turks, Arabs, Mongols, etc. origin. The Aryans evolved a relatively developed system of local administration and certain ideas and institutions. They consolidated and organised social and religious system of *Smriti literature*. They built an economic structure based essentially on productive system managed and controlled on 'caste system'. With the pressure of a superior social and techno- economic organisation of the Indo-Aryans, the indigenous tribes were obliged to move bit by bit into remoter areas, the relatively more inaccessible regions of forests and hills.

Alongside this process, the process of integration and assimilation into the Hindu fold went on simultaneously. At the end product, we find tribes who for centuries lived far away from the mainstream, in the relatively isolated, inaccessible, less fertile and less agriculturally productive regions of forests, hills and mountains. "[5] When British Rule spread into the hill tracts, "many developmental schemes such as roads, rest-sheds, schools and dispensaries were constructed there and with the opening up of the interiors, many people of the plains infiltrated into these areas as contractors, money- -lenders, merchants and brokers."[6]

In the pre-Independence era, "Adivasis were dubbed as aborigines or tribals. Both the words convey the import of primitiveness and seclusiveness. The foreign governments kept these honest and simple people under this category with malafide intention. As these people are by nature freedom loving and liked to have their own way of living, the foreign government wished to degrade them by using the epithet 'aborigines'."[7] Initially the use of the word 'tribe' had a different purpose. "Purely for the sake of classification and enumeration the British Government in India introduced the category of 'tribe' (with occasional qualifying prefixes like 'hill and jungle', 'aboriginal, 'indigenous' to designate these people. It is significant to note that unaffected by its usage in India, British social Anthropologists like Radcliffe-Brown, Evans-Pritchard, Fortes and Nadel have used the word tribe to refer to an autonomous political unit which lives on its own territory and possesses its own distinctive way of life."[8]

Attempts have been made to find out the common denominators or features of the 'tribe' in Indian context. Eight such features were listed in the report of the Commissioner for Scheduled Castes and Scheduled Tribes for the year 1952. They are "*(i)* They live away from the civilised world in the inaccessible parts lying in the forests and hills, *(ii)* They belong to either one of the three stocks — Negritos, Australoids or Mongoloids, *(iii)* They speak the same tribal dialect, *(iv)* Profess primitive religion known as "Animism" in which the worship of ghosts and spirits is the most important element; *(v)* Follow primitive occupation such as gleaning, hunting, and gathering of forest product, *(vi)* They are largely carnivorous or flesh and meat eaters, *(vii)* They live either naked or semi-naked using tree-barks and leaves for clothing, and *(viii)* They have nomadic habits and love for drink and dance."[9]

As per the classification of Ethnologists, the tribes of India are divided into four major groups. While, "the tribes of NEFA and Eastern India belong to the Mongoloid ethnic stock, the tribes of Bihar and Orissa are Proto-Australoids, the tribes of Western and Central Himalayas are Mediterranean-Nordic, and the tribes of South India have strains of Australoid, Negroid and Alpine. What is significant in this connection is the fact that none of these constitutes a product by itself but shares the ethnic traits in some measure with its neighbouring non-tribal populations."[10] From linguistic points of view, the tribes of India are broadly classified into four categories, namely, (1) Indo-Aryan speakers, (2) Dravidian speakers, (3) Tibeto-Burmese speakers, and (4) Austric speakers. There are some 400 tribal languages which means that most of the tribes have their own language. However, in majority of cases, these languages are unwritten ones. In Orissa, the speakers of the Tibeto-Burmese language family are absent and therefore, Orissan tribes belong to other three language families."[11]

As per, "1991 Census Reports, the Scheduled Tribes have been listed in each State/Union Territory separately under the Presidential Order 'the Scheduled Castes and the Scheduled Tribes lists (Modification Order 1956)' as amended from time to time. No Scheduled Tribe has been listed in Haryana, Punjab, Chandigarh, Delhi, and Pondicherry as per this Presidential Order ... 67.76 million persons were counted in 1991 Census as belonging to Scheduled Tribes in different States/Union

Territories in India, excluding Jammu & Kashmir, constituting 8.08 per cent of the total population. The percentage of Scheduled Tribes has marginally increased from 7.83 per cent in 1981 to 7.95 per cent in 1991. (While making the comparison between 1981 and 1991, both Assam and Jammu & Kashmir are excluded as census was not taken in Assam in 1981 and Jammu & Kashmir in 1991). The Scheduled Tribe population has increased by 25.67 per cent during the decade 1981-1991 .This growth rate is more than the growth rate of the total population of the country (23.79 per cent)."[12]

Excluding Jammu & Kashmir, the total Scheduled Tribe population of India spread under 573 tribes of the country was 67,758,380 out of the total population of 838,583,988 as per 1991 Census. The total population of India including the projected figure of Jammu & Kashmir was 846,302,688 as per the said Census. But, "in some of the states and Union Territories, the population was predominantly Scheduled Tribe. For example, in Mizoram 94.75 per cent of the total population belongs to Scheduled Tribes. The other states/ Union Territories with predominantly Scheduled Tribe population were: Lakshadweep (93.15 per cent), Nagaland (87.70 per cent), Meghalaya (85.53 per cent), Dadra and Nagar Haveli (78.99 per cent), and Arunachal Pradesh (63.66 per cent). Manipur and Tripura also had substantial proportion of population as Scheduled Tribes, the respective proportions being 34.41 and 30.95 per cent. Among the major states, Madhya Pradesh had the largest proportion of Scheduled Tribe population (23.27 per cent) followed by Orissa (22.21 per cent). Gujarat, Assam and Rajasthan were the other three major States in which more than 10 per cent of the population belonged to Scheduled Tribes, the respective percentages being 14.92, 12.82, and 12.44. Of the total Scheduled Tribe population of 67.76 million counted in different States/ Union Territories in India, 22.73 per cent are in Madhya Pradesh, 10.80 per cent in Maharashtra -and 10.38 per cent in Orissa, Thus, roughly 44 per cent of the Scheduled Tribe population of India live in these three states only. Going a little further, 71 per cent of the Scheduled Tribe population in India live in six states, viz., Madhya Pradesh, Maharashtra, Rajasthan, Gujarat, Bihar, and Orissa."[13]

Only, "29.60 per cent of the Scheduled Tribe population in the age- group of 7 years and above is found to be literate as per the 1991 Census, the literacy rate being 40.65 for males and 18.19 for females. These figures are much lower than the corresponding figures for the total population of India. In fact, these figures are even lower than the corresponding figures for the Scheduled Caste population. If we were to take out the population of North- Eastern states like Nagaland, Mizoram, Meghalaya and Manipur which have a predominantly Scheduled Tribe population and very high literacy rates, the literacy rates of the Scheduled Tribe population would become much lower. That is, the literacy levels among the Scheduled Tribe population in other states are extremely low. In Andhra Pradesh, the literacy rate of the Scheduled Tribe population was just 17.16 per cent. In Rajasthan it was 19.44 per cent. In case of females, the literacy rates for Scheduled Tribe population are extremely low in Rajasthan (4.4), Andhra Pradesh (8.7), Orissa (10.2), Madhya Pradesh (10.7), Bihar (14.8) and Uttar Pradesh (15.0)."[14] The total number of Scheduled Tribe literates was 16,008,547 out of the 359,284,417 total literates of the country who constituted 52.21 per cent of the total population of India excluding the population in the age-group of 0-6 years.

But, "the work participation rate (total workers as percentage of total population) of the Scheduled Tribe population is 49.30 per cent which is much higher than that for the general population (37.46) and also for the Scheduled Caste Population (39.45). This is primarily due to very high percentage rates among the Scheduled Tribe women. In case of males, the work participation rate of

Table 1

State/Union Territorywise Total Population, Number of Scheduled Tribes, Total Scheduled Tribe population and Percentage of Scheduled Tribe Population to Total Population in India as per 1991 Census

Sl.	States	Total Population	Number of Scheduled Tribes	Total Scheduled Tribe Population	Percentage of total Scheduled tribe Population to Total Population
1.	Andhra Pradesh	66,508,008	33	4,199,481	6.31
2.	Arunachal Pradesh	864,558	12	550,351	63.66
3.	Assam	22,414,322	14	2,874,441	12.82
4.	Bihar	86,374,465	30	6,616,914	7.66
5.	Goa	1,169,793	05	376	0.03
6.	Gujarat	41,309,582	29	6,161,775	14.92
7.*	Haryana	16,463,648	...	...	...
8.	Himachal Pradesh	5,170,877	08	218,349	4.22
9.	Jammu & Kashmir	...	08	...	...
10.	Karnataka	44,977,201	49	1,915,691	4.26
11.	Kerala	29,098,518	35	320,967	1.10
12.	Madhya Pradesh	66,181,170	46	15,399,034	23.27
13.	Maharashtra	78,937,187	47	7,318,281	9.27
14.	Manipur	1,837,149	29	632,173	34.41
15.	Meghalaya	1,774,778	17	1,517,927	85.53
16.	Mizoram	689,756	14	653,565	94.75
17.	Nagaland	1,209,546	05	1,868,822	87.70
18.	Orissa	31,659,736	62	7,032,214	22.21
19.*	Punjab	20,281,969	...	...	...
20.	Rajasthan	44,005,990	12	5,474,881	12.44

Table 1 contd.

21.	Sikkim	406,457	02	90,901	22.36
22.	Tamil Nadu	55,858,946	36	574,194	1.03
23.	Tripura	2,757,205	19	853,345	30.95
24.	Uttar Pradesh	139,112,287	05	287,901	0.21
25.	West Bengal	68,077,965	38	3,808,760	5.59
	Union Territories				
1.	Andaman & Nicobar Islands	280,661	06	26,770	9.54
2.*	Chandigarh	642,015	...	...	...
3.	Dadra & Nagar Haveli	138,477	07	109,380	78.99
4.*	Daman & Diu	101,586	05	11,724	11.54
5.*	Delhi	9,420,644	...	...	...
6.*	Lakshadweep	51,707	#	48,163	93.15
7.*	Pondicherry	807,785	...	...	...
	*INDIA***	*8,38,583,988****	*573*	*67,758,380*	*8.08*

Source: Union Primary Census (1991) Abstract of Total Population and Scheduled Tribe Population, Series - I of 1992 & 1993, Govt of India, New Delhi.

* Does not have any Scheduled Tribe

** Except the Number of Scheduled Tribes, the figures of Jammu & Kashmir have not been included as census was not conducted there in 1991.

*** The Total population of India as per 1991 Census including the projected figure of Jammu & Kashmir is 846,302,688

\# Inhabitants of Lakshadweep who, and both of whose parents were born in Lakshadweep have been treated as Scheduled Tribes.

Table - 2

State/Union-Territorywise Total Literacy and Scheduled Tribe Literacy in India as per 1991 Census**

Sl. No.	State	No of Literate Persons: Total	No of Literate Persons: Scheduled Tribe	Percentage of Literacy: Total Population	Percentage of Literacy: Scheduled Tribe Population
1.	Andhra Pradesh	24,487,559	572,411	44.09	17.16
2.	Arunachal Pradesh	283,610	147,833	41.59	35.45
3.	Assam	9,516,393	1,124,556	52.89	49.16
4.	Bihar	26,402,898	1,415,687	38.48	26.78
5.	Goa	779,596	124	75.51	42.91
6.	Gujarat	21,131,400	1,828,365	61.29	36.45
7.*	Haryana	7,449,012	...	55.85	...
8.	Himachal Pradesh	2,765,409	84,598	63.86	47.09
9.	Jammu & Kashmir	...	...	...	...
10.	Karnataka	21,013,193	559,509	56.04	36.01
11.	Kerala	22,686,461	156,061	89.21	57.22
12.	Madhya Pradesh	23,465,301	2,599,380	44.20	21.54
13.	Maharashtra	42,447,139	2,153,241	64.87	36.79
14.	Manipur	916,692	282,940	59.89	53.63
15.	Meghalaya	678,105	545,868	49.10	46.71
16.	Mizoram	461,930	437,173	82.27	82.71
17.	Nagaland	617,736	538,848	61.65	60.59
18.	Orissa	12,915,917	1,272,863	49.09	22.31
19.*	Punjab	9,932,116	...	58.51	...
20.	Rajasthan	13,549,088	836,722	38.55	19.44
21.	Sikkim	188,920	44,001	56.94	59.01
22.	Tamil Nadu	30,336,235	134,072	62.66	27.89
23.	Tripura	1,365,980	275,256	60.44	40.37
24.	Uttar Pradesh	46,144,196	81,723	41.60	35.70
25.	West Bengal	32,609,397	852,134	57.70	27.78
	Union Territories				
1.	Andaman & Nicobar Islands	171.086	12,586	73.02	56.62
2.*	Chandigarh	425,060	...	77.81	...
3.	Dadra & Nagar Haveli	44,834	24,104	40.71	28.21
4.	Daman & Diu	61,096	5,110	71.20	52.91
5.*	Delhi	5,882,297	...	75.29	...
6.	Lakshadweep	34,548	31,382	81.78	80.58
7.*	Pondicherry	521,213	...	74.74	...
	*INDIA****	*359,284,417*	*16,008,547*	*52.21*	*29.60*

Source: Union Primary Census (1991) Abstract of Total Population and Scheduled Tribe Population, Series - I of 1992 & 1993, Govt. of India, New Delhi.

* Does not have any Scheduled Tribe.

** Excludes Population in the age-group of 0-6 years.

*** Does not include the figures of Jammu & Kashmir where Census was not conducted in 1991.

Table 3

Percentage of Main Workers among Total Population and Scheduled Tribe Population in India and Orissa as per 1991 Census

	Primary Sector		*Secondary Sector*		*Tertiary Sector*	
	Total Population	*Scheduled Tribe Population*	*Total Population*	*Scheduled Tribe Population*	*Total Population*	*Scheduled Tribe Population*
INDIA*	67.53	90.03	11.97	3.85	20.50	6.12
ORISSA	75.83	91.48	7.51	3.83	16.66	4.69

Source: Union Primary Census (1991) Abstract of Total Population and Scheduled Tribe Population, Series - I of 1992 & 1993, Govt of India, New Delhi and Statistical Outline of Orissa, 1995, Govt. of Orissa, Bhubaneswar.

* Excludes figures of Jammu and Kashmir where Census was not conducted in 1991.

Table 4

Percentage of Total Workers and Scheduled Tribe Workers in India and Orissa as per 1991 Census

	Total Population			Scheduled Tribes Population		
	Total	Males	Females	Total	Males	Females
INDIA*	37.46	51.55	22.25	49.30	54.74	43.71
ORISSA	37.53	53.79	20.79	49.36	58.94	39.81

Source: Union Primary Census (1991) Abstract of Total Population and Scheduled Tribe Population, Series - I of 1992 & 1993, Govt of India, New Delhi and Statistical Outline of Orissa, 1995, Govt. of Orissa, Bhubaneswar.

* Excludes figures of Jammu and Kashmir where Census was not conducted in 1991.

the Scheduled Tribe population is 54.74 per cent which is somewhat higher than that of the total population (51.55) as well as Scheduled Caste population (51.48). But the female work participation rate among the scheduled Tribes is 43.71 per cent as against 25.98 per cent for the Scheduled Castes and 22.25 per cent for the total population of the country. ... 90.03 per cent of the main workers among the Scheduled Tribes are in the primary sector, 3.85 per cent in the secondary sector and 6.12 per cent in the Tertiary sector. The corresponding figures for 1981 were 90.71, 4.57 and 4.72. Thus, there has been a very-marginal decline in the primary sector, but there has been a considerable decline in the secondary sector leading to a substantial increase in the proportion in tertiary sector. There appears to be a clean shift away from the secondary sector to the tertiary sector. Within the agricultural sector, 54.51 per cent of the Scheduled Tribe main workers have reported as cultivators, while 32.69 per cent have reported as agricultural labourers."[15]

Orissa

Lying in the shadows of the Eastern Ghats, Orissa, a littoral state of India on the Bay of Bengal which became a separate province on 1st April, 1936 has maintained its political identity by the same name in independent India. Spread over a geographical area of 1,55,707 square kilometres, it has now 30 revenue districts, 58 sub-divisions, 147 Tehsils, 314 Blocks and 424 police stations. Out of its total 51,057 villages, 46,989 are inhabited and the rest 4068 are uninhabited. The villages have been organised under 5263 Grampanchayats. There are altogether 102 urban local bodies in the State in the form of two Municipal Corporations, 30 Municipalities and 70 Notified Area Councils. The state has also 22 census towns. By 1993-94, out of the total forest area of 57,183 square kilometres of Orissa, 27,087 square kilometres were declared as reserve forests and 16,113 square kilometres as protected forests. By 1990-91 the state had a total cattle population of 135,77,157. The state had a total of 143,774 kilometres of surface road and 2157 kilometres of railroad by 1993-94. By the same period there were 41,604 primary schools, 12,762 Middle Schools, 4,921 Secondary schools and 677 general education colleges in the state. 1,05,340 primary teachers, 41,123 Middle school teachers, 44,305 Secondary school teachers and 13,749 general college teachers worked in these institutions of the state. Taking a total figure of all hospitals, dispensaries, public health centres, etc., the figures for the said period were 1,543 in Allopathic branch, 444 in Homeopathic branch and 512 in Ayurvedic branch. The state has 147 Assembly constituencies out of which 22 are reserved for the scheduled castes and 34 reserved for the scheduled tribes. Similarly, the state has a share of 21 seats in Lok Sabha and 10 seats in Rajya Sabha. The scheduled castes and the scheduled tribes of the state have a share of 3 seats and 5 seats respectively in Lok Sabha.

Orissa has a total population of 31,659,736 as per 1991 census as against 263,70,271 in 1981 Census. As per 1991 Census the total population of Orissa constituted 3.88 per cent of the total population of India. The decennial (1981-91) growth rate of population of the state is 20.06. This growth rate is a little higher than the rate of 19.72 of the preceding decade (1971-81). 203 persons live in every square kilometre of the state, on an average. The 1991 Census shows that there are 971 females for every 1000 males. This rate has gradually decreased from 988 in 1971 and 982 in 1981. This shows that the growth rate of females in relation to males is constantly decreasing. The average size of operational holding in the state is 1.34 hectares as per 1990-91 Survey. By religion, the people of Orissa are Hindus by 94.67 per cent, Christians by 2.10 per cent and Muslims by 1.83 per cent. The rest are Sikhs, Buddhists and Jains. As per the Scheduled Castes and Scheduled Tribes Orders

Table 5
District-wise Total and Scheduled Tribe Demographic Stastics of Orissa as per 1991 Census

Sl. No.	Name of District	Area in sq. Kms.	No. of Blocks	No. of Gram-Pachayats	Total Population	Decennial Growth rate of Population (1981-1991)	Percentage of District Population to state's Total Population	Densityof Population per Sq. km. (No. of Persons)	Sex ratio of Females per 1000 males	Total ST Population	Percentage of ST Population to total Population of the District	Percentage of ST Population of the District to Total Population of the state
(1)	(2)	(3)	(4)	(5)	(6)	(7)	(8)	(9)	(10)	(11)	(12)	(13)
1	Balasore	3705.8	12	256	16.96.583	24.96	5.36	458	955	1.79,289	10.57	2.55
2	Bhadrak	2787.9	7	166	11,05,834	23.55	3.49	397	985	18.703	1.69	0.27
3	Bolangir	6551.5	14	241	12.30.938	15.94	3.89	188	987	2.71.511	22.06	3.86
4	Sonepur	2284.4	6	80	4.76.815	19.99	1.51	209	979	45.286	9.50	0.64
5	Cuttak	3915.2	14	262	19.72.739	19.58	6.23	504	919	68.858	3.49	0.98
6.	Jagatsinghpur	1739.4	8	181	10.14.242	17.70	3.20	583	977	6.232	0.61	0.09
7	Kendrapara	2565.6	9	205	11.49.501	17.15	3.63	448	1.007	4.552	0.40	0.06
8.	Jajpur	2884.9	10	242	13.86.177	22.01	4.38	480	977	1.02.546	7.40	1.46
9	Dhenkanal	4597.1	8	172	9.47.870	18.92	2.99	206	954	1.20.226	12.68	1.71
10.	Angul	6347	8	181	9.61.037	22.31	3.04	151	942	1.12.293	1 1 .68	1.60
11.	Ganjam	6070.6	22	444	27.04.056	19.25	8.54	335	1 .006	79.120	2.93	1.13
12.	Gajapati	3016.8	7	106	4.54.708	13.00	1.44	151	1.027	2.17.725	47.88	3.10
13.	Kalahandi	81 97.4	13	195	11.30.903	19.47	3.57	138	999	3.26.648	28.88	4.64
14.	Nuapada	3407.6	5	93	4.69.482	19.58	1.48	138	1.002	1.68.777	35.95	2.40
15.	Keonjhar	8303	13	244	13.37.026	19.95	4.22	161	974	5.95.184	44.52	8.46
16.	Koraput	8379.3	14	197	10.29.986	19.89	3.25	123	991	5.21.849	50.67	7.42
17.	Rayagada	7584.7	11	140	7.13.984	17.29	2.26	94	1.012	4.00,097	56.04	5.69
18.	Malkangiri	6115. 3	7	77	4,21,917	25.88	1.33	69	985	2.46.214	58.36	3.50
19.	Nabarangpur	529O.1	10	148	8,46,659	24.33	2.68	160	989	4,67.919	55.27	6.65
20.	Mayurbhanj	10418	26	316	18,84,580	19. 14	5.95	181	979	10,90,626	57,87	15.51

21.	Phulbani	5484.9	12	144	5,46.281	21.69	1.73	100	999	2.81.386	51.51	4.0
22.	Boudh	5444.5	3	58	3.17.622	18.35	1.00	92	981	41.022	12.92	0.58
23.	Puri	3054.6	11	204	13.05.365	18.33	4.12	427	970	3,481	0.27	0.05
24.	Khurda	2887.5	10	153	15.02.014	32.39	4.75	520	903	77.242	5.14	1.10
25.	Nayagarh	3954. 2	8	143	7.82.647	14.52	2.47	198	958	46.624	5.96	0.66
26.	Bargarh	5831.6	12	196	12.07.172	16.93	3.81	207	979	2.36.072	19.56	3.36
27.	Sambal pur	6704	9	133	8.09.017	18.50	2.56	121	956	2.83.801	35.08	4.04
28.	Jharsuguda	2203.2	5	63	4.46.726	21.31	1.41	203	938	1.42,418	31.88	2.03
29.	Deogarh	2781.7	3	53	2.34.238	18.50	0.74	84	982	78,032	33.31	1.11
30.	Sundargarh	9712	17	170	15.73.617	17.62	4.97	162	936	7,98.481	50.74	11.35
	ORISSA	1,55,707	314	5,263	31,659,736	20.06	100.00	203	971	70,32,214	22.21	100.00

Source: Statistical Outline of Orissa, 1995 and the Department of Welfare, Govt. of Orissa. Bhubaneswar

(Amendment) Act, 1976 (No. 108 of 1976, dated the 18th September, 1976), the Government of India have recognised 62 tribes in Orissa. This is the highest number of tribes found in any state. As per 1991 Census the Scheduled Tribe population in the state was 7,032,214 which constituted 22.21 per cent of the total population of 3 1,659,736 for the State. The Scheduled Tribe population of the state is 10.84 per cent of the total Scheduled Tribe population of India. The Scheduled Tribe population of the state as per 1981 Census was 59,15,067. As per 1991 Census, out of the total 12,915,917 literates of the state 1,272,863 belong to Scheduled Tribes who constitute 22.31 per cent of the Scheduled Tribe literates of the state.

The tribals are, in lesser or greater degrees, present in all the districts of Orissa. While seven districts such as Malkanagiri (58.36), Mayurbhanj (57.87), Rayagada (56.04), Nabarangpur (55.27), Phulbani (51.51), Sundargarh (50.74), and Koraput (50.67) have a tribal concentration of more than 50 per cent of their respective total population; six districts such as Gajapati (47.88), Keonjhar (44.52), Nuapada (35 95), Sambhalpur (35.08), Deogarh (33.31) and Jharsuguda (31.88) have recorded a tribal concentration of more than 30 per cent of their respective total population as per 1991 Census. Thus, the heavy tribal concentration of Orissa is seen in southern, western and north-western parts of the state. These parts comprising the above 13 revenue districts out of the total 30 districts of the state constitute more than 75 per cent of the total tribal population of the state. The tribal population in all the districts of Orissa has increased steadily over the years since 1961 Census to 1991 Census.

By July, 1997 there were 930 non-residential *sevashramas* (class I to class V), 135 residential *sevashramas*, 147 *ashram* schools, 213 high schools, totalling 1,425 schools exclusively for educational opportunities of the tribal students of the state.

Table 6

District-wise Total Population and ST Population of Orissa from 1961 Census to 1991 Census

(Fig in '000)

Sl. No.	Name of the district (Undivided)	1961 Census		1971 Census		1981 Census		1991 Census*	
		Total	ST	Total	ST	Total	ST	Total	ST
1.	Balasore	1,416	96	1,831	129	2,253	154	2,803	198
2.	Bolangir	1,069	221	1,264	249	1,469	280	1,708	316
3.	Cuttack	3,060	86	3,824	111	4,629	145	5,522	183
4.	Dhenkanal	1,029	143	1,294	167	1,583	194	1,909	232
5.	Ganjam	1,873	189	2,294	229	2,670	253	3,158	297
6.	Koraput	1,498	912	2,043	1,151	2,484	1,371	3,013	1,636
7.	Kalahandi	1,010	335	1,167	341	1,339	419	1,600	496
8.	Keonjhar	743	350	950	449	1,115	500	1,337	595
9.	Mayurbhanj	1,204	730	1,134	840	1,582	912	1,884	1,091
10.	Puri	1,865	67	2,341	86	2,291	101	3,591	128
11.	Phulbani	514	214	622	251	717	279	864	322
12.	Sambalpur	1,509	439	1,845	519	2,281	612	2,697	740
13.	Sundargarh	759	441	1,131	550	1,338	686	1,574	798
	ORISSA	17,549	4,223	21,945	5,072	26,370	5,914	31,660	7,032

Source: Compiled from different Census Reports and the Department of Welfare, Govt of Orissa, Bhubaneswar.

* District Figures for 1991 Census have been converted from present 30 Districts into the fold of their parent districts as given in the table.

Table 7
District-wise Percentage of Literacy among the Total and ST Population in Orissa as per 1991 Census

Sl. No.	*Name of Districts*	*Percentage of Total Literacy*			*Percentage of ST Literacy*		
		Male	*Female*	*Total*	*Male*	*Female*	*Total*
1.	Balasore	71.23	43.40	57.64	30.08	7.37	18.91
2.	Bhadrak	74.62	46.35	60.54	20.25	4 91	12.87
3.	Bolangir	55.64	21.30	38.63	41.17	8 65	24.86
4.	Sonepur	61.48	23.38	42.62	43.42	11.38	27.44
5.	Cuttack	77.30	52.47	65.44	32.83	8.24	21.03
6.	Jagatsingh-pur	78.4I	52.94	65.78	35.35	13.33	24.87
7.	Kendra-pada	76.82	50.67	63.61	26.02	6.25	16.86
8.	Jajpur	70.50	45.29	58.00	26.07	5.60	16.04
9.	Dhenka-nal	68.82	40.33	54.92	35.01	9.28	22.40
10.	Angul	67.64	34.32	51.52	40.01	11.13	25.77
11.	Ganjam	63.88	29.87	46.72	32.69	7.02	19.98
12.	Gajapati	41.76	17.44	29.37	25.66	6.75	15.88
13.	Kalahandi	46.85	15.28	31.08	32.00	5.48	18.54
14.	Nuapada	42.31	12.78	27.52	32.00	5.18	18.49
15.	Keonjhar	59.04	30.01	44.73	38.01	11.74	24.89
16.	Koraput	29.42	15.15	24.64	14.61	2.14	8.34
17.	Rayagada	36.53	15.63	26.01	17.73	3.40	10.39
18	Malkana-giri	28.22	11.69	20.04	11.21	2.32	6.77
19.	Nabarang-pur	28.10	9.01	18.62	17.50	1.80	9.66
20.	Mayurbh-anj	51.84	23.68	37.88	37.74	10.50	24.10
21.	Phulbani	54.68	12.82	37.23	43.93	11.56	27.49
22.	Boudh	60.61	21.01	40.98	48.41	9.30	28.88
23.	Puri	76.83	49.41	63.30	52.45	22.77	38.94
24.	Khurda	78.74	55.39	67.72	41.66	13.41	28.11
25.	Nayagarh	73.00	40.74	57.20	50.14	13.88	32.05
26.	Bargarh	63.78	31.21	47.65	47.08	14.61	30.85
27.	Sambalpur	.65.94	36.48	51.56	47.10	16.83	32.06
28.	Jharsug-uda	67.21	37.01	52.64	50.95	18.37	34.87
29.	Deogarh	59.43	29.26	44.45	41.25	13.73	27.47
30.	Sundar-garh	65.41	39.60	52.97	50.13	24.52	37.34
	ORISSA	63.09	34.68	49.09	34.44	10.21	22.31

Source : Statistical Outline of Orissa, 1995 and the Department of Welfare, Govt. of Orissa, Bhubaneswar.

Table 8

District-wise Forest Area cover, average size of operational holdings and Main Workers of Orissa

Sl. No	Name of the District	Percentage of Forest area to State's total Forest area (1992-93)	Average size of operational Holdings in Hectares (1990-91)	Percentage of Main workers to the District's Total Population (1991)	Percentage of District's main Workers to the State's Main Workers (1991)
1.	Balasore	0.40	0.97	27.89	4.56
2.	Bhadrak	0.05	1.45	25.70	2.74
3.	Bolangir	1.94	1.69	34.57	4.10
4.	Sonepur	0.57	1.39	36.19	1.66
5.	Cuttack	1.14	0.94	28.58	5.43
6.	Jagatsinghpur	0.15	0.94	26.52	2.59
7.	Kendrapada	0.51	1.16	24.31	2.69
8.	Jajpur	1.20	1.17	25.49	3.40
9.	Dhenkanal	3.25	1.19	29.99	2.74
10.	Angul	6.08	1.25	32.84	3.04
11.	Ganjam	4.65	1.05	39.02	9.18
12.	Gajapati	7.63	0.97	41.94	1.84
13.	Kalahandi	6.72	1.94	37.68	4.11
14.	Nuapada	3.15	1.77	36.95	1.67
15.	Keonjhar	4.35	1.28	32.91	4.24
16.	Koraput	2.46	1.83	41.08	4.08
17.	Rayagada	7.54	1.61	41.25	2.84
18.	Malkanagiri	2.71	1.81	37.39	1.52
19.	Nabarangpur	2.76	1.55	38.78	3.16
20.	Mayurbhanj	9.18	1.25	37.28	6.77
21.	Phulbani	7.92	1.38@	38.98	2.05

Table 8 Cont...

22. Boudh	1.95	1.38@	37.99	1.16
23. Puri	0.54	1.03	28.19	3.55
24. Khurda	2.06	1.02	29.03	4.20
25. Nayagarh	3.13	0.96	30.23	2.28
26. Bargarh	2.04	1.80	37.02	4.31
27. Sambalpur	6.96	1.63*	38.12	2.97
28. Jharsuguda	0.31	1.63*	33.52	1.44
29. Deogarh	1.69	1.63*	36.59	0.83
30. Sundargarh	6.96	1.73	32.29	4.90
ORISSA	100.00	1.34	32.78	100.00

Source : District Statistical handbook — Kandhamal, 1993 and the Statisticval Outline of Orissa 1995, Directorate of Economics and Statistics, Govt. of Orissa, Bhubaneswar.

@ Relates to Undivided Phulbani District

* Relates to undivided Sambalpur District.

As per, "the Constitution (the Scheduled Areas Order, 1977) the scheduled area in the state of Orissa comprises of the districts of Mayurbhanj, Sundargarh and Koraput (Undivided); Kuchinda Tahasil of Sambalpur (Undivided); Telkoi; Keonjhar, Champua and Barbil Tahasils of Keonjhar district; Kandhamals, Baliguda and G.Udayagiri Tahasils of Phulbani District; R.Udayagiri Tahasil, Gumma Block and Rayagada Block, Suruda Tahasil excluding Gazalbadi and Gochha *Grampanchayats* of Ganjam (Undivided) district; and Thuamul-Rampur Block and Lanjigarh Block of Kalahandi (Undivided) district; and Nilgiri Block of Balasore District.

According to the Constitution, Scheduled Tribes Order 1950 as amended by the Scheduled Castes and Scheduled Tribes Orders (Amendment) Act, 1976 there are 62 Scheduled Tribes in Orissa."[16] According to 1981 Census, the total population of the Scheduled Tribes of Orissa constituted 22.43 per cent of total population of the State while they constitute 22.21 per cent of the total population of the state according to 1991 Census. This implies a slight decrease of the percentage of population growth of the Scheduled Tribes of the State in relation to the total population of the State over the decade 1981-91. Among the Scheduled Tribes the decennial growth rates of population over the decades are fluctuating implying instability, migration and mortality among them. While their growth rate during 1961-71 was 20.08 per cent, it was decreased to 16.68 per cent during 1971-81, but again rose to 18.86 per cent during 1981-91. There are 35.13 lakh males and 35.19 lakh females among the Scheduled Tribes of the State as per 1991 Census. Only 22.31 per cent of the scheduled tribes of the State are literate. It shows a steady growth over the decades 1961-71 and 1971-81 where the percentages of Scheduled Tribe literacy in the State were 9.46 and 13.96 respectively. However, the literacy percentage of 22.31 is much lower than the State's general percentage of literacy of 49.09 which itself is lower than the national total literacy percentage of 52.21 as per 1991 Census. 34.44 per cent of Scheduled Tribe males of the State are literate as against 63.09 per cent of literates among the total males of the State. This is a very wide gap. This gap is still wider in case of women literacy. Only 10.21 per cent of Scheduled Tribe women of the State are literate as against the corresponding percentage of 34.68 for the total women of the state..

Table 9

Percentage of Total and Tribal Literacy in Orissa from Census to Census

Census year	*State's Total* Males	Females	Total	*Scheduled Tribes* Males	Female	Total
1961	34.7	8.6	21.66	13.00	1.8	7.36
1971	30.3	13.09	26.02	16.4	2.6	9.46
1981	47.10	21.12	34.75	23.27	4.76	13.96
1991	63.09	34.68	49.09	34.44	10.21	22.31

Source: Adivasi, Vol. XXXIII, Nos. 3 & 4 September-December, 1993, Bhubaneswar and Department of Welfare, Govt. of Orissa, Bhubaneswar.

Table 10

Tribal Schools in Orissa and Phulbani District (as on July, 1997)

Sl. No.	*Category of School*	*Total Nos. in the State*	*Total Nos. in Phulbani District*
1.	Non-residential Sevashramas	930	86
2.	Residenital Sevashramas	135	08
3.	Ashram Schools	147	06
4.	High Schools	213	15
	Total	1425	115

Source : Department of Welfare, Govt. of Orissa, Bhubaneswar.

The main workers of the state constitute 32.78 per cent of the total population of the state. The Scheduled Tribes of the State are more dominant in the primary sector. Their high degree of participation in this sector by 91.48 per cent is even higher than the corresponding national percentage of 90.03. But their percentage (91.48) far exceeds the State's and even nation's averages of total population in the said sector which are 75.83 per cent and 67.53 per cent respectively. However, the Scheduled Tribes of the State are less prominent in the secondary and tertiary sectors. In the secondary sector, the percentage of Scheduled Tribe participation is 3.83 which is lower than the corresponding national percentage of 3.85 and also the State's percentage of total participation in the said sector which is 7.51.

Similarly, in the tertiary sector the percentage of participation of the Scheduled Tribes is 4.69 which is also lower than the corresponding National percentage of 6.12 and drastically lower than the State's percentage of total participation in the concerned sector which is 16.66. Taking total work participation into consideration it is found that the Scheduled Tribes have a dominant share althrough. Their percentage of work participation in the State which is 49.36 is a little higher than the corresponding national percentage of 49.30. This percentage is much higher than the state's and nation's percentages of total population which are 37.53 and 37.46 respectively. The Scheduled Tribe male workers of the State constitute 58.94 per cent of the total Scheduled Tribe population which is higher than the state's corresponding percentage of total population i.e., 53.79. Similarly, the Scheduled Tribe female workers constitute 39.81 per cent of the total Scheduled Tribe population. Of course, this is a little lower than the corresponding national percentage of 43.71. But this percentage is much higher than the State's, even the nation's corresponding percentages of total workers which are 20.79 per cent and 22.25 per cent respectively. This implies that Scheduled Tribe females are more industrious than the other females of the country.

Table 11

Tribe-wise Population of Orissa and Phulbani District according to 1991 Census

Sl. No.	*Name of the Tribe*	*Population in Orissa*	*Population in Phulbani District*
1.	Bagata	4,806	16
2.	Baiga	1,556	1

3.	Banjara or Banjari	12,843	115
4.	Bathudi	1,71,074	4
5.	Bhottuda or Dhotada	3,04,137	14
6.	Bhuiya or Bhuiyan	2,46,537	49
7.	Bhumia	1,09,538	Nil
8.	Bhumiji	1,78,214	64
9.	Bhunjia	11,276	1
10.	Binjhal	1,19,929	15
11.	Binjhia or Benjhoa	8,128	Nil
12.	Birhor	825	10
13.	Bondo Paraja	7,315	Nil
14.	Chenchu	275	Nil
15.	Dal	19,867	Nil
16.	Dasua Bhumiji	1,880	Nil
17.	Dhartua	11,512	51
18.	Didayi	5,471	Nil
19.	Gadaba	67,138	Nil
20.	Gandia	3,588	1
21.	Ghara	1,553	86
22.	Gand, Gando	7,01,139	13,619
23.	Ho	50,892	58
24.	Holva	13,662	16
25.	Jatapo	9,139	11
26.	Juang	35,665	Nil
27.	Kandha Gouda	19,278	3,523
28.	Khawar	9,582	1
29.	Kharia or Kharian	168,407	752
30.	Kharwar	3,280	13
31.	Kondh or Kandha, Sita Kandha	11,40,374	2,90,388
32.	Kisan	266,371	166
33.	Kol	5,777	218
34.	Kolh-kol-loharas	12,321	264
35.	Kolha	4,04,864	661
36.	Koli including Malhar	5,093	131
37.	Konda Dora	19,235	110
38.	Kora	10,313	262
39.	Korua	1,989	32
40.	Kotia	28,607	4,653
41.	Koya	1,41,927	Nil
42.	Kulia/Kulis	6,526	96
43.	Lodha	7,458	4
44.	Madia	1,439	1
45.	Mahali	13,585	11
46.	Mankidi	1,150	Nil
47.	Mankirdia	1,491	12
48.	Matya	13,226	Nil
49.	Mirdhas	30,853	739
50.	Munda, Munda-Lohara, Munda, Mahalis	3,96,561	888

Table 11 Contd...

Sl. No.	Name of the Tribe	Population in Orissa	Population in Phulbani District
51.	Mundari	31,147	64
52.	Omanatya	25,915	382
53.	Oran/Oraon	2,57,829	26
54.	Parenga	5,843	Nil
55.	Paraja/Paroja	3,53,336	2
56.	Pentia	11,399	22
57.	Rajaur	3,146	2
58.	Santal	6,29,782	95
59.	Saora, Sahara Savar or Saura	4,03,510	3,941
60.	Shabar or Lodha	3,73,545	790
61.	Sounti	96,251	1
62.	Tharua	1,595	24

Source : Cenus of India, 1991, Series -19-Orissa, part - VIII (II) volume - 1, special Tables on STs.

Society, Economy and Development

Clear and distinctive features appear between the tribal and the non-tribal societies in India in the sense that, "the former are more homogenous, kin-based and community-oriented. They have their distinctive language and culture. However, tribal societies remained static over the years and with the passage of time, some changes have occurred in the culture of the tribal communities for various reasons. Nevertheless, they differ considerably from one another with regard to primitivism and modernity. Diversity among them is all reflected in their life style due to their peculiar geographical locations and concentration in hilly and forest areas. They continue to veer around their age-old occupational categories excepting those who have changed their occupation due to modernisation and/or migration to urban and industrial areas in search of livelihood. There are 74 primitive tribal communities who are still at the food-gathering, hunting and shifting cultivation stage. Rest others are depending upon either settled agriculture or pastoralism or artisanry However, the economy of the tribal communities, by and large, is undifferentiated, because a majority of them depend on several economic pursuits to overcome the stark problem of survival."[17]

They face, "insurmountable problems because of the erosion of their traditional rights on forest and forest land. In the name of development, they are evicted from their forest habitat. The growth of communication facilities have created opportunities for some non-tribals to grab the meagre assets of the tribals. Exposure of backward tribes to exogenous forces has impoverished them. They, particularly the vulnerable ones, are withering under the irresistible aggressive thrust of neo-colonial modern forces."[18]

Societies of tribal communities are, "kin-based, segmentary and homogenous. They encourage common values, norms, and mutual cooperation, and foster a strong sense of collectivism. Amongst them, natural resources are owned by the community. Tribal traditions and institutions are all community oriented. But the process of development promotes individualism amongst them. Now they are exposed to a culture which values individualism and promotes competition. Being unable to cope up with the culture of self and rising aspirations, tribal communities dwindle away and disintegrate by falling easy prey to land alienation, loss of assets and consequential exploitation. Land alienation is taking place because of the lacunae in the existing legislations. Sometimes, non-tribal men marry tribal women with an ulterior motive to grab land and house sites."[19]

In expressing the anxiety on the experiments over tribal value system, their culture and tradition it may be further added that, "tribal's homestatic personality system, collective social system and homogenous cultural systems are being twisted in the present process of development because development planning does not take into consideration the tribal value system and ideological system. Many development schemes flop as they run counter to the value system of the beneficiaries. Sudden and unplanned exposure of the primitive and weak tribals to the individualistic urban and industrial cultures and capitalistic market economy does not lead to their development, rather it leads to their gradual disintegration and degradation ... Their traditions, customs, norms and values cherished for generations fade away under the impact of modernism. Norms and values are bound to change slowly with the passage of time as the personality, social and cultural system are dynamic entities. Functionally, they are both promotive and regulative. Therefore, when the existing norms and values get eroded without being replaced by better ones, there will be anomie and alienation which are social pathological symptoms."[20]

About the derailment and exploitation of tribals it is again observed that, "Tribal development efforts do not seem to be resiting on firm commitment and dedication. Often funds earmarked for the development of tribals are diverted for the benefits of non-tribals. Several studies have pointed out that only 10 to 15 per cent of the allotted funds are actually spent for the benefit of the tribals. Migrant and uprooted tribals do not come within the purview of any specific development package. They are forced to earn their living in urban and industrial areas as unskilled labour. Minimum wages are not paid to them and thus, they lead a life of deprivation and destitution... Educated tribals foster a feeling that the state social policy in tribal areas is more anti-tribal as the poor tribals are exposed to open exploitation and penury. In several areas tribals are in the midst of an identity crisis. Hence, the rise of socio-politico movements in tribal belts. In several tribal pockets, the tribals are being outnumbered by non-tribals and steadily loosing their resource base. Their apprehension is that slowly they will lose their language, culture and identity... The tendency toward consumerism is fast growing among the exposed tribals, and the demonstration effects have been enticing them to emulate the style of life of non-tribal elites This attitude prompts them to spend their income on such goods that carry status symbols."[21]

Elaborating more on this aspect Bhupinder Singh

observes that, "the tribal communities which lived in comparative isolation for long periods of history began to come into contact in later times with non-tribals particularly the Hindu peasants, artisans, traders, money-lenders, etc. The establishment of British administration had a profound political and economic effect. The system of land rent was introduced and with it the landlord-tenant system which was hitherto unknown in hilly areas came to be introduced. Jagirdars and Zamindars were the direct result. Lands began to pass more and more from tribal to non-tribal hands. Some of the intermediaries turned into money-lenders and traders. The immigrant jagirdars and zamindars forced many of the tribals to pay high rents or to render unlimited amount of forced labour. When some reluctance was shown, the tribals were ejected out of their free-holds. The tribals lost ownership rights over their lands, were converted into mere tenants and were subjected to serious forms of exploitation. The new class of landlords looked on the tribals as uncivilised savages. Deep discontent arose among the tribals. There were a series of rebellions and movements in the 18th and 19th centuries. Rajmahal rebellion of 1772, Tamar rebellion of 1795–1800, Ganganarayan Hangama of 1832 amongst the Bhumij, Kol rebellion of 1832, the Santal rebellion of 1857-58, the Sardar Larai of 1885, the Birsa movement of 1895-1900, Tana Bhagat movement of 1915-16. Following these tribal rebellions or otherwise, there were a series of reform movements emulating the cultural pattern of the higher Hindu castes. As a result, some of their inter-tribal political associations have emerged and movements for separate tribal states like Jharkhand for Chhotanagpur and Orissa, hill state of Assam, Adisthan movement among Bhils have been in evidence in recent decades. There were also violent secessionist movements amongst the tribals located on the international frontier, the Nagaland movement, the Mizo National Front movement, etc... Thus, it would be seen that although during British times, new channels of communication were opened, mines and industries were established and the volume of non-tribal migration into these regions increased, the illiterate and economically backward tribals lost large portions of their lands to non-tribals. The Britishers were more concerned with maintenance and expansion of their empire and throughout their regime they evolved a policy of keeping the tribals away from the mainstream, perhaps largely for minimising their problems. However, after an initial phase of repression, the British Government initiated a series of protective legislation and administrative devices for tribals."[22]

To highlight the predicament of the tribals, he explains that, "there is the striking factor of economic backwardness among the weaker communities. Depending on land, agriculture is the mainstay for an overwhelming percentage. They had been driven to impoverished, infertile tracks, where productivity is low and irrigation almost absent. Wherever secondary occupations like industry and mining have been established, the role of the original tribal and scheduled caste inhabitant has been reduced to that of servitor. On the other hand, they have been dispossessed of land and if they got compensation money it has been frittered away. Secondly, the non-tribal who intruded into the tribal land, more often than not assumed the role of an exploiter. Always living on subsistence economy and perpetually in want, the outsider has taken advantage of the tribal predicament and snatched away his land. The money-lender has been a particularly vicious parasite and has often reduced them to a state of serfdom. Bonded slavery is in evidence in varying degrees as *Kamia* system in Bihar, *Sagri* system in Rajasthan, *Hali* system in Gujarat, *Chanamalu* system in Andhra Pradesh and *Goti* system in Orissa."[23]

For the welfare of tribals, four different methods have been suggested and even followed at various periods. "The first and earliest one is the policy of isolation, the second one is the policy of assimilation, the third one is the policy of revivalism and re-vitalisation and the fourth one which is in operation is the policy of integration and development. The last approach is the best because it aims at the development of tribals along with their integration with the national mainstream. Through this policy, special attention is being paid to primitive tribal groups, individual tribal families and to sectoral as well as integrated development."[24]

Jawaharlal Nehru, the first PrimeMinister of the country summed the policy of tribal development in the following words, "We can not allow matters to drift in the tribal areas or just not take interest in them ... At the same time we should avoid over-administering the areas and in particular sending too many outsiders into their territory. It is between the two extreme positions we have to function."[25]

For community development programme in the country, "43 special multi-purpose tribal development projects were established in 1954. The Community Development approach was multi-sectoral and lacked penetrative thrust and proved to be a failure as far as tribals were concerned. As a result, a model of Tribal Development Block was evolved. The norms for the constitution of tribal development block comprised of 150 to 200 sq. miles and a population of 25,000. It did not prove to be an effective instrument of tribal development mainly because the administrative and protective aspects of tribal life remained largely unattended. However, by the end of the Third Five Year Plan, 500 such blocks has emerged covering 40 per cent of the total tribal population of the country.. In the Fourth Five Year Plan (1969-74) during 1970-71 a special programme for the development of selected tribal areas was initiated. It was an additive programme with focus on specific target groups/areas in Bihar, Orissa, Madhya Pradesh and Andhra Pradesh. Six pilot development agencies were set up, each being registered under the Registration of Societies Act, 1860.

In these programmes the tribals had to give their shares. Poor tribals failed to derive benefits from the programmes as they were unable to pay their own share."[26]

From the Fifth Five Year Plan the tribal sub-plan strategy started operation. "The main objectives were socio-economic development and protection against exploitation of tribals particularly the weak and the vulnerable ones. Sixteen (later on it became seventeen) tribal sub-plans were formulated covering 63 per cent of the tribal population in the country in 17 states and 2 Union territories. The tribal sub-plan areas were divided into 191 Integrated Tribal Development Projects for operational purposes. In these areas concentration of tribal population is 50 per cent or more. But the minimum Scheduled Tribe population threshold of about 20,000 was adopted in delineating tribal sub-plan areas in Maharashtra, Andhra Pradesh and Assam. In the case of Tamil Nadu and Kerala the population norms were further reduced to the Scheduled Tribe population of about 10,000. In West Bengal and Tripura groups of villages with more than 50 per cent concentration of tribal population were included under the sub-plan strategy. In Uttar Pradesh and Karnataka where the Scheduled Tribe population is dispersed and small, family-based approach was adopted. The sub-plan approach aimed at the reduction of the gap between the levels of development of tribal and non-tribal areas and improving the quality of life of the tribals by alleviating them from abject indigence... During the Sixth Five Year Plan Modified Area Development Approach (MADA) was introduced to cover small areas of tribal concentration having 10,000 population or less out of which not less than 50 per cent should be tribals. By end of the Seventh Five Year Plan there were already 268 MADA pockets covering 15,080 villages and 45.82 lakhs population in 9 states and 74 cluster pockets covering 1,219 villages and 3.36 lakh population in 7 states. There were 74 special projects for primitive tribal groups in 15 states/Union Territories...

During the Eighth Five Year Plan the sub-plan strategy continued... The strategy for tribal development has been refined during the successive plan periods and from the Fifth Five Year Plan the sub-plan strategy together with its ITDA/ITDP instrument has been the major agency for implementation of tribal development programmes in terms of comprehensive coverage of tribal population."[27]

It is pertinent here to mention the vital observations of the two important committees set up by the Government of India on tribal development. The Elwin Committee (1960) stressed the participation and involvement of the tribals in the implementation of the development programmes. It recommended enactment of legislations to curb the exploitation of tribals by private money-lenders and make provision of adequate Government sources of credit for the tribals. It also suggested measures to redeem tribals from chronic loans, and discharge tribal bonded labourers from bonded labour contracts.[28] The Report of the Dhebar Committee (1963) pointed out that the protective measures were sporadic and inadequate to ameliorate complex tribal problems. It felt that the process of tribal development in the tribal areas was slow due to meagre financial investment.

Coming to Orissa, the features of the tribal economy can be broadly classified into following four points, "(1) The tribal people mostly depend on two kinds of occupations, shifting cultivation and the exploitation of forest products. Shifting cultivation is most uneconomic in character: it is not only subsistence agriculture where hardly any investment is made for the improvement of productivity of land and therefore yield of land is awfully low, which is hardly sufficient to meet the basic requirements of life, it is also self-destructive in character: it destroys the fertility of the soil and what is worse, it destroys the forest products on which the tribal people depend for their subsistence. There has been hardly any change in the technology of such primitive occupations. Consequently, the tribal people are outside the fringe of modem civilisation.

(2) The tribal economy is not only unorganised, it is also non-monetised. In case of India, probably 65 to 70 per cent of the economy is unorganised whereas the non-monetary sector will come to about 30 to 35 per cent. Since the tribal people are concentrated in a few regions, and non-monetised sector has become more or less synonymous with the tribal sector. The non-monetised economy has given rise to all kinds of exploitations; they cannot get a good price for the forest products that they sell in the markets, they are cheated in weights and measures and further, they are not actuated by monetary incentives to produce more so as to get the benefits of economic motivation. Monetary economy, in spite of all its evils, helps in promoting economic incentives and generalising purchasing power with a view to making a smooth transaction from a primitive economy to modern economy. This has not happened in tribal areas.

(3) Exploitation is rampant in tribal areas. The tribal people require credit mostly for consumption and ritual purposes. Since they do not have any durable productive enterprises, they have to fall on the money-lenders for meeting their financial requirements during the loan period. Their productive loan is limited as they do not have either scientific agriculture or industrial enterprises requiring heavy capital or other inputs for investment. Their agriculture is just a way of life. Most of the tribals are ridden with a number of rituals which require substantial amount of family budget to be spent for purchasing liquor or goats and buffaloes for sacrifice. Marriage, death or other religious ceremonies are also observed in several tribal communities with quite a great deal of pomp and ceremony with liquor, meat etc. All these depress the economy of tribal communities. It is said that *'panas'* and *'domas'* who belong to scheduled castes generally play the role of money-lenders charging high rate of interest. They live in the tribal villages and

form a part of the tribal life and exploit them to the fullest extent.

(4) Tribal people are scattered in small villages. The average size of a tribal village in the interior inaccessible areas comes to hardly 20 to 25 households, in some cases it constitutes 3 to 4 households. Due to lack of development of communication or transport facilities, these people have remained almost excommunicated from the other plain people. Lack of contact with the other so-called civilised people and absence of basic minimum facilites of life have made them terribly exclusive and primitive in their outlook. They have almost no aspirations to look forward for a better life which is considered to be a *sine qua non* of economic progress."[29]

Shifting cultivation as a technique of agriculture has a major role in tribal economy. "The shifting cultivation as opposed to settled cultivation as a major productive technique is prevalent among many primitive tribes at present. This is regarded as the oldest method of agriculture from time man learnt the use of land and fire... Primarily the tribes were primitive food gatherers collecting fruits, roots and tubers from jungle to keep their body and soul together. The agriculture they were practicing was very cruel and primitive in nature. [30]

Bhupinder Singh gives a list of economic activities generally being undertaken by the tribals of Orissa. "Apart from the forest usufruct and fuel obtained by the tribal, the minor forest produce is second only to the agriculture produce for the sustenance of the tribal. In the category of minor forest produce fall various items like *Kendu* leaf, *siali* leaf, broom sticks, medicinal herbs, honey, resins, macrobalam, tamarind, arrow-root, *sal, karanj* and *kusum* seeds. In some parts of the state, they have also taken to sericulture of *Asan* trees. The *kendu* leaves provide them considerable employment from January to June every year. *Mohua* flower is collected abundantly during February and April and is used for food and liquor. Tamarind is collected for pulp and seeds and sold to the traders. The main problem is organising and collection, processing and in marketing ensuring a fair deal to the tribals. They are often exploited by private traders and money-lenders, the *usual modus operandi* being advancing of consumption loans against forward contract."[31]

The land owning pattern of the tribals shows the nature of their economy. As per the Universal Bench-mark survey (1978-80) the data based on the study of 15 major tribes of Orissa shows peculiar features of tribal land owning pattern of the state. Though the data refers to a period almost 17 years back still this is to be relied upon as comprehensive and upto-date data on the desired line are lacking. The survey shows that the 22.68 per cent of the total tribal households were landless and only 77.32 per cent of them owned land. Of the land-owning class 53.47 per cent of households were marginal farmers having upto 2.5 acres of land, and 27.65 per cent households were small farmers having a land range of 2.6 to 5.0 acres. Together these two groups constituted 81.12 per cent of the total tribal households. Only 18.88 per cent of households are big farmers. This shows that the tribals are generally very poor or even landless. The tribes such as *Shabar, Lodha, Paraja, Saora, Kandha* etc., have a large number of landless households. The marginal farmers and the small farmers who constitute together 81.12 per cent of total tribal households occupy only 48.87 per cent of land of the community. This strengthens the point that the tribals are poor as to possession of agricultural land.

In Orissa the worst way of tribal exploitation is indebtedness to which the tribals were and are still exposed. "The size of the problem is enormous. It has various aspects—psychological, social and economic. It is difficult to estimate the psychological burden; for some, at least, all happiness and peace of mind is lost, while others so burdened seem to sink into a dull and hopeless apathy. Often the debt descends from father to son and even to the third generation. Generally speaking, the tribals appear to accept indebtedness as a normal, almost inescapable aspect of their existence. On the social side, the custom of marriage, death, and hospitality are deeply ingrained in their culture. It is true that these customs provide occasions for the tribals to escape from the dull routine of village life, but on the economic side, they rely entirely upon the money-lender for the settlement of his dues. His faith and trust in him is quite astonishing. One reason is that the money-lender gives easy credit when it is needed most. He has no idea of defending himself in a court of law nor in distrusting the money-lender's word. The cumulative result of this three sided oppression is crushing."[32]

Table 12

Categories of Land Owners Among the 15 Major Tribes of Orissa

Sl.	Category of Land owning Household	No. & Percentage to Total Land owning House-hold	Percentage of Land Owned to Total Land	Average size of land per landowning household (in acres)
1	Marginal farmer (Upto 2.5 acres)	267,368 (53.47)	20.15	1.36
2	Small farmer (From 2.6 to 5 acres)	138,286 (27.65)	28.72	3.76
3	Big Farmer:-			
(a)	Sub-category I (5.1 to 7.5 acres)	41,417 (8.28)	14.39	6.30
(b)	Sub-category II (7.6 to 12.5 acres)	36,305 (7.26)	19.11	9.55
(c)	Sub-category III (12.6 to 25 acres)	14,398 (2.88)	13.21	16.65
(d)	Sub-category IV (25 acres and above)	2,294 (0.46)	4.42	34.98

Source : Adibasi, Vol. XXXIII, No.2, June, 1993, Bhubaneswar, p. 5.

In order to develop the tribal regions of the state the total scheduled areas of Orissa except the Suruda Tehsil are covered under the tribal sub-plan area. In the tribal sub-plan area 21 Integrated Tribal Development Projects

Table 13

Tribewise Number and Percentage of Household belonging to different categories of farmers among the 15 major Tribes of Orissa

Sl.	Name of the Tribe	Total House-holds	No. and percentage of landless households	No. and percentage of landowning house-holds	Number and Percentage of Landowning Households					
					Marginal Farmers (upto 2.5 acres)	Small Farmers (2.6 to 5 acres)	Big Farmer(1) (5.1 to 7.5 acres)	Big Farmers (ii) (7.6 to 12.5 acres)	Big Farmers (iii) (12.6 to 25 acres)	Big Farmers (iv) (25 acres & above)
(1)	(2)	(3)	(4)	(5)	(6)	(7)	(8)	(9)	(10)	(11)
1.	Khond, Kond, Kondha	145.803 (100%)	44,454 (30.49)	101,349 (69.51)	54,318 (53.59)	27,815 (27.44)	8,004 (7.90)	7,280 (7.18)	3,299 (3.26)	633 (0.63)
2.	Gond, Gondo	41,298 (100%)	7,317 * (17.72)	33,981 (82.28)	15,135 (44.54)	10,828 (31.86)	3,691 (10.86)	3,024 (8.90)	1,144 (3.37)	159 (0.47)
3.	Santal	81,006 (100%)	8,296 (10.24)	72,710 (89.76)	39,877 (54.84)	21,304 (29.30)	5,461 (7.51)	4,752 (6.54)	1,198 (1.65)	118 (0.16)
4.	Saora, Savar Saura, Sahara	45, 403 (100%)	14.126 (31.11)	31,277 (68.89)	21,780 (69.64)	6,283 (20.09)	1,573 (5.03)	1,121 (3.58)	441 (1.41)	78 (0.25)
5.	Munda. Munda Lohara	30,524 (100%)	7,730 (25.32)	22,794 (74.68)	10,681 (46.86)	6,567 (28.81)	2,523 (11.07)	2,102 (9.22)	813 (3.57)	108 (0.47)
6.	Shabar, Lodha	4,129 (100%)	1,550 (37.54)	2,579 (62.46)	1,886 (73.13)	459 (17.80)	125 (4.85)	86 (3.33)	19 (0.74)	4 (0.15)
7.	Kolha	52,562 (100%)	9,340 (17.77)	43,222 (82.23)	25,417 (58.81)	10,997 (25.44)	3,183 (7.36)	2,666 (6.17)	843 (1.95)	117 (0.27)
8.	Paroja	50,544 (100%)	18,523 (36.65)	32,021 (63.35)	14,589 (45.56)	9,456 (29.53)	2,813 (8.79)	3,011 (9.40)	1,785 (5,57)	367 (1.15)
9.	Bhottada, Dhotada	43,504 (100%)	8,938 (20.55)	34,566 (79.45)	17,208 (49.78)	10,794 (31.23)	2,769 (8.01)	2,593 (7.50)	1,023 (2.96)	179 (0.52)
10.	Kisan	24,292 (100%)	3,886 (16.00)	20,406 (84.00)	9,821 (48.13)	6,410 (31.41)	2,033 (9.96)	1,576 (7.72)	507 (2.49)	59 (0.29)

11. Oraon	26,405	2,757	23,648	.7,118	7,898	3,611	3,285	1,545	191
	(100%)	(10.44)	(89.56)	(30.10)	(33.40)	(15.27)	(13.89)	(6.53)	(0.81)
12. Bhuiya,	33,307	5,270	28,037	15,556	7,017	2,330	2,091	875	168
Bhuiyan	(100%)	(15.82)	(84.18)	(55.48)	(25.03)	(8.31)	(7,46)	(3.12)	(0,60)
13. Bhumij	25,102	6,321	18,781	13,766	3,500	697	639	147	32
	(100%)	(25.18)	(74.82)	(73.30)	(18.64)	(3.71)	(3.40)	(0.78)	(0.17)
14. Bathudi	23,386	3,121	20,265	13,425	4,787	1,052	801	190	10
	(100%)	(13.35)	(86.65)	(66.25)	(23.62)	(5.19)	(3.95)	(0.94)	(0.05)
15. Kharia,	19,494	5,602	14,432	6,791	4,171	1,552	1,278	569	71
Kharian	(100%)	(25.97)	(74.03)	(47.06)	(28.90)	(10.75)	(8.86)	(3.94)	(0.49)
	646,759	146,691	500,068	267,368	138,286	41,417	36,305	14,398	2,294
TOTAL	(100%)	(22.68)	(77.32)	(53.47)	(27.65)	(8.28)	(7.26)	(2.88)	(0.46)

Source : Adibasi, Vol.XXXIII, No.2, June, 1993, BBSR, PP 8-15.

* Figures within the brackets indicate respective percentages.

covering 118 blocks in 12 districts are at work. It includes all the 26 blocks of Mayurbhanj, all the 17 blocks of Sundargarh, all the 11 blocks of Rayagada, all the 14 blocks of Koraput, all the 7 blocks of Malkanagiri, all the 10 blocks of Nawrangpur and all the 12 blocks of Phulbani. As per 1991 census, a total population of 87,28,422 live under the 21 ITDA project areas. Out of them 75,52,373 are in rural areas and 11,76,049 are urbanites. Of the total population under ITDA project areas of the state 47,49,355 persons— 45,23,742 rural dwellers and 2,25,613 urbanites are scheduled tribes who constitute together 54.41 per cent of the total population within such areas. Among the scheduled tribes under ITDA project area, 59.89 per cent live in rural areas and 19.18 per cent live in urban areas.

Table 14

Statement showing Name of Revenue Division/ District/ITDA Blocks covered under Tribal sub-Plan Area of Orissa

Name of Revenue Division	*Name of District*	*Name of Integrated Tribal Development Agency (ITDA)*	*Name of Blocks covered under ITDA*
(1)	(2)	(3)	(4)
Central Division	1. Balasore	1 . Nilagiri	1. Nilagiri
	2. Mayurbhanj	2. Baripada	2. Baripada
			3. Badasahi
			4. Sanakhunta
			5. Betanati
			6. Rasgobindapur
			7. Morda
			8. Bangriposhi
			9. Sarasakana
			10. Kuliana
			11. Suliapada
		3. Kaptipada	12. Khunta
			13. Khunta II (Gopabandhunagar)
			14. Kaptipada
			15. Udala
		4. Karanjia	16. Karanjia
			17. Raruan
			18. Jashipur

			19. Thakurmunda
			20. Sukruli
		5. Rairangpur	21. Bisoi
			22. Bijatola
			23. Kusumi
			24. Rairangpur
			25. Tiring
			26. Bahalda
			27. Jamda
Northern Division	3. Keonjhar	6. Champua	28. Joda
			29. Champua
			30. Jhumpura
		7. Keonjhar	31. Patna
			32. Ghatgaon
			33.. Keonjhar
			34. Saharpada
			35. Harichandanpur
			36. Telkoi
			37. Bansapal
	4. Sambalpur	8. Kuchinda	38. Kuchinda
			39. Gobindapur (Bamra)
			40. Jamankira
	5. Sundargarh	9. Bonai	41. Bonaigarh
			42. Lahunipada
			43. Gurundia
			44. Koira
		10. Panposh	45. Kuanrmunda
			46. Bisra
			47. Nuagaon
			48. Lathikata
		11.Sundargarh	49. Sundargarh
			50. Subdega
			51. Ballisankara
			52. Lephripada
			53. Badagaon
			54. Tangarpalli
			55. Hemagiri
			56. Kutra
			57. Rajgangpur
Southern Division	6. Gajapati	12. Parlakhem-undi	58. Gumma
			59. Rayagada
			60. Mohana
			61. R. Udayagiri
			62. Nuagada
	7.Kalahandi	13. Th. Rampur	63. Thuamul Rampur
			64. Lanjigarh
	8. Rayagada	14. Gunupur	65. Gunupur

Table 14 Contd...

		66. Gudari
		67. Padmapur
		68. Ramanaguda
		69. Bissam Cuttack
		70. Muniguda
		71. Chandrapur
	15. Rayagada	72. Rayagada
		73. Kolnara
		74. Kashipur
		75. Kalyansingpur
9. Koraput	16. Jeypur	76. Jeypur
		77. Boriguma
		78. Kotpad
		79. Baipariguda
		80. Kundra
	17. Koraput	81. Koraput
		82. Semiliguda
		83. Pottangi
		84. Nandapur
		85. Dasmanthpur
		86. Lamtaput
		87. Narayanpatna
		88. Laxmipur
		89. Bandhugaon
10. Malkanagiri	18. Malkangiri	90. Malkangiri
		91. Korkunda
		92. Kalimela
		93. Podia
		94. Khairput
		95. Kudumuluguma
		96. Mathili
11. Nawarangpur	19. Nawarang-pur	97. Nawarangpur
		98. Tentulikhunti
		99. Papadahandi
		100. Nandahandi
		101. Kosagumuda
		102. Raighar
		103. Umerkote
		104. Chandahandi
		105. Jharigaon
		106. Dabugaon
12. Phulbani	20. Balliguda	107. Balliguda
		108. Nuagaon
		109. Daringbadi
		110. Tumudibandh
		111. Kotagarh
		112. Tikabali

		113. G. Udayagiri
		114. Raikia
		115. Chakapada
	21. Phulbani	116. Phulbani
		117. Phiringia
		118. Khajuripada

Source : Department of Welfare, Govt. of Orissa, Bhubaneswar.

Many of the 62 tribes of Orissa reside beyond the sub-plan area. Such areas are called Modified Area Development Approach (MADA) pockets. There are altogether 46 MADA pockets in 47 blocks spread over 17 districts of the State and cover 2553 villages. 10,48,588 number of persons live within the MADA pockets out of which 56,7,071 are scheduled tribes who constitute 54.08 per cent of the total population thereof. Govt. of India have recognised 13 primitive tribes in Orissa. Some of them are in tribal sub-plan area and few are outside the sub-plan area. 17 Micro Projects are functioning for all-round developments of these primitive tribes in 12 districts of the State covering 537 villages in total. 61,240 persons belonging to primitive tribes live within these project areas as per 1991 census. Together they constitute for a literacy percentage of 24.20 of the total population within such areas.

The amount of financial assistance from state as well as Central Government has been on the increase from 5th Plan to 8th Plan so far as Tribal Sub-plan in the state is concerned. In terms of percentages of state assistance to tribal sub-plan to the total plan outlay of the state, it was on the increase upto 6th Plan but gradually decreased thereafter. While the percentage of T.S.P. assistance from total state plan outlay was 19.58 during 5th Plan (1974-78), it has reached only at 23.52 during 8th Plan (1992-97). Though amount-wise the assistance from the state and the Centre may seem higher, still such assistance is not proportional to tribal development. Thus, the slogan for tribal development seems to be only in words.

Constitutional and Legal Safeguards

In the pre-independence era some Acts were made in

Table 15

ITDA wise Total Population and Scheduled Tribe Population of Orissa as per 1991Census

Sl. No.	ITDA	Total Population			Scheduled Tribe Population			% of ST Population to Total Population		
		Total	Rural	Urban	Total	Rural	Urban	Total	Rural	Urban
1.	Nilagiri	106,468	93,668	12,800	53,080	50,463	2,617	49.85	53.87	20.44
2.	Baripada	857,884	788,644	69,240	429,281	419,081	10,200	50.03	53.13	14.73
3.	Kaptipada	287,989	276,700	11,289	188,223	184,975	3,248	65.35	66.85	28.77
4.	Karanjia	330,226	312,603	17,623	209,454	204,184	5,270	63.42	65.31	29.90
5.	Rairangpur	408,481	390,384	18,097	263,668	261.072	2,596	64.54	66.87	14.34
6.	Keonjhar	646,857	600,478	46,379	354.605	342,557	12,048	54.81	57.04	25.97
7.	Champua	328,437	238,220	90,217	152,986	127,037	25,949	46.58	53.32	28.76
8.	Kuchinda	225,086	212,925	12,161	125,741	121,603	4,138	55.86	57.11	34.02
9.	Bonai	243,188	238,589	4,599	163,142	162,225	917	67.08	67.99	19.93
10.	Panposh	712,421	261,916	450,505	271,056	182,423	88,633	38.04	69.64	19.67
11.	Sundargarh	618,008	548,107	69,901	364,283	347,552	16,731	58.94	63.40	23.93
12.	Paralakhem-undi	287,799	287,799	...	195,497	195,497	...	67.92	67.92	...
13.	Thuamul-Rampur	116,751	116,751	...	60,874	60,874	...	52.14	52.14	...
14.	Koraput	553,187	460,037	93,150	294,718	277,009	17,709	53.27	60.21	19.01
15.	Jeypore	476,799	398,244	78,555	227,131	216,742	10,389	47.63	54.42	13.22
16.	Rayagada	356,465	292,067	64,398	204,779	195,913	8,866	57.44	67.07	13.76
17.	Gunupur	357,519	332,591	24,928	195,318	192,884	2,434	54.63	57.09	9.764
18.	Malkanagiri	421,917	387,489	34,428	246,214	241,724	4,490	58.35	62.38	13.04
19.	Nawarangpur	846,659	804.542	42,117	467,919	463,003	4.916	55.26-	57.54	11.67
20.	Balliguda	386,076	337,568	8,508	204,799	202,932	1,867	53.04	53.74	21.94
21.	Phulbani	160,205	133,051	27,154	76,587	73,992	2,595	47.80	55.61	9.556
	TOTAL	8,728.422	7,552,373	1,176,049	4,749,355	4,523,742	225,613	54.41	59.89	19.18

Source : Department of Welfare, Govt of Orissa, Bhubaneswar.

Table 16

MADA wise Total and ST Population of Orissa as per 1991 Census

Sl. No.	District	Name of Block	Name of MADA Pockets	No. of villages covered	Total Population	ST Population	% of ST Population to total Population
1	2	3	4	5	6	7	8
1.	Jajpur	1. Sukinda	1. Sukinda - 1,	33	23,543	13,552	57.56
			2. Sukinda - II	12	14,375	7,339	51.05
			3. Sukinda -III	24	19,161	9,931	51.83
		2. Danagadi	4. Danagadi	23	24,189	13,268	54.85
2.	Khurda	3. Banapur } 4. Ranapur }	5. Banapur-} Ranapur	82	17,052	10,330	60.58
3.	Nayagarh	5. Nuagaon	6. Nuagaon	107	11,248	7,863	69.91
		6. Gania } 7. Dassapalla}	7. Gania-Dassapalla	196	28,906	13,155	45.51
4.	Balasore	8. Jaleswar	8. Jaleswar	31	24,259	13,588	56.01
5.	Keonjhar	9. Anandapur	9. Anandapur - I	55	24,362	19,633	80.59
			10. Anandapur - II	29	23,623	13,952	59.06
		10. Hatadihi	11. Hatadihi	28	20,199	10,673	52.84
		11. Ghasipura	12. Ghasipura	33	20,978	13,022	62.07
6.	Anugul	12. Pallahara	13. Pallahara	145	51,034	24,434	47.88
		13. Athamallik	14. Athamallik	56	15,933	7,755	48.67
7.	Dhenkanal	14. Kankadahad	15. Kankadahad	52	36,482	17,614	48.28
8.	Ganjam	15. Patrapur	16. Turubudi	90	12,611	5,981	47.43
9.	Gajapati	16. Kasinagar	17. Kasinagar	34	11,290	6,847	60.65
10.	Boudh	17. Boudh	18. Boudh	149	17,458	8,179	46.85
11.	Bolangir	18. Khaprakhole	19. Khaprakhole	56	26,216	13,118	50.04

Table 16 Contd...

1	2	3	4	5	6	7	8
		19. Tureikela	20. Tureikela	22	13,202	6,818	51.64
		20. Gudvela	21. Tentulikhunti	38	15,824	7,863	49.69
		21. Deogaon} 22. Patnagarh}	22. Deogaon-Patnagarh	31	16,137	8,851	54.85
		23. Saintala } 24. Muribahal}	23. Saintala-Muribahal	47	20,690	10,728	51.85
12.	Sambalpur	25. Dhanakouda	24. Dhanakauda	24	19,430	11,031	56.77
		26. Jujumura	25. Jujumura	92	47,947	25,363	52.90
13.	Jharsuguda	27. Kolabira } 28. Rengali }	26. Kolabira-Rengali	41	33,958	19,016	56.00
		29. Lakhanpur	27. Lakhanpur	19	14,793	8,042	54.36
		30. Jharsuguda	28. Jharsuguda-Lakhanpur	35	21,278	10,394	48.85
		31. Laikera } 32. Kirmira	29. Laikera-Kirmira	45	29,688	19,049	64.16
14.	Bargarh	33. Paikamal	30. Paikamala	30	16,779	8,445	50.33
		34. Jharbandh	31. Paikamala-Jharbandh	45	34,301	16,721	48.75
15.	Deogarh	35. Barkote	32. Barkote	44	18,696	8,004	42.81
		36. Tileibani	33. Tileibani	162	35,184	19,301	54.86
16.	Kalahandi	37. Bhawanipatna	34. Bhawanipatna	95	19,781	11,298	57.09
		38. Kesinga	35. Kesinga	17	13,995	7,727	55.21
		39. Junagarh	36. Junagarh	41	14,160	8,234	58.15
		40. Madanpur-Rampur	37. Madanpur-Rampur	157	24,710	14,218	57.54
		41. Jayapatna	38. Jayapatna	24	19,064	11,144	58.46

Table 16 Contd...

1	2	3	4	5	6	7	8
		42. Narla	39. Narla	23	11,219	5,504	49.06
17.	Nawapara	43. Komna	40. Komna	73	48,923	27,465	56.14
		44. Boden	41. Boden	50	38,931	20,881	53.64
		45. Nawapara	42. Nawapara- I	36	19,531	9,761	49.98
			43. Nawapara - II	41	32,316	16,330	50.53
		46. Khariar	44. Khariar -I	16	12,277	7,208	58.71
			45. Khariar-II	27	14,248	7,618	53.47
		47. Sinapali	46. Sinapali	44	18,607	9,823	52.79
		TOTAL		2,553	10,48,588	5,67,071	54.08

Source : Department of Welfare, Govt. of Orissa, Bhubaneswar.

Table 17

List of Micro Projects in Orissa and Their Location with Population

District	*Covered under*	*Part of blocks covered*	*Sl. No.*	*Name of Micro Project*	*Name of Primitive Tribe*	*Year of Establishment of Micro projct*	*No. of Villages covered*	*Primitive tribal population as per 1991 Census*	*% of literacy*
1	2	3	4	5	6	7	8	9	10
Angul	Non-TSP	Pallahara	1	PaudiBhuyan Development Agency, Jamardihi	Paudi-bhuyan	1978-79 17.5.78	27	5,433	70.02
Deogarh	Non-TSP	Barkote	2	Paudi Bhuyan Development Agency, Rugudakudar	-do-	1993-94 01.05.93	19	2,467	14.07
Ganjam	Non-TSP	Patrapur	3	Thumba Development Agency, Thumba	Lanjia Saora	1978-79 20.05.78	55	3,057	26.79
Kuapada	Non-TSP	Komna	4	Chuktia-Bhunjia Dev. Agency, Sunabeda	Chuktia-Bhunjia	1994-95 30.09.94	17	1,579	8.11
Sundergarh	Bonai	Lahunipada	5	Paudi Bhuyan Development Agency, Khuntagaon	Paudibhu-yan	1978-79 25.05.79	21	3,026	16.36
Malkanagiri	Malkanagiri	Khairput	6	Bonda Development Agency, Mudulipada	Bonda	1976-77	35	5,050	4.79
-do-	-do-	Khudumul-		Didayi Development	Didayi	1986-87	38	5,990	39.93

contd...

Table 17 contd...

1	2	3	4	5	6	7	8	9	10
		uguma, Khairput	7	Agency, Bayapada		05.08.86			
Rayagada	Gunupur	Bissam-Cuttack & Muniguda	8	Dongaria Kondh Dev. Agency, Kurli	Dongaria Kandha	1978-79	63	5,181	29.11
-do-	Rayagada	K.Singpur	9	Dongaria Kondha Development Agency, Parsali.	-do-	1987-88 07.12.87	49	2,485	7.32
Rayagada	Gunupur	Gunpur	10	LanjiaSaura Development Agency. Puttasingi	Lanjia Saura	1984-85 01.04.84	19	3,544	33.86
Gajapati	Parlakhe-mundi	Gumma	11	Lanjia Saora Dev. Agency, Seranga	-do-	1978-79 21.03.78	21	4,043	9.42
Gajapati	Parlakhe-mundi.	Mohana	12	Saura Development Agency, Chandragiri	Saora	1978-79 01-04.78	26	3,420	13.86
Phulbani	Balliguda	Tumuddi-bandha	13	Kutia Kandh Dev. Agency, Belghar	Kutia Kandh	1978-79	69	4,578	18.00
Kalahandi	Th.Rampur	Lanjigarh	14	Kutia Kandh Dev. Agency, Lanjigarh	-do-	1986-87 13.08.86	I7	1,901	27.72
Keonjhar	Keonjhar	Bansapal	15	Juang Development Agency, Gonasika	Juang	1978-79 10.03.78	32	5,774	12.24
Mayurbhanj	Baripada	Suliapada & Murda	16	Lodha Development Agency, Murda	Lodha	1985-86	8	2,052	22.66

contd...

Table 17 contd...

1	2	3	4	5	6	7	8	9	10
-do-	Karanjia	Jashipur & Karanjia	17	Hill-Kharia and Mankirdia Dev. Agency, Gudugudia	Kharia and Mankirdia	1986-87 10.02.87	21	1,660	27.71
						TOTAL	537	61,240	24.20

Source:- Department of Welfare, Government of Orissa, Bhubaneswar.

Table 18

State and Central Assistance to Tribal Sub-plan (T. S. P.) in Orissa during various Plan Periods
(Rupees in Lakhs)

Plan Period	*Total State Plan Outlay*	*STATE PLAN T. S. P Flow from State Plan*	*% of Flow to T.S.P. from state plan outlay*	*Central/ Centrally Sponsored Plan*	*Special Central Assistance (ITDP)*	*Total (3+5+7)*
5th Plan (1974-78)	46279.00	9065.10	19.58	2316.57	1467.31	12848.98
Annual Plan (1978-80)	40098.00	10667.14	26.60	2186.61	1822.18	14675.93
6th Plan (1980-85)	141939.75	48094.24	33.88	10941.86	8944.62	68631.08
7th Plan (1985-90)	324822.63	90821.64	27.96	33780.57	9134.71	133736.92
Annual Plan (1990-92)	213531.51	50462.97	23.63	16336.31	4868.88	71668.16
8th Plan (1992-97)	700552.00	164770.77	23.52	54112.00	19858.37	238741.14

Source : Department of Welfare, Govt. of Orissa, Bhubaneswar.

different provinces for protection of the interests of tribals. The Bengal Tenancy Act, 1885, the Central Province Tenancy Act, 1898 and 1920, the Chhotanagpur Tenancy Act, 1908 and the C.P. Land Alienation Act, 1918 covered a few segments of the Indian Tribals.

But the constitution of independent India showed its commitment towards security and welfare of the tribals. The Government of India and the Governments of the Indian states are making, from time to time, necessary concurring provisions towards fulfilment of the noble declarations of the constitution regarding tribals.

As to who are tribals or scheduled tribes the constitution is very clear. Article 342 of the constitution deals with identification and enlistment of scheduled tribes. Article 342(1) reads:- "The President may with respect to any state or union territory and where it is a state, after consultation with the Governor thereof, by public notification, specify the tribes or tribal communities or parts or groups within tribes or tribal communities which shall for the purposes of this constitution be deemed to be scheduled tribes in relation to that state or union territory, as the case may be".[33] Article 342(2) reads:- "Parliament may by law include in or exclude from the list of scheduled tribes specified in a notification issued under clause (1) any tribe or tribal community or part thereof or group within any tribe or tribal community, but save as aforesaid a notification issued under the said clause shall not be varied by any subsequent notification."[34]

The Constitution (first Amendment) Act, 1951 added sub-clause 4 to Article 15 for making special provisions for backward classes of citizens including the scheduled tribes in spite of the fact that Article 15 as a guarantor of fundamental right to equality prohibits discrimination on grounds of religion, race, caste, sex or place of birth. Making an exception to it, Article 15(4) reads:- "Nothing in this Article (Art. 15) or in clause (2) of Article 29 shall prevent the state from making any special provision for the advancement of any socially and educationally backward classes of citizens or for the scheduled castes and the scheduled tribes."[35] Similarly while Article 16 guarantees the fundamental right to equality of opportunity in matters of public employment, Article 16 (4) makes an exception to it and reads : "Nothing in this article shall prevent the state from making any provision for the reservation of appointments or posts in favour of any backward class of citizens which, in the opinion of the state, is not adequately represented in the services under the state".[36] Corollary to this, Article 335 declares:- the claims of the members of the scheduled castes and the scheduled tribes shall be taken into consideration, consistently with the maintenance of efficiency of administration, in the making of appointments to services and posts in connection with the affairs of the union or of the state. Taking these two articles into consideration, the Government of India and the various state Governments have made a series of statutory measures for reservation of posts in various services for the scheduled tribes, the opportunity which they continue to avail till now since after the inauguration of the constitution.

Article 17 dealing with the fundamental right to equality abolishes untouchability and declares that its practice in any form is forbidden. The enforcement of any disability arising out of 'untouchability' shall be an offence punishable in accordance with law. The scheduled castes and the scheduled tribes, for long, were treated as untouchables. However, with a deference to Article 17, the Government of India enacted the Untouchability (Offences) Act, 1955 towards a great relief of such communities. However, this was renamed later on as Protection of Civil Rights Act, 1955.

Article 46 as a Directive Principle of State Policy speaks for promotion of educational and economic interests of scheduled castes, scheduled tribes and other weaker sections. It declares: "The state shall promote with special care the educational and economic interests of the weaker sections of the people, and in particular, of the scheduled castes and scheduled tribes, and shall protect them from social injustice and all forms of exploitation.[37]" According to Article 37, the provisions including that in Article 46 contained in Part IV of the constitution dealing with Directive Principles of State Policy shall not be enforceable by any court, but the principles therein laid down are nevertheless fundamental in the governance of the country and it shall be the duty of the state to apply these principles in making laws.[38] True to its spirit, both the central government and the state governments have made special provisions for promotion of education of the scheduled tribes. In Orissa special T.R.W. residential schools are in operation with their full cost of expenditure being borne by the Govt. Besides, provisions have been made for reservation of seats in schools, colleges and universities receiving aid out of the state fund.

Part XVI of the constitution has made special provisions relating to certain classes including the scheduled tribes. Article 330 provides proportionate reservation of seats for scheduled castes and scheduled tribes in the House of the People (Lok Sabha). Article 330(2) reads: "The number of seats reserved in the state or union territory for the scheduled castes or the scheduled tribes under clause (1) shall bear, as nearly as may be, the same proportion to the total number of seats allotted to the state or union territory in the House of the People as the population of the scheduled castes in the state or union territory or of the scheduled tribes in the state or union territory, as the case may be, in respect of which seats are so reserved, bears to the total population of the state or union territory."[39] In the same manner Article 332 provides proportionate reservation of seats for scheduled tribes in the Legislative Assemblies of the state. Article 334 originally made provision for the reservation of seats, *inter alia*, for the scheduled tribes in the house of the people (Lok Sabha) and in the Legislative Assemblies (Vidhan Sabhas) of the states for a period of ten years. But this period has been extended from time to time by various constitution Amendment Acts. The Constitution (Sixty-second Amendment) Act, 1989 extended such reservation for a period of ten years enhancing the total period of reservation to 50 years expiring on 20.12.1999.[40*]

Part X of the constitution deals with the scheduled and tribal areas. Article 244(1) declares:- "The provisions of the Fifth Schedule shall apply to the administration and control of scheduled areas and scheduled tribes in any State other than the states of Assam, Meghalaya, Tripura and Mizoram."[41] Article 244(2) reads: "The provisions of the sixth schedule shall apply to the administration of the tribal areas in the states of Assam, Meghalaya., Tripura and Mizoram."[42] According to Article 339 the President of India has the power to appoint a commission to report on the administration of the Scheduled Areas and the welfare of the scheduled tribes in the states. Under clause 2 of the same Article the executive powers of the Union extends to the giving of directions to a state for welfare of scheduled tribes in the state.[43]

The Constitution (Sixty-fifth Amendment) Act, 1990 has restructured Article 338 to create a National Commission for the scheduled castes and scheduled tribes.[44] It shall be the duty of the said commission to investigate and monitor all matters relating to the safeguards provided for the scheduled castes and scheduled tribes under the constitution or under any law for the time being in force or under any order of the Government and to evaluate the working of such safeguards. It shall also inquire into specific complaints with respect to the deprivation of rights and safeguards of the scheduled castes and scheduled tribes besides

* The constitution (Seventy-ninth Amendment) Act, 1999 further extended the period to 60 years till 25.1.2010.

participating and advising on the planning process of socio-economic development of the scheduled castes and scheduled tribes and evaluating the process of their development under the Union and any state. The commission has been empowered to report upon the working of constitutional and legal safeguards for scheduled castes and scheduled Tribes from time to time with suggestions for remedial measures that the Union or the states can take.

In the state of Orissa, Regulations[45] have been promulgated for bonded labour, land alienation, debt relief and regulations of money-lenders much towards checking tribal exploitation and promotion of tribal welfare. Such regulations are as follow:-

(1) The Orissa Debt Bondage Abolition Regulation, 1948
(2) The Orissa Scheduled Area Transfer of Immovable Property (by Scheduled Tribes) Regulations, 1956
(3) The Orissa Scheduled Areas Debt Relief Regulation, 1967.
(4) The Orissa (scheduled areas) Money-Lenders Regulation, 1967

In spite of all those, "the searches for the essence of tribal life are very often carried to absurd ends, laying emphasis on the superficial and losing sight of the essential. The principle 'means justifies ends' should always prevail... Everything that is tribal is idealised and glorified. This sort of mentality tries to keep the tribes isolated from the whole world and preserve them in primitive poverty. This perverted outlook on the tribes is sometimes wrongly attributed to the anthropologists, no reputed anthropologist ever held such an opinion. It has been strongly condemned as an unscientific proposition, but the idea has taken root among some administrators and planners. It should be strongly emphasised that radical changes should be introduced among the tribes. They require all the technological achievements available to modern civilisation and the best is only good enough as these have been denied to them uptil now...Introduction of modern technology to improve the material condition of the tribal people, preservation and vitalisation of the care of their society and culture, assimilation of their patterns of human relationship by our society : these are then our problems. And these are not disparate problems. They should be tackled as an integrated whole. To this task our scientists, planners and administrators should address themselves, in all seriousness."[46]

Phulbani District - A Bird's Eye View

After this project was undertaken with 'Phulbani District' specifically mentioned as the study area, the district was divided and even the original district was renamed as Kandhamal. Thus, for the purpose of this research project, as clarified in the Preface, 'Phulbani' and 'Kandhamal' will generally carry the same meaning and weight and shall be used interchangeably. However, 'Phulbani' district will also refer to the undivided district of Phulbani or Boudh - Khondhmals, wherever necessary.

The district of Phulbani renamed as Kandhamal is a totally landlocked district, lying in the very heartland of Orissa. It has been created out of the erstwhile parent district of Boudh-Khondmals which was a centrally located district of Orissa and lay "between 19°48´N and 20°54´N latitudes and between 83° 30´ E and 84° 48´ E, longitudes... "The district of Boudh-Khondmals was created in the year 1948 with two sub-divisions, viz., Boudh and Khondmals, with headquarters at Phulbani. The former sub-division was an ex-state which merged with Orissa on the 1st January, 1948 and the latter had formerly formed a part of the district of Ganjam. Unlike most of the districts of Orissa it does not derive its name from the name of its headquarters town although it is popularly known as Phulbani district. To some, it is even known as Boudh-Phulbani district. In many of the Government publications the district is also wrongly identified".[47]

As its ruler, "the Raja of Boudh had suzerainty over Khondmals from early times. But in the middle of the 19th century when the Khonds rose in rebellion under Chakra Bisoyee, the Raja failed to bring order in that territory and later the Khondmals were brought under the administration of the British in February, 1835. The Khondmals were made a sub-division of the district of Angul in 1891 and in 1904 Phulbani was made the sub-divisional headquarters. When Orissa was made a separate province on 1st April, 1936 the Khondmals sub-division was incorporated in the district of Ganjam. On the 1st January, 1948 the district of Boudh-Khondmals was constituted with the ex-state of Boudh and Khondmals sub-division. Subsequently, in 1949 (1.4.1949) the Baligurha subdivision of Ganjam Agency consisting of the Taluks of G. Udayagiri and Baligurha was transferred to the district."[48]

In the process of reorganisation of districts in the state during 1993-94 whereby the original 13 districts were reconstituted into 30 districts, the Government of Orissa in Revenue and Excise Department under notification No. 56408/R., dated 22nd December, 1993 bifurcated the ex-Boudh-Khondmals district into two separate districts such as 'Boudh' and 'Phulbani'. While out of the two constituent parts of the parent 'Boudh-Khondmals' district, the former part, i.e., 'Boudh' retained its original name in the form of a new district, the name in the latter part, i.e., 'Khondmals' was withdrawn in favour of 'Phulbani' which was declared a separate district under such order probably due to the fact that the parent district was popularly known by this name, i.e., 'Phulbani'. The newly carved out 'Phulbani' district was constituted of 'Khondmals' and Baligurha subdivisions. "The Khondmals (Khond or Kandha—a hill tribe, *Mals*-in Oriya signify a hill tract) which imply a hilly habitat of the Khonds, seems to have derived its name from this particular hill tribe who are predominant in the area".[49] The abolition from the administrative use, the name

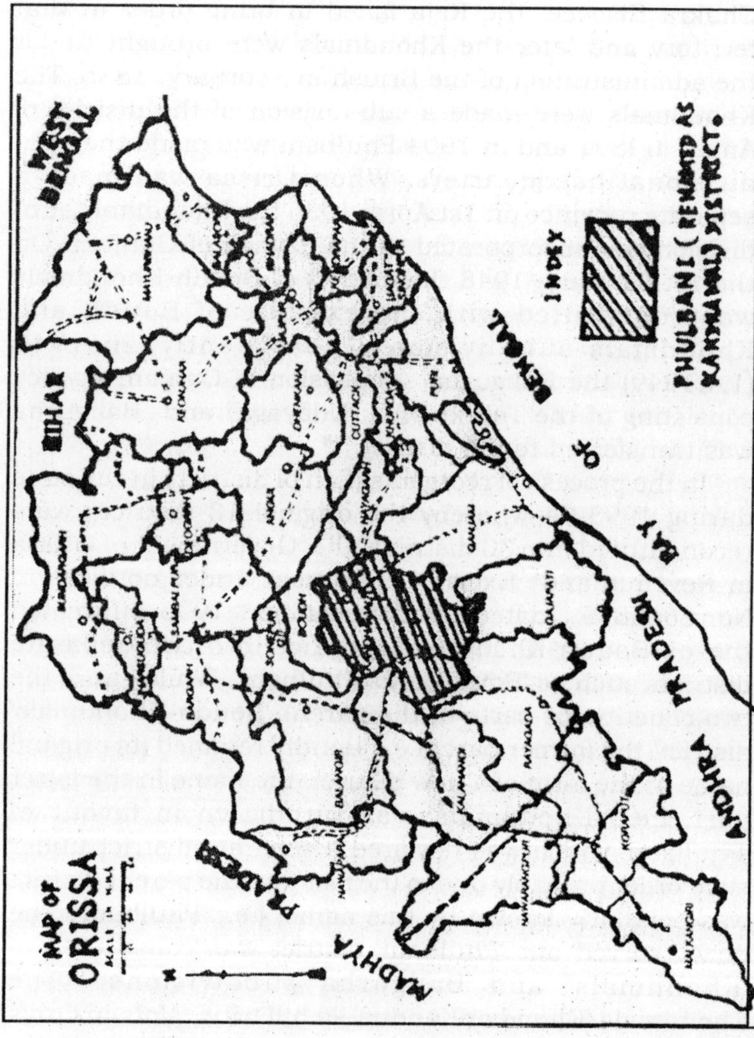
MAP OF
ORISSA
WEST BENGAL
BIHAR
MADHYA PRADESH
ANDHRA PRADESH
BAY OF BENGAL
INDEX
PHULBANI (RENAMED AS KANDHAMAL) DISTRICT.

Fig. 1

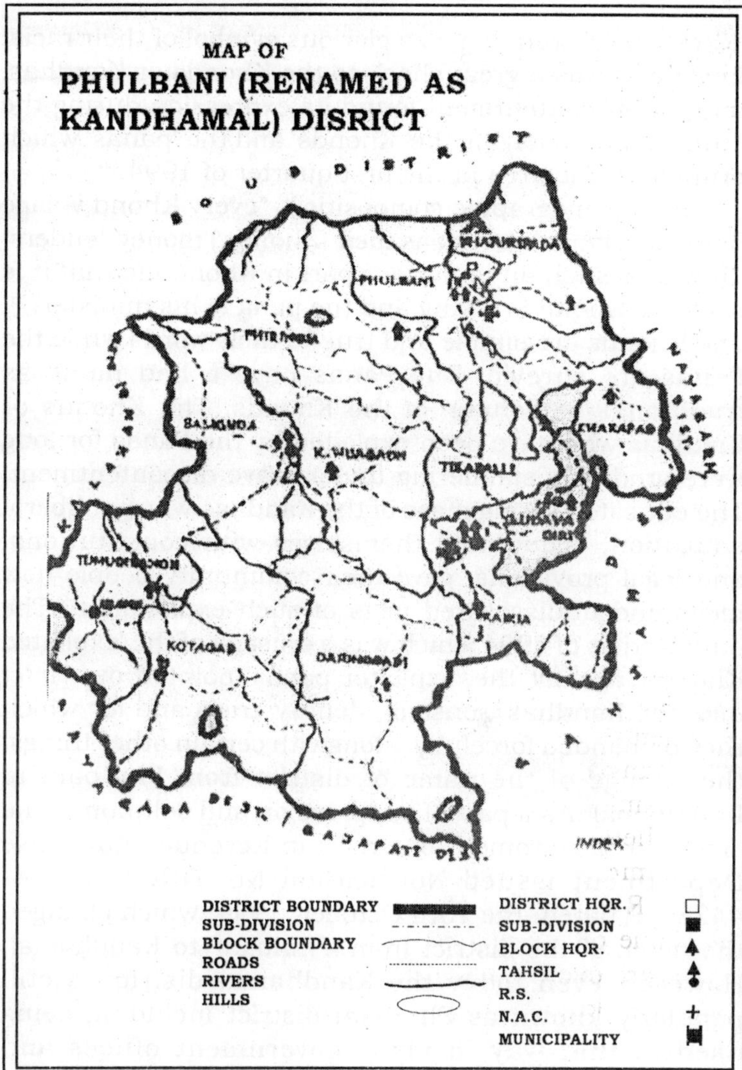
MAP OF
PHULBANI (RENAMED AS KANDHAMAL) DISRICT
PHULBANI
PHIRINGIA
BALIGUDA
K. NUAGAON
TIKABALI
CHAKAPAD
KOTAGAD
DARINGIBADI
RAIKIA
INDEX
DISTRICT BOUNDARY
SUB-DIVISION
BLOCK BOUNDARY
ROADS
RIVERS
HILLS
DISTRICT HQR.
SUB-DIVISION
BLOCK HQR.
TAHSIL
R.S.
N.A.C.
MUNICIPALITY

Fig. 2

'Khondmals' standing as a glorious symbol of their racial homeland was a great shock to the Khonds or Kandhas, and the discontentment found its expression during the ethnic crisis involving the 'Khonds' and the 'panas' which erupted in the area in the first quarter of 1994.[50]

As to demographic composition, "every Khond village has a few panas who act as their (Khonds') money-lenders. They play such an important part in Khond life that it is said 'the Khond is a king and the pana is his minister."[51] The Khonds are simple and true to their words while the Panas are shrewd. The Panas have a bad name as traditional 'exploiters' of the Khonds. The Khonds or Kandhas who have been exploited by the Panas for long were gradually simmering under grave discontentment. The educated young mass of the Kandhas who got liberal education, acquainted themselves with constitutional and legal provisions, gave their community people new ideas and undiscovered facts of such exploitation. The ethnic crisis of 1994 which was a crusade of the 'exploited Khonds' against the 'exploiter panas' pointed out, *inter alia*, the Kandhas' sense of identity crisis and for which they demanded forcefully, alongwith certain other things, the change of the name of district from Phulbani to Kandhamal. As a part of suppression and solution of the crisis the Government of Orissa in Revenue and Excise Department issued Notification No. DRC/136/94-44250/R dated, the 13th October, 1994, which changed the name of the district from 'Phulbani' to Kandhamal. However, even today the Kandhamal district is still popularly known as Phulbani district including being used in that way in many government offices and documents. Thus, for this research project Phulbani district means the same as Kandhamal district after having been divided and renamed. It will also refer to the undevided Phulbani or Boudh-Khondmals district wherever necessary.

Table 19

Phulbani District at a Glance

Sl. No.	Items	Area	Magnitude in Nos.
1.	Geographical Area	5,464.9 sq. kms	
2.	Sub-divisions		2
3.	Tehsils		4
4.	CD. Blocks		12
5.	Towns (with N.A.C)		2
6.	Police Stations		15
7.	Gram-Panchayats		144
8.	Villages:		2,515
	a) Inhabited		2,336
	b) Uninhabited		179
9.	Fire Stations		3
10.	Assembly Constituencies		3

Source: District Statistical Handbook, Kandhamal, Directorate of Economics and Statistics, Govt. of Orissa, Bhubaneswar, 1993

The district of Phulbani which covers an area of 5,464.9 square kilometres is bounded on the north by the district of Boudh, on the east by the district of Nayagarh, on the south-east by the district of Ganjam, on the south by the district of Gajapati, on the south-west by the district of Rayagada and on the west by the districts of Kalahandi and Bolangir.

The Phulbani district has 2 sub-divisions, i.e., Kandhamal (Phulbani) and Balliguda : 4 tehsils such as Phulbani, G. Udayagiri, Balliguda and Daringbadi. It has 12 community development Blocks, 2 UB towns—Phulbani and G.Udayagiri each having a Notified Area Council. It has 15 police stations, 144 Grampanchayats, 3 fire stations and 3 Assembly constituencies such as Phulbani (SC), Baliguda (ST) and G.Udayagiri (ST). The district has total 2,515 villages out of which 2,336 are inhabited and the rest 179 are uninhabited. Out of the total 1,21,459 households, only 1,20,690 are residential houses. Of the total district area, 29.24 sq. km is covered by the urban areas of the district where there are 7,619 households of which 7,549 are inhabited.

Table 20

Area, Number of Residential Houses, Households and Census Villages in Different Blocks/ Towns of Phulbani District as per 1991 Census

Sl. No.	Block/ Town	Date of Inception	Area in Sq. Km.	No. of Residential Houses	No. of House-holds	Number of villages		
						Inhabited	uninhabited	Total
1.	Balliguda	October, 1956	434.30	11,258	11,386	239	19	258
2.	Chakapad	April, 1957	244.45	8,050	8,087	138	18	156
3.	Daringbadi	April,1963	769.68	15,694	15,786	259	15	274
4.	G. Udayagiri	April, 1956	137.97	6,377	6,407	76	6	82
5.	Khajuripada	April,1958	372 49	9,352	9,416	237	11	248
6.	Kotagarh	April, 1961	323.60	7,465	7,484	142	5	147
7.	Nuagaon	October,1956	396.39	9.108	9,152	173	39	212
8.	Phiringia	October,1962	632.66	13,148	13,223	390	20	410
9.	Phulbani	October,1955	307.32	6,694	6,727	205	13	218
10.	Raikia	April, 1958	238.30	9,253	9,300	138	11	149
11.	Tikabali	April,1957	259.07	9,919	10,020	133	12	145
12.	Tumudibandha	April,1969	257.24	6,823	6,852	206	10	216
	URBAN							
1.	G. Udayagiri (NAC)	February, 1981	13.24	1,790	1,799			
2.	Phulbani (NAC)	February, 1963	16.00	5,759	5,820			
	*DISTRICT TOTAL		5,464.9	1,20,690	1,21,459	2,336	179	2,5 1 5

Source : District Statistical Handbook, Kandhamal - 1993, Directorate of Economics and Statistics, Govt. Of Orissa, Bhubaneswar.

* The District total is not additive.

Out of the total population of 5,46,281 for the district 2,73,234 are males and 2,73,047 are females. Of the total population 35,662 persons -18,994 males and 16,668 females live in Urban areas. The rest, i.e., 5,10,619 constituting 2,54,240 males and 2,56,379 females live in rural areas. Similarly out of the total 2,81,386 scheduled tribe population for the district 1,38,808 are males and 1,42,578 are females who belong to 43 tribes found in the district out of the 62 tribes found in the state. A total of 4,462 scheduled tribe persons covering 2,327 males and 2,535 females live in the urban areas of the district. The scheduled tribe population forms 51.51 per cent of the total population of the district. It proves that the district is predominantly tribal.

Of the 62 tribes notified as scheduled tribes for the state as many as 43 tribes are found in this district. Of these, five tribes, viz., *Gond, Kandha, Saora, Kandha-Gauda,* and *Kotia* are numerically important. These five tribes together constituted 96.21 per cent of the total tribal population of the district in 1971. Kandhas alone constituted 89.11 percen! of the total tribal population. As per 1971 Census the tribal population of the district accounted for 40.31 per cent of the total population of the district as against 23.11 per cent in Orissa state and 6.94 per cent in India as a whole. In 1981 the growth rate of scheduled tribe population came down to 38.94 from 40.31 in 1971 but again it rose upto 51.51 in 1991. The 1991 figure refers to separate and divided Phulbani district. Due to separation of Boudh from the district the scheduled tribe percentage rose to this level.

Looking at the population growth of the district from 1901 census to 1991 census, it is found that the Decadal growth rate shows a fluctuating trend over the censuses. Except over the decade (1911-21) where the growth rate is in the negative direction showing — 0.45, the growth rates at the rest other decades have a positive trend. However, almost alternatively the decadal growth rate goes up and down. It has also gone down very sharply

Table 21

Block/town wise Total Population and S.T. Population of Phulbani District as per 1991 Census.

Sl. No.	*Block/Town*	*Total Population*			*S.T. Population*			*% of S.T. Population to Total Population*
		Males	*Female*	*Total*	*Males*	*Female*	*Total*	
1.	Baliguda	26,536	25,873	52,409	11,870	11,907	23,777	45.37
2.	Chakapad	18,012	18,156	36,168	8,531	8,551	17,082	47.23
3.	Daringbadi	36,010	37,678	73,688	20,572	22,000	42,572	57.77
4.	G. Udayagiri	13,436	13,826	27,262	8,566	8,880	17,446	63.99
5.	Khajuripada	21,363	21,199	42,562	10,912	10,931	21,843	51.32
6.	Kotagarh	16,222	16,091	32,313	9,128	9,173	18,301	56.64
7.	Nuagaon	20,081	20,178	40,259	10,181	10,407	20,588	51.14
8.	Phirigia	29,665	30,015	59,680	17,190	17,820	35,010	58.66
9.	Phulbani	15,448	15,361	30,809	8,538	8,601	17,139	55.63
10.	Raikia	20,863	21,331	42,194	10,981	11,617	22,598	53.56
11.	Tikabali	21,414	21,501	42,915	11,512	11,814	23,326	54.35
12.	Tumudibandha	15,190	15,170	30,360	8,500	8,742	17,242	56.79
	Urban							
1.	G. Udayagiri (NAC)	4,257	4,251	8,508	883	984	1,867	21.94
2.	Phulbani (NAC)	14,737	12,417	27,154	1,444	1,551	2,595	9.56
	District Total	273,234	273,047	546,281	138,808	142,578	281,386	51.51

Source: District Statistical Handbook, Kandhamal - 1993, Directorate of Economics and Statistics, Govt. of Orissa, Bhubaneswar.

from +9.33 in 1931- 41 to only + 1.52 in 1941-51. For the 1981-91 decade the growth rate is 19.70 which is as nearly as the state's growth rate of 20.06. But the sex ratio of the district over the censuses shows a very peculiar trend of almost constantly going downwards particularly after 1931. From 1901 to 1931 it had an increasing trend of 1013 females per 1000 males in 1901 to 1022 females per 1000 males in 1931. But from 1941 till 1991 it has gone down gradually. While in 1941 it was 1021 females for 1000 males, it was 1015 in 1951, 1012 in 1961, 1004 in 1971, 1000 in 1981 and 998 in 1991, in all cases the constant is 1000 males. It shows that while for a quite good period the females outnumbered the males.

Table 22

Growth of Population in Phulbani District from Census to Census

Census Year	*Males*	*Females*	*Total*	*Decadal Variation*	*% of Decadal Variation*	*Sex Ratio of Females per 1000 Males*
1901	165,955	168,081	334,036	– —	– —	1013
1911	187,789	190,250	378,039	+ 44,003	+ 13.17	1013
1921	186,534	189,821	376,355	– 1,684	– 0.45	1018
1931	203,618	208,051	411,669	+ 35,314	+ 9.38	1022
1941	222,690	227,369	450,059	+ 38,390	+ 9.33	1021
1951	226,733	230,157	456,895	+ 6,836	+ 1 52	1015
1961	255,685	258,742	514,427	+ 57,532	+ 12.59	1012
1971	310,233	311,442	621,675	+ 107,248	+ 20.85	1004
1981	358,862	358,418	717,280	+ 95,605	+ 14.65	1000
1991	429,809	428,744	858,553	+ 141,273	+ 19.70	998

Source : District Gazetteer, Boudh - Khondmals, 1983 and Census of India Reports, 1981 & 1991.

Literacy and Education

As per 1991 census, the total number of literates of the district is 1,64,877 which includes 1,20,968 males and 43,909 females. In urban areas of the district there are 23,366 literate persons including 14,344 males and 9,022 females. Excluding the population in the age group of 0-6 yrs,the percentage of literacy in the district is 37.23. In the said age group the male literacy is 54.68

and the female literacy is 19.82. This shows that the females are very poor in literacy not only in comparison with the males of the district, but also as compared to the total females of the state who account for a literacy rate of 34.68. The male literacy of the district, though lower than the state's corresponding percentage of 63.09 is competing. However, the total literacy percentage of the district which is 37.23 is also lower than the percentage of literacy of state's total population, i.e., 49.09.

Table 23

Block/Town Wise Literacy in Phulbani District As per 1991 Census

Sl. No.	Block/ Town	Total No. of Literates			Percentage of Literacy*		
		Males	Females	Total	Males	Females	Total
1.	Baliguda	10,116	3,595	13,711	46.98	17.36	32.46
2.	Chakapad	8,950	2,760	11,710	60.09	18.10	38.84
3.	Daringbadi	11,889	3,873	15,762	43.43	13.28	27.87
4.	G. Udayagiri	7,252	3,242	10,494	66.15	28.22	46.74
5.	Khajuripada	11,495	3,212	14,707	64.72	18.12	41.45
6.	Kotagarh	3,961	1,087	5,048	31.54	8.69	20.14
7.	Nuagaon	9,065	2,860	11,925	56.19	17.53	36.75
8.	Phiringia	10,824	2,580	13,404	44.53	10.50	27.42
9.	Phulbani	7,834	2,071	9,905	61.58	16.31	38.96
10.	Raikia	10,634	4,604	15,238	62.30	26.50	44.24
11.	Tikabali	10.623	3,952	14,575	60.45	22.32	41.3I
12.	Tumudibandha	3,981	1,051	5,032	32.87	8.75	20.86
	URBAN						
1.	G. Udayagiri (NAC)	3,132	2,330	5,462	87.53	64.90	76.20
2.	Phulbani (NAC)	11,212	6,692	17,904	88.56	63.93	77.41
Distrcit Total		1,20,968	43,909	1,64,877	54.68	19.82	37.23

Source : District Statistical Handbook, Kandhamal - 1993, Directorate of Econimics and Statistics, Govt. of Orissa, Bhubaneswar.

* Excludes population in the age group of 0-6 years.

As to educational infrastructure and opportunities of the district, it is found that during 1992-93 there were total 1,315 primary schools having enrolled 70,168 students of which (upto standard V) 41,241 were boys

Table 24
Education in Phulbani District During 1992-93

Sl. No.	School/ College	Rural (R) Urban(U) Total (T)	No. of Schools/ Colleges	Number of Teachers				Number of Students				
				Male		Female						
				Trained	Untrained	Trained	Untra-ined	Boys	Girls	Total	SC	ST
1	2	3	4	5	6	7	8	9	10	11	12	13
1	Primary School	R	1292	1818	119	376	36	41,241	28,927	70,168	18,051	36,953
		U	23	31	...	52	...	NA	NA	NA	NA	NA
		T	1315	1,849	119	428	36	41,241	28,927	70,168	18.051	36,953
2.	Middle School	R	208	674	47	130	18	12,463	6,307	18,770	5,846	8,764
		U	10	38	...	38	01	1,458	1,350	2,808	652	571
		T	218	712	47	168	19	13,921	7,657	21,578	6,498	9.335
3 .	Secondary School	R	60	477	51	103	08	8,220	3,670	11,890	3,161	5,350
		U	06	51	01	55	02	1,606	1,424	3,030	646	823
		T	66	528	52	158	10	9,826	5,094	14,920	3,807	6,173
		NUMBER OF TEACHERS										
4	General College	R	04	35(M)	03(W)	38(T)		1,048	275	1,323	249	369
		U	04	89(M)	16(W)	105{T)		2,003	767	2,770	448	604
		T	08	124(M)	19(W)	143(T)		3,051	1,042	4,093	697	973

Source : District Statistical Hand Book, Kandhamal, Directorate of Economics & Statistics, Orissa. Bbubaneswar, 1993.

Table 25

Work Participation in Phulbani District as Per 1991 Census

Sl. No,	Block/Town	Total Workers Male	Total Workers Female	Total Workers Total	Main Workers Male	Main Workers Female	Main Workers Total	Marginal Workers Male	Marginal Workers Female	Marginal Workers Total	Non-Workers Male	Non-Workers Female	Total
1	2	3	4	5	6	7	8	9	10	11	12	13	14
1.	Balliguda	15,077	9,461	24,538	14,303	5,806	20,109	774	3,655	4,429	11,459	16,412	27,871
2.	Chakapad	10,466	7,067	17,533	10,279	4,909	15,188	187	2,158	2,345	7,546	11,089	18,635
3.	Daringbadi	19,653	16,293	35,946	19,260	9,432	28,692	393	6,861	7,254	16,357	21,385	37,742
4.	G. Udayagiri	7,237	6,569	13,806	6,990	3,975	10,965	247	2,594	2,841	6,199	7,257	13,456
5.	Khajuripada	11,918	8,659	20,577	11,306	5,219	16,525	612	3,440	4,052	9,445	12,540	21,985
6.	Kotagarh	9,365	6,554	15,919	8,921	3,759	12,680	444	2,795	3,239	6,857	9,537	16,394
7.	Nuagaon	11,512	9,258	20,770	11,194	5,718	16,912	318	3,540	3,858	8,569	10,920	19,489
8.	Phiringia	8,798	11,195	28,548	16,592	5,546	22,138	761	5,649	6,410	12,312	18,820	31,132
9.	Phulbani	8,798	6,655	15,453	8,603	4,940	13,543	195	1,715	1,910	6,650	8,706	15,356
10.	Raikia	11,732	9,698	21,430	11,248	5,574	16,822	484	4,124	4,608	9,131	11,633	20,764
11.	Tikabali	12,022	9,498	21,520	11,797	5,515	17,312	225	3,983	4,208	9,392	12,003	21,395
12.	Tumudibadha	8,864	5,310	14,174	8,533	3,365	11,898	331	1,945	2,276	6,326	9,860	16,186
	URBAN												
1.	G.Udayagiri (NAC)	1,916	556	2,472	1,827	373	2200	89	183	272	2,341	3,695	6,036
2.	Phulbani (NAC)	6,810	1,380	8,190	6,740	1,222	7,962	70	158	228	7,927	11,037	18,964
	District	1,52,723	1,08,153	2,60,876	1,47,593	65,353	2,12,946	5,130	42,800	47,930	1,20,511	1,64,894	2,85,405

Source : District Statistical Hand Book, Kandhamal, Directorate of Economics & Statistics, Orissa, Bhubaneswar, 1993.

Table 26

Classification of Main Workers in Different Blocks/Towns of Phulbani District as per 1991 Census

Sl. No.	Block/Town	Cultivators	Agricultural labourers	Live Stock, forestry fishing, hunting, planting and allied activities	Mining and quarring	Manufacturing, processing, servicing and repairs: Household Industries	Manufacturing, processing, servicing and repairs: other than Household Industries	Construction	Trade and commerece	Transport Storage and communications	Other services
1	2	3	4	5	6	7	8	9	10	11	12
1.	Balliguda	9,004	7,215	362	1	617	185	162	804	113	1,646
2.	Chakapad	6,845	6,496	187	1	363	86	28	330	48	804
3.	Darigbadi	14,097	11,761	126	1	282	151	71	713	103	1,387
4.	G.Udayagiri	5,215	3,191	171	...	504	103	70	497	71	1,143
5.	Khajuripada	7,688	6,842	205	5	252	60	46	214	56	1,157
6.	Kotagarh	6,510	5,154	86	...	105	40	24	220	31	510
7	Nuagaon	8,768	6,118	211	5	524	73	32	332	45	804
8.	Phiringia	12,754	6,813	227	2	514	194	27	423	58	1,126
9.	Phulbani	7,949	3,899	223	8	249	84	54	251	48	778
10	Raikia	8,673	4,975	341	2	575	160	81	605	106	1,304
11.	Tikabali	7,771	6,650	254	2	454	153	86	698	82	1,162
12.	Tumudibandha	6,952	3,536	149	24	159	50	35	212	44	737
	URBAN										
1.	G.Udayagiri (NAC)	262	360	190	1	40	100	28	430	89	700
2.	Phulbani (NAC)	441	717	553	11	93	479	292	1,365	430	3,581
District Total		1,02,929	73,727	3,285	63	4,731	1,918	1,036	7,094	1,324	16,839

Source : District Statistical Hand Book, Kandhamal, Directorate of Economics & Statistics, Orissa, Bhubaneswar, 1993,

and 28,927 were girls. Among these 36,953 students belonged to scheduled tribe communities. The total number of teachers in such schools was 2432 including 464 females. At the middle school stage (standard VI & VII) there were 218 schools with 946 teachers including 187 females. The total enrolment of students was 21,578 with 13,921 boys and 7,657 girls. Among them 9,335 were scheduled tribes. For secondary school education (standard VIII to X) there were 66 schools with 748 teachers including 168 females. The total enrolment of students in these schools was 14,920 with 9,826 boys and 5,094 girls. 6,173 of these students were scheduled tribes. At the college level from standard XI to Post Graduation, there were only 8 colleges for General Educalion. There were 143 teachers for total 4,093 students including 3051 boys and 1042 girls enrolled for college education. Out of these students 973 belonged to the scheduled tribes. It is seen that while district's education upto secondary school stage is primarily rural-based, college education is dominantly urban-centred. By July 1997, there were altogether 115 tribal schools - 6 residential Ashram schools (Class I to VII), 8 residential sevashrams (Class I to V), 86 non-residential sevashrams and 15 high schools exclusively for tribal students of the district.

Work Participation

According to 1991 census figures 2,60,876 persons — 1,52,723 males and 1,08,153 females constitute the total workers of the district. Out of them 2,12,946 persons — 1,47,593 males and 65,353 females are main workers; 47,930 persons — 5,130 males and 42,800 females are marginal workers; 2,85,405 persons — 1,20,511 males and 1,64,894 females are non-workers. Thus, the total non-workers are more than the total workers of the district. Men outnumber the women as total workers. But the reverse is the position in case of non-workers. As main workers, the numerical strength of males is more than double of the females. But as marginal workers the females have a numerical strength of more than eight times of the males.

The main workers of the district as classified into different sectors show a trend of heavy concentration as cultivators. The cultivators alone claim a share of nearly half of the total main workers. Next come the agricultural labourers. The cultivators and the agricultural labourers together constitute more than 80 per cent of the total main workers. Thus, the district proves to be primarily agriculture-based. Main workforce in other sectors seem to be very insignificant. Mining and quarrying is almost absent. The third category of main workers are in trade and commerce who constitute a workforce of 7,094 persons.

Land, Climate, Forest, Irrigation, Agriculture and Livestock.

As to the nature of land in the district, it is "highly uneven and undulating comprising hill slopes, plateaus, valleys and plains with varying slopes. The agricultural land in the district has been classified into four broad divisions depending on the gradients of the land *(i) Att, (ii) Mal, (iii) Berna and (iv) Bahal.* Berna and Bahal are low-lying lands which are mostly used for paddy cultivation. Mal (locally called Majhikhandia) is medium land and Att (locally called *Dhepaketa* or *Dhipa*) is high land. Att and Mal are suitable for light crops like pulses, millets, oil-seeds and root crops. In the hilly areas of Khondmals, Balligurha and G. Udayagiri tahasils, the high lands lying on the hill tops or on the slopes of the hills are known as *Dongar* and are used for cultivation of dry crops like turmeric, oil-seeds (niger, castor, mustard, gingelly, etc.) and minor millets like maize, bajra, ragi, etc. The low-lying land in the valley between two hill ranges are called *Jhola* where water is available for wet crops like paddy. Jhola lands are the best cultivable lands in these areas."[52]

One can find that "the district has mostly red soil which is generally deficient in nitrogen, humus and lime.

The soil in Khondmals, Balliguda and G.Udayagiri Tahasils is sandy loam and of red laterite type which is poor in organic contents. The red soil favours growth of maize, jawar, bajra, ragi, turmeric, arhar, niger, groundnuts, early paddy and fruits like guava, mango, papaya, lemon and pineapple. In laterite soils, jowar, maize, paddy niger and fruit plants like mango, jack-fruit, guava, pine-apple, papaya and sapeta are grown."[53]

The Annual normal rainfall of the district is 1597.1 mm. But in 1993 the actual rainfall was 1271.0mm.; the highest being 323.0 mm in July and the lowest being 0.8 mm in March of that year. The highest rainfall recorded at any place in the year was 533.8 mm in July at Balliguda and the lowest was 4.0 mm recorded in March at Daringbadi. Block-wise the total highest rainfall recorded was 1,807.0 mm at Phiringia and the lowest was 777.0 mm at Khajuripada. In 1993 the highest temperature recorded at Phulbani town was 45.6 degree centigrade in May and the lowest was 2.0 degree centigrade in December of that year there.

As on 1.4.1993 the district had a total forest cover of 4534.32 square kilometres. The total forest of the district constituted nearly 83 per cent of the total area of the district. This shows that the district accounts for an extensive forest cover with little land left for habitation and agriculture. This is another reason for less number of population in the district. Out of the total forest area, 2010.06 sq.kms. are reserved forest, 1832.45 sq.km. are demarcated protected forest, 689.98 sq.km. are undemarcated protected forest and 1.99 sq.km as unclassified forest.

The Irrigation Potential in the district can be divided into four categories such as (1) major and medium irrigation projects, (2) minor irrigation projects (flow), (3) lift irrigation projects and other sources. The total irrigation potential for the district in Kharif is 20,573 hectares and for Rabi is 11,549 hectares accounting for a gross total of 3,212 hectares. The total irrigation coverage by major and medium irrigation projects is 2,866 hectares, 6,465 hectares by minor irrigation projects, 4,416 hectares by lift irrigation projects and 18,375 hectares by other sources. The first three sources which are modern and large-scale irrigation systems together cover only 13,747 hectares of land. This is far less than the irrigation coverage of 18,375 by the other sources. The latter constitutes around 57 per cent of the total irrigation potential. Thus, it is seen that the irrigation potential in the district is still traditional and not modernised in a big way.

For agriculture purpose a very limited land is available in the district. After excluding the Urban Areas, Reserve forests, Protected forests. Project Area Hill Blocks, villages submerged under river, an estimate was prepared for land utilisation pattern in the district for the year 1992-93 which is shown as below:

Table 27

Land Utilisation Pattern in Phulbani District During 1992-93

Sl. No.	*Land Pattern*	*Area in Hectares*
1.	Forest Area	1,42,497
2.	Miscellaneous tree crops and groves not included in the net area sown	1,063
3.	Permanent pasture and other grazing lands	9,164
4.	Culturable Waste	13,864
5.	Land put to non-agricultural uses	15,287
6.	Barren and un-cultivable land	1,31,258
7.	Current follows	23,878
8.	Other follows	17,307
9.	Net area sown	82,852

Source : District Statistical Handbook, Kandhamal - 1993, Directorate of Econimics and Statistics, Govt. of Orissa, Bhubaneswar.

Taking a look into the number and area of operational holdings in the undivided Phulbani district for the year 1990-91, it is found that out of the total 1,22,578 number of operational holdings 1,21,735 are in rural areas and only 843 are in urban areas. The total number of marginal operational holdings of 65,233, each having an operational holding not exceeding 1 (one) hectare constitute nearly 53 per cent of the total number of operational holdings. The total number of marginal and

Table 28

Classwise Number and Area of Operational Holdings of Phulbani District for the Year 1990-91

Sl. No.	Class in Hectares	All Social Groups						Scheduled Tribes					
		Number			Area			Number			Area		
		Rural	Urban	Total	Rural	Urban	Total	Rural	Urban	Total	Rural	Urban	Total
1	2	3	4	5	6	7	8	9	10	11	12	13	14
1.	Below.0.02	635	4	639	10	NA	10	91	...	91	2	...	2
2.	0.02-0.5	32,790	452	33,242	9,006	103	9,109	11,957	90	12,047	3,505	37	3,542
3.	0.5-1.0	31,212	140	31,352	23,004	102	23,106	14,230	63	14,293	10,498	48	10,546
	Marginal (1+2+3)	64,637	596	65,233	32,020	205	32,225	26,278	153	26,431	14,005	85	14,090
4.	1.0-2.0 (Small)	31,293	136	31,429	44,343	181	44,524	16,317	84	16,401	23,375	109	23,484
5.	2.0-3.0	14,659	47	14,706	34,852	116	34,968	7,518	26	7.544	17,769	65	18,034
6.	3.0-4.0	4,665	24	4,689	15,933	78	16,011	2,453	9	2,462	8,370	31	8,401
	Semi medium (5 + 6)	19,324	71	19,395	50,785	194	50,979	9,971	35	10,006	26,339	96	26,435
7.	4.0-5.0	3,015	7	3,022	13,118	35	13,153	1,687	4	1,691	7,347	14	7,361
8.	5.0-7.5	2,071	28	2,099	12,301	147	12,448	987	4	991	5,719	20	5,739
9.	7.5-10.0	877	2	879	7,308	11	7,319	404	...	404	3,386	...	3,386
	Medium (7+8+9)	5,963	37	6,000	32,727	193	32,920	3,078	8	3,086	16,452	34	16,486
10.	10.0-20.0	442	3	445	5,695	41	5,736	172	...	172	2,205	...	2,205
11.	20.0 & above	76	...	76	2,179	...	2,179	15	...	15	342	...	342
	Large(10+11)	518	3	521	7,874	41	7,915	187	...	187	2,547	...	2,547
	Total	1,21,735	843	1,22,578	1,67,749	814	1,68,563	55,831	280	56,111	82,718	324	83,042

Source: District Statistical Handbook, Kandhamal - 1993. Directorate of Econimics and Statistics, Govt. of Orissa, Bhubaneswar..

small operational holdings together numbering 96,662 constitute nearly 80 per cent of the total number of operational holdings of the district. In terms of area, the marginal farmers occupy 32,225 hectares of operational holding which is only about 19 per cent of the total area of operational holding for the district, i.e., 1,68,563. Thus, 53 per cent of total operational holdings claim only 19 per cent of total area of operational holding. Otherwise, the total number of marginal and small operational holdings taken together, which constitute nearly 80 per cent of the total number of operational holdings, claim only around 45 per cent of the total area of operational holding. This proves that majority of the people in the district are poor so far as operational holding is concerned.

Similarly, the total number of operational holdings belonging to the scheduled tribes was 56,111 which constituted more than 50 per cent of the total operational holdings of the state. This shows that tribals have predominantly taken to agriculture. But the total number of marginal and small operational holdings of the scheduled tribes which together constitute about 77 per cent of the total operational holdings claim only about 45 per cent of the total area of operational holdings. This proves that the scheduled tribes of the district are very poor in this regard.

In agriculture, "the principal crops grown in the district are paddy, ragi, maize, wheat, minor millets (jowar, bajra, kudo, gurji, etc.) and pulses like arhar, *Mung* and black gram. Among the commercial crops turmeric, potato, tobacco, fruits and vegetables are important. Turmeric is the chief commercial crop; the district is noted for turmeric cultivation in the state The Khonds of Khondmals, Baligurha and G. Udayagiri tahsils widely cultivate turmeric which is their hereditary crop. The district is also noted for some oil-seeds like niger, mustard, ginjelly, groundnut and castor."[54]

During 1993-94 the total production of cleaned rice in the district was 6,15,422 quintals. The total area under paddy cultivation during the year was 52,648 hectares and the yield rate of dry paddy with husk during the said period was 17.71 quintals per hectare. Similarly, from 4,399 hectares of Maize cultivation, the total production was 41,416 quintals at the yield rate of 941 kg/hect. From 4,860 hectares of mustard cultivation, the total production was 8,741 quintals at the yield rate of 180 kg/hect. From 1796 hectares of horsegram cultivation, the total production was 6,204 quintals at the yield rate of 345 kg/hect. From 420 hectares of potato cultivation, the total production was 26,546 quintals at the yield rate of 6,321 kg/hect. From 359 hectares of groundnut cultivation, the total production was 2,248 quintals at the yield rate of 626 kg/hect. The other important crops were ragi, greengram, blackgram, til.

As per livestock census of 1991, there were in the district 3,03,199 cattle population out of which 3,01,320 were of indigenous breed. Besides this, there were 52,705 buffaloes, 5,124 sheep, 1,69,891 goats, 42,049 pigs. As to poultry population, there were 4,35,526 fowls and 670 ducks. During 1992-93 the district had produced 346 metric tons of fresh water fish.

Table 29

Cultivation Area, Yield Rate and Production of Different Crops in Phulbani District During 1993-94

Sl. No.	*Name of the Crops*	*Area under Cultivation (in hectares)*	*Yield in (Kilograms per Hectare)*	*Total Production (in quintals)*
1.	Paddy	52,648	1771	6,15,422
2.	Maize	4,399	941	41,416
3.	Mustard	4,860	180	8,741
4.	Horsegram	1,796	345	6,204
5.	Potato	420	6,321	26,546
6.	Groundnut	359	626	2,248
7.	Til	486	184	894
8.	Blackgram	206	189	390
9.	Green gram	188	122	229
10.	Ragi	122	484	591
11.	Sugar cane	04	52,667	2,107

Source : District Statistical Handbook, Kandhamal, Directorate of Economics and Statistics, Govt. of Orissa, Bhubaneswar, 1993.

Economic Trends

As on 31 3.1993 there were in the district 24 agricultural credit cooperative societies with membership of 84,719 and working capital of Rs.392.50 lakhs; 10 non-agricultural credit co-operative societies with 1,796 members and working capital of Rs. 294.52 lakhs. Also upto the said date there were 3 wholesale and 14 primary consumer cooperative stores with membership of 2,830 and 44,128 respectively.

During the year 1992-93 there were in the district only 5 industries with 527 employees, Rs. 19,56,000 fixed capital and Rs. 6,67,000 working capital. Besides that, there were 21 small scale industries with 181 employees and a capital investment of Rs. 2,585,000. This shows that the district is industrially too backward.

During 1993-94, the collection of land revenue in the district was Rs.3,020,000 which was 115 per cent of the amount demanded for the period, i.e., Rs.2,627,000. This shows the honesty of the people as tax payers.

During 1992-93 the total number of documents registered was 1604 and the value of the movable and immovable properties transferred was Rs. 138.22 lakhs.

As on March 1993, there were in the undivided Phulbani district a total number of 70 branches of various banks including 24 branches of regional rural banks and 46 other scheduled commercial banks. Together they employed 570 employees and accounted for Rs.5,389 lakhs of deposits and created credit of Rs.2,844 lakhs with credit deposit ratio of 52.77.

By the end of the year 1993 the total number of persons (unemployed) placed in the live register was 16,044 which included 2,309 women and 3,225 scheduled tribes. Out of the total number, 6,216 were under-matriculates. However, the placement during the year was only 233 including 45 women and 34 scheduled tribes. This shows the grave unemployment problem in the district.

During the year 1992-93 the average daily wage in rural areas of the district for a skilled labour ranged between Rs. 37.64 and Rs.45.63. For an unskilled rural male labourer in agricultural or other works the average wage ranged between Rs.19.48 and Rs. 20.07 while for the same work it ranged between Rs. 13.66 and Rs. 13.82 for a woman labourer. For a child labourer in the same unskilled work, the average daily wage varied from Rs. 14.86 to Rs. 15.06. This proves that the wage pattern in the district is not only low but also discriminatory.

Under public distribution system, there were 465 retail shops — 446 in rural areas and 19 in urban areas of the district as on 31.3.1993. For distribution of essential commodities 18,509.0 metric tons rice, 1,922.6 metric tons wheat, 2,084.0 metric tons sugar, 3,093 kilo-liters Kerosene oil and 53,175 Kg. imported edible oil was allotted for the district during the year 1992.-93.

Under poverty alleviation programme of Integrated Rural Development Programme (IRDP), a total number of 4,145 beneficiaries covering 1,226 in primary sector 1,813 in secondary sector and 1,106 in tertiary sector of the district were benefited during the year 1992-93. These beneficiaries include 1,830 scheduled tribes and 1,812 women.

Table 30

Blockswise Rural Families Below Poverty Line Having Annual Income of Rs. 11,000 in Phulbani District as Per 1992 Survey

Sl. No.	*Name of Block*	*Total Rural Families*	*Income groupwise number of rural families below poverty line*				
			Below Rs. 4000	*Rs. 4001 to Rs. 6000*	*Rs. 6001 to Rs. 8500*	*Rs. 8501 to Rs.11000*	*Total*
1	Balliguda	10,453	2,607	4,948	1,272	357	9,184
2	Chakapad	7,239	3,310	3,080	721	128	7,239
3	Daringbadi	14,813	4,755	6,354	2,293	894	14,296
4	G. Udayagiri	6,261	4,308	1,086	149	87	5,630
5	Khajuripada	2,262	5,265	1,931	823	256	8,275
6	Kotagarh	6,983	4,448	1,582	325	75	6,430
7	Nuagaon	9,476	3,395	3,944	954	406	8,699
8	Phiringia	12,991	6,107	4,079	1,778	513	12,477
9	Phulbani	6,158	3,369	1,533	747	344	5,993
10	Raikia	9,275	1,802	3,078	2,746	788	8,414

11	Tikabali	9,315	3,160	3,702	1,099	242	8,203
12	Tumudiban-dha	6,037	3,180	1,699	725	301	5,875
	District Total	1,08,263	45,706	36,986	13,632	4,391	1,00,715

Source : District Statistical Handbook, Kandhamal, Directorate of Economics and Statistics, Govt. of Orissa, Bhubaneswar, 1993.

As per 1992 Survey out of total 1,08,263 rural families of the district as many as 1,00,715 families constituting around 92 per cent of the total rural families of the district were below poverty line, i.e., Annual income range of Rs. 11,000 or less per family. The survey has pointed out that all the 7,239 families in Chakapad block are below the poverty line. Thus, there is 100 per cent poverty in the Block. Besides, about 82 per cent of the total families below poverty line have an annual income not exceeding Rs. 6,000 per family. This shows the abject poverty of the people in the district.

Health Sector

During 1992-93 in the Allopathic wing there were 9 Hospitals, 6 Dispensaries, 12 Primary Health Centres, 1 Community Health Centre, 17 Additional Primary Health Centres, 1 Medical Aid Centre, 3 Subsidiary Health Centre, 2 Mobile Health units in the district with 396 beds and a treatment report of 72,447 indoor and 8,38,448 outdoor patients. In the Homeopathic wing 8 Dispensaries with 5 doctors had treated around 87,000 patients. In the Ayurvedic wing 11 Dispensaries with 6 Doctors (Kaviraj) had treated around 70,000 patients. During 1993-94 the total number of births and deaths registered were 11,926 and 2,718 respectively. The latter figure includes 556 infant deaths.

Power, Transport and Communication

Upto the year 1993-94 as many as 940 villages of the district constituting 40.2 per cent of total villages of the district were electrified. As on 31.3.1994 a total number of 850 Lift Irrigation Points were energised. During 1992-

93 the total electricity consumption in the undivided Phulbani district was 39.683 million units out of which 6.610 million units were for industrial purposes, 11.035 million units for Agriculture and Irrigation purposes, 14.887 million units for Domestic purposes and 5.739 million units for commercial purposes.

Upto the year 1993-94, there were in the district 5,609.4 k.m. length of Gram Panchayat roads, 340.5 km. length of state highways, 173.1 km. length of major district roads, 62.8 Km length of other district roads, 90.5 Km (upto 1992-93) length of Municipal roads and 324.1 Km (1991-92) length of forest roads. Upto 31.3.1993 the total number of registered vehicles in the district was 2,764 out of which only 1,781 were on road.

As on 31.3.1993, the district had a total number of 262 post officies with 31 sub-post offices, 22 public call offices and 1,259 working telephone connections.

Police, Crime and Judiciary

In the undivided Phubani district as on 31.12.1993 there were 1 sub-divisional police office, 3 police circles, 21 police stations, 11 outposts, 2 town outposts and 5 Beat houses, 351 Armed Police Reserve force and 503 unarmed police force. During the year 1993, there were 1620 incidents of crime including 17 cases of death due to dowry and atrocity on women.

As on 31.12.1993 there were total 8 judges in the district. By the said date there remained pending 9,558 criminal cases after disposal of 4,165 such cases during the year 1992-93. Similarly, the number of civil cases by end of the year 1991-92 which remained pending was 471 after disposal of 604 such cases during the said year.

It may be said that the district of Phulbani is backward in many fields. Though it possesses abundant resources, human as well as material, they are underutilised. This district needs careful planning, dogged pursuit in implementation of plans and projects and a special care in financial front.

References

1. L. P. Vidyarthi, ; and B.K. Rai; *The Tribal Culture of India,* Concept Publishing Company, New Delhi, 1985, p.25.
2. A. L. Basham, ; *The Wonder that was India,* Rupa & Co., Calcutta, 1992, p. 199.
3. *Ibid.*
4. P. K . Bhowmick. ; *Adibasi,* Vol. XXIV, Nos. 3 & 4. 1984-85. Bhubaneswar p. 5.
5. B. Singh, ; *Adibasi,* Vol. XIV, .No. 4, January, 1973, pp. 2-10.
6. N. Patnaik, and P.S. Daspatnaik; *The Kondh of Orissa,* Tribal and Harijan Research -cum- Training Institute, Bhubaneswar, 1982, p.245.
7. T. Sanganna. ; *Adibasi,* No. 1, 1963-64, Bhubaneswar, p. 3.
8. K. S. Mathur. ; 'Tribe in India : A problem of identification and Integration' in *Tribal Situation in India* (Ed.), Vol. 13. S.K. Singh. Indian Institute of Advanced Study, Simla, 1972. p,459.
9. *Ibid.*
10. *Ibid.,* p. 458
11. N. K. Behura. ; 'Tribal Societies in Orissa' in *Tribes of Orissa,* Tribal & Harijan Welfare Department, Orissa, Bhubaneswar, 1990. p. 11,
12. *Primary Census (1991) Abstract for Scheduled Castes and Scheduled Tribes* (Paper - I of 1993), Series- I. Govt. of India, New Delhi, pp.6-9.
13. *Ibid.*
14. *Ibid.*
15. *Ibid.*
16. G. N. Satpathy, ; 'Orissa Tribes and their Homeland' in *Tribes of Orissa,* Tribal and Harijan Welfare Department, Govt. of Orissa. Bhubaneswar. 1990, pp. 1-9.
17. N. K. Behura, ; *Adibasi* (Special Issue), Vol. XXXII, No. 4. December, 1992, Bhubaneswar, p. 15.
18. *Ibid.,* p. 18.
19. *Ibid.*
20. *Ibid.*
21. *Ibid.* , pp. 18-19.
22. B. Singh, *loc. cit.,* No. 5
23. *Ibid.*
24. N. K. Behura, ; *loc. cit.,* No. 17, pp. 16-19.
25. As quoted in the *Report of the Committee on Special Multi-purpose Tribal Blocks (Elwin Committee Report),* Ministry of Home Affairs. Govt. of India. New Delhi, 1960, p. 13.
26. N. K. Behura, ; *loc.cit.,* No. 17, pp. 16-19
27. *Ibid.*
28. *Elwin Committee Report, op.cit.,* No. 25.
29. B. Mishra, ; *Adibasi* (Special issue). Vol. XXXII, No. 4, December, 1992, Bhubaneswar, pp.20-21.
30. P. R. Chandra, ; *Adibasi,* Vol. XII, Nos. 1-4, 1970-71, Bhubaneswar, p. 3.

31. B. Singh, ; *loc.cit.*m No. 5.
32. P. R. Chandra, ; *loc. cit.* p .5.
33. *The Constitution of India,* Ministry of Law, Justice and Company Affairs, Govt. Of India, New Delhi, 1991, p. 95.
34. *Ibid.*
35. *Ibid.*, p. 5.
36. *Ibid.*
37. *Ibid.*, p. 14.
38. *Ibid.*
39. *Ibid.*, p. 92.
40. *Ibid.*, p. 93.
41. *Ibid.*, p. 67.
42. *Ibid.*
43. *Ibid.*, p. 196.
44. *Ibid.*
45. B. Singh, ; *loc. cit.*, No. 5.
46. T. Sanganna, ; *Adibasi,* No.2, November, 1963, Bhubaneswar, p. 4.
47. Gazetteer of India-Orissa-Boudh-Khondmals, Department of Revenue, Govt. of Orissa, Bhubaneswar, 1983, p.2
48. *Ibid.*, p. 3.
49. Gazetteer of India-Orissa-Boudh-Khondmals , *op. cit.*, p. 2.
50. All India Radio Cuttack on 12. 06. 1994 Broadcast an hour-long programme named 'Dukhini Phulbani' (sorrowed Phulbani) from 7.30 P.M . to 8.30 P.M. in the network programme 'Aaji Sandhyare' (today evening). This programme dealt in details about this ethnic crisis with direct interviews of the parties concerned, the administrative authorities, the intelligentsia, the journalists and the public. Besides, the issue had come up as a major and important news item in the headlines of both National and Regional newspapers of the time.
51. Gazetteer of India-Orissa-Boudh-Khondmals, *op.cit.*, p. 1.
52. *Gazeeter of India* - Orissa - Boudh-Khondamals, *op. cit.*, p. 100.
53. *Ibid.*, p. 99.
54. *Ibid.*, p. 100.

2
The Urban Panorama

Genesis and Evolution

According to Encyclopaedia of the Social Sciences, "urbanisation is characterised by movements of people from small communities concerned chiefly or solely with agriculture to other communities, generally larger, whose activities are primarily centred in Government, trade, manufacture or allied interests. Although there were earlier eras, as for example, in Greece during the age of Pericles and during the later Roman Empire, when the movement of people to the cities presented serious social problems, the phenomenon has become specially important since the onset of the industrial revolution. Urbanisation depends largely on the extent to which industrial and mercantile products are divorced from agriculture."[1]

The time "when Paleolithic man moved from his cave into the shelters he constructed of boughs and leaves, he was making the first step towards urbanisation."[2] In fact, "man was a gregarious being. He sought the companionship of his fellowmen and devised group entertainment and sports. The stronghold of the village became an appropriate sanctuary for the altar of his deity. It provided a place for worship, a meeting place for assembly, and a centre for trade. The environment became popular, and urbanisation had begun"[3]. Gradually, "the village brought something new to the lives of primitive man. It introduced the necessity for mutual responsibility and cooperation. There were various interests common to all the inhabitants, and they were merged into a form of society, a social and political organisation"[4].

In modern times the origin and growth of towns and cities have been seen differently by the scientific socialists or the modern communists. Basing on the economic interpretation of history and society, Karl Marx and Frederick Engels have written thus : "The bourgeoisie has subjected the country to the rule of the towns. It has created enormous cities, has greatly increased the urban population as compared with the rural, and has thus rescued a considerable part of the population from the idiocy of rural life."[5]

In this regard Kingsley Davis observes that, "the great impetus to the development of cities came with the industrial revolution. The application of mechanical power to textile and metal industries in the latter part of the eighteenth and early part of the nineteenth centuries enormously increased the economic surplus available for the support of urban populations. The new power could best be utilised with large machines and large plants; hence the factory with its requirement of numerous workers created the factory town and factory city. At the same time the agriculture system, stimulated by a rising urban market, constantly improved its techniques. And the application of mechanical power to water and land transportation enabled the agricultural produce to reach the cities quickly and cheaply. Improved transportation also facilitated the circulation of people and information. The introduction of the power press and machine manufacture of paper made possible an enormous increase in printed matter, thus facilitating technical education, scientific progress, and further innovation in all fields. The development of canning and refrigeration, of telegraph, telephone, and radio; of electric railways, automobiles, and airplanes— these and countless other inventions enormously increased the number and potential size of cities. Everywhere the urban population grew faster than the rural; everywhere the city increasingly set the pattern of life, becoming the chief diffusion centre as well as the main offspring of the new mechanical era."[6]

About growth of cities in Europe, Nehru writes, " the age of faith declined, and with it the building of churches and cathedrals. Men's thoughts turned in other directions, to their business and trade, to their civic life. Instead of cathedrals, city halls began to be built. So we find from the beginning of the fifteenth century beautiful Gothic town-halls or guild-halls scattered over northern and western Europe... The old cities were waking up, and new towns were growing.There was a change all over Europe, and everywhere town life was increasing. In the old days of the Roman Empire there were, of course, great towns all round the Mediterranean coast."[7]

Expansion of suburban areas "was encouraged by the growing urban population, but it did not drain off the excess population from the centre of cities. People responded to their natural desire to live near their work, and employment opportunities were concentrated in the city centre. Then the nature of these opportunities changed from the pre-factory system. Stable industrial employment was uncertain. With expanding commercial enterprise the tendency to shift from job to job extended to movement from city to city. Mobility of the family offered advantages over fixed tenure... The urban population thus became transient in character. Freedom to move was not desirable but it was necessary. The rental apartment satisfied this requirement and it became popular."[8]

In its proper sense, "urban development implies a continuing responsibility, all forces acting together and interdependently. The degree to which these forces are integrated reflects the aspirations, ambitions and convictions of a community, and the initiative and responsibility of the citizenship in whole and in each of its parts. When the forces that contribute to city building are unbalanced, inequities develop and the city declines".[9]

Focusing on the characteristics of urbanism and the urbanised man, Nels Anderson writes, "urbanism as a way of life was once fairly restricted within the walls of the city and, within the city, it was limited to certain sections. The urbanised man remains oriented in the crowd. He is not disturbed by the coming and going of people, hence he is always making new acquaintances and forgetting the old ones; transiency is one of his characteristics. He cannot know all persons about him well and he may not wish to. Thus, again to use a term from Wirth, international relations are marked by superficiality. Since the urbanised man cannot know all people and may not wish to, he acquires the ability to move in the crowd caring who the people are about him, and he does not invite their approaches; anonymity is still a third characteristic... But urbanism is not merely a way of thinking and behaving. The urbanised man, wherever he may be, is ever adjusting to the new and changing. As he is congenial to initiative, he may also be intolerant of tradition if tradition stands in the way of getting things done. He is not only mobile himself, but he accepts the mobility of others. He may be loyal to his immediate family but he tends lo lose contact with other relatives. As he tends to be more urbanised he is also more the individual than is possible in non-urban-society."[10]

Karl Mannheim adds, "merely moving a man to the city does not necessarily urbanised him (although it helps), while another rural man may be very much urbanised and never leave his rural work or habitat. Urbanisation involves basic changes in the thinking and behaviour of people and changes in their social values. It is not merely a matter of an individual or group changing from one kind of work to another, but involves changes in attitudes toward work, and it means entering a new and ever-changing division of labour."[11]

In contrast to rural life, "Urbanisation denudes the household of economic functions as we have seen, and throws the individual into associational relations determined by specific interests of work and temperament. In drawing the contrast, however, between the self - determination of the urbanite and the subjection to family and communal mores of the country dweller, we must avoid the bias of personal predilection. The city dweller is no less a socialised being because his family relationships are less inclusive and because many of his contacts are more impersonal. The scale and variety of his relationships are extended so that they can range from the most superficial to the most intimate and binding. If relationships in rural life gain in quality because they are more persistent, they gain similarly in the city because they are the more definite choice of the individual."[12]

To distinguish the phenomenon, "now the question arises to what extent is the urban way of life limited to the urban population ? To what extent do the physical and the social definitions of urban correspond ? The answer is that there is a causal connection between the two but not a one-to-one correspondence. The city, as a place where population is concentrated inevitably gives rise to and depends upon certain features of social organisation that we regard as urban. By its very nature it throws people into close contact with strangers, facilitates the rapid diffusion of news and fashions, permits a high degree of individualisation, stimulates invention, social mobility, secularisation, etc. At the same time it depends on a complex economic system which makes possible the quick transfer of goods and services, an elaborate division of labour and a high degree of rational enterprise. But once these things have arisen, once we have actual cities, their influence can be carried far beyond the city boundaries and can thus characterise people who do not actually dwell in cities. In this way rural areas can become highly urbanised."[13]

To put it otherwise, "among the factors that are indicative of lack of urbanisation the following stand out prominently : (1) lack of occupations in the secondary sector, (2) Lack of pull-factor in the towns, (3) social customs relating to marriage, (4) Absence of a Railway link in the district, (5) Lack of voluntary social organisation, (6) Lack of facilities for stay of visitors and public eating places."[14]

The percentage of urban population in India has always been on the increase since the first census was undertaken in 1881. "The only break in the continuously increasing proportion of the urban population to the total population was in 1911. This was possibly due to the prevalence of plague at the time of that census which had led to a considerable efflux of people from the cities as a precaution against catching the infection. For all practical purposes the trend was unbroken though the tempo of increase was very slow upto 1931. It has since accelerated."[15]

Table 1

Towns in India as per 1991 Census

Sl. No.	*States*	*No. of Towns*	*No. of Urban Agglomerations (Excluding Urban Outgrowths)*
1	2	3	4
1.	Andhra Pradesh	264	213
2.	Arunachal Pradesh	10	10
3.	Assam	93	87
4.	Bihar	271	211
5.	Goa	31	26
6.	Gujarat	264	227
7.	Haryana	94	90
8.	Himachal Pradesh	58	55
9.	*Jammu & Kashmir	...	...
10.	Karnataka	306	254
11.	Kerala	197	109
12.	Madhya Pradesh	465	433
13.	Maharashtra	336	291
14.	Manipur	31	30
15.	Meghalaya	12	07
16.	Mizoram	22	22
17.	Nagaland	09	09
18.	Orissa	124	119
19.	Punjab	120	120
20.	Rajasthan	222	215
21.	Sikkim	08	08
22.	Tamil Nadu	469	260

Table 1 Contd...

1	2	3	4
23.	Tripura	18	18
24.	Uttar Pradesh	753	702
25.	West Bengal	382	160
	UNION TERRITORIES		
1.	Andaman & Nicobar Islands	01	01
2.	Chandigarh	05	01
3.	Dadra & Nagar Haveli	01	01
4.	Daman and Diu	02	02
5.	Delhi	32	07
6.	Lakshadweep	04	04
7.	Pondicherry	11	07
	TOTAL	4,615	3,699

Source: NICNET - Census Service, Govt. of India, New Delhi, 1993.

* Figures of Jammu and Kashmir not included as Census was not conducted there in 1991.

In fixing criteria, "the census report of 1961 laid down the following test. For defining an 'Urban area'; (1) population of 5,000, (2) density of not less than 1,000 persons per square mile or 400 persons per square kilometre, (3) at least three-fourths of the male working population being engaged in non-agricultural occupations.

Earlier censuses have applied different criteria for purposes of defining an urban area. This change in stance on the part of the census injects avoidable confusion and, what is worse, renders comparison over a period of years very difficult. The census report of 1981 has slightly varied the criteria of judging the people as urban. In the earlier censuses, the male workers in activities like fishing, livestock, plantations etc. were treated as engaged in agricultural activities. In 1981 census, these activities were treated as agricultural activities."[16] Excluding 74 towns of Jammu & Kashmir,there were 4,615 towns and 3,699 Urban Agglomerations (excluding urban outgrowths) and towns in India as per 1991 Census. In Orissa, the corresponding numbers were 124 and 119.

Table 2

Percentage of Urban Population to Total Population in India From Census to Census

Census year	*1881*	*1891*	*1901*	*1911*	*1921*	*1931*	*1941*	*1951*	*1961*	*1971*	*1981*	*1991*
Percentage of Urban Population to Total Population	9.3	9.4	10.9	10.4	11.2	12.0	13.9	17.3	17.89	19.87	23.34	25.73

Source : Compiled from different Census Reports; S.R Maheshwari, *Local Government in India*, Laxmi Narain Agarwal, Agra, 1992-93, p. 169 and N.V. Sovani, *Urbanisation and Urban India*, Asia Publishing House, Bombay, 1965, p. 34.

Table 3

State/Union Territory Wise Total and Scheduled Tribe Population with their respective percentages Living in Urban Areas of India as Per 1991 Census

Sl. No.	State	Total Population		Scheduled Tribe Population		
		No. of Persons	Percentatge of Total Population	No. of Persons	Percentage to Total Urban Population	Percetage to Total Population
1.	Andhra Pradesh	17,887,26	26.89	319,227	7.60	1.78
2.	Arunachal Pradesh	110,628	12.80	32,129	5.84	29.04
3.	Assam	2,487,795	11.10	97,133	3.38	3.90
4.	Bihar	11,353,012	13.14	463,225	7.00	4.08
5.	Goa	479,752	41.01	287	76.33	0.06
6.	Gujarat	14,246,061	34.49	498,597	8.09	3.50
7.	*Haryana	4,054,744	24.63	...	...	...
8.	Himachal Pradesh	449,196	8.69	5,409	2. 48	1.20
9.	**Jammu & Kashmir	...	...	...	...	...
10.	Karnataka	13,907,788	30.92	286,195	14.94	2.06
11.	Kerala	7,680,294	26.39	11,203	3.49	0.15
12.	Madhya Pradesh	15,338,837	23.18	746,304	4.85	4.87
13.	Maharashtra	30,541,586	38.69	912,467	12.47	2.99
14.	Manipur	505,645	27.52	53,243	8.42	10.53
15.	Meghalaya	330,047	18.60	205,834	13 56	62.37
16.	Mizoram	317,946	46.10	295,452	45.21	92.93
17.	Nagaland	208,223	17.21	127,677	12.04	61.32
18.	Orissa	4,234,983	13.38	361,708	5.14	8.54
19.	*Punjab	5,993,225	29.55	...	...	...

Table 3 Contd...

20.	Rajasthan	10,067,1 13	22.88	254,332	4.65	2.53
21.	Sikkim	37,006	9.10	7,415	8.16	20.04
22.	Tamil Nadu	19,077,592	34. 15	68,986	12.01	0.36
23.	Tripura	421,721	15.30	14,081	1.65	3.34
24.	Uttar Pradesh	27,605,915	19.84	16,873	5.86	0.06
25.	West Bengal	18,707,601	27.48	196,312	5.15	1.05
	UNION TERRITORIES					
1.	Andaman & Nicobar Islands	74,955	26.71	502	1 88	0.67
2 .	*Chandigarh	575,829	89 69	...	...	...
3.	Dadra & Nagar Haveli	11,725	8.47	3,516	3.21	29.99
4.	Daman and Diu	47,543	46.80	2,532	21.60	5.33
5.	* Delhi	8,471,625	89 93	...	...	...
6.	Lakshadweep	29,114	56.31	26,685	55.41	91.66
7.	* Pondicherry	516,985	64.00	...	...	...
	INDIA	*** 213,283,817	25.73	5,007,354	7.39	2.32

Source : Primary Census (1991) Abstract - General and Scheduled Tribe Population, Series I of 1992 and 1993, Govt. of India, New Delhi.

* Has no Scheduled Tribe. ** Census was not conducted in Jammu & Kashmir in 1991.

*** The Total Urban Population of India including the projected figure of Jammu & Kashmir as per 1991 Census is 217,611,012.

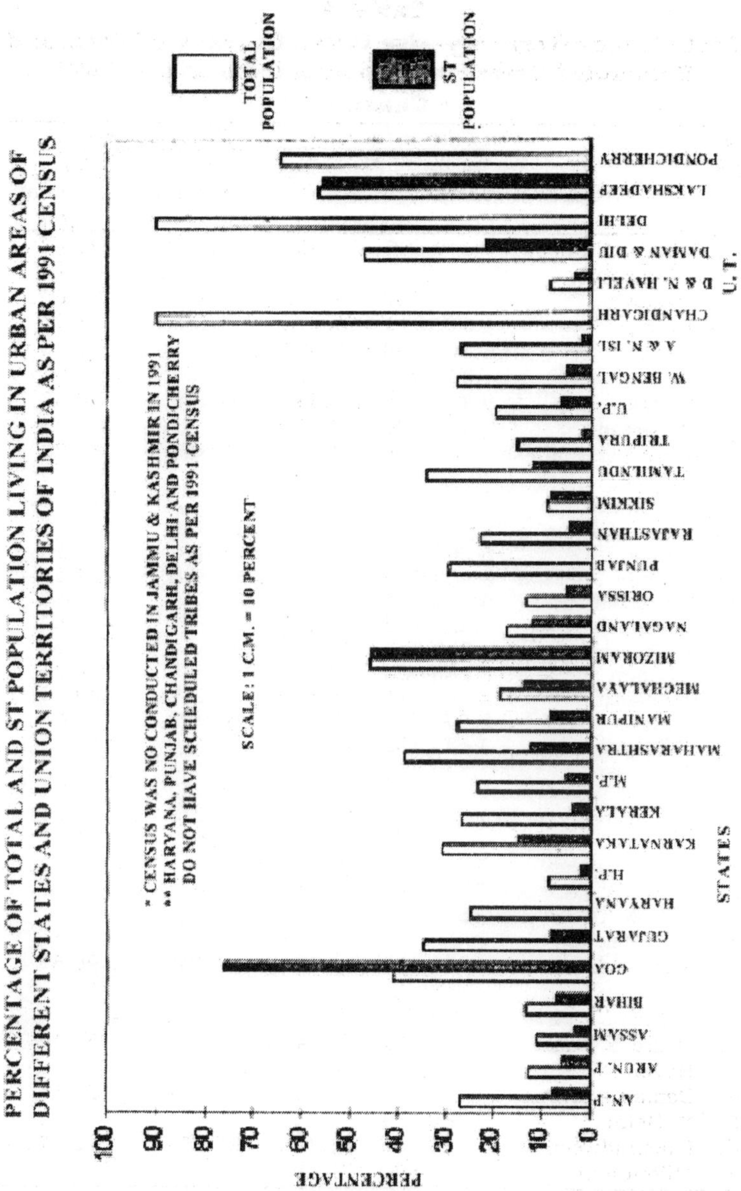
PERCENTAGE OF TOTAL AND ST POPULATION LIVING IN URBAN AREAS OF DIFFERENT STATES AND UNION TERRITORIES OF INDIA AS PER 1991 CENSUS
TOTAL POPULATION
ST POPULATION
* CENSUS WAS NO CONDUCTED IN JAMMU & KASHMIR IN 1991
** HARYANA, PUNJAB, CHANDIGARH, DELHI AND PONDICHERRY DO NOT HAVE SCHEDULED TRIBES AS PER 1991 CENSUS
SCALE: 1 C.M. = 10 PERCENT
PERCENTAGE
100
90
80
70
60
50
40
30
20
10
0
AN. P
ARUN. P
ASSAM
BIHAR
GOA
GUJARAT
HARYANA
H.P.
KARNATAKA
KERALA
M.P.
MAHARASHTRA
MANIPUR
MEGHALAYA
MIZORAM
NAGALAND
ORISSA
PUNJAB
RAJASTHAN
SIKKIM
TAMILNDU
TRIPURA
U.P.
W. BENGAL
A & N. ISL
CHANDIGARH
D & N. HAVELI
DAMAN & DIU
DELHI
LAKSHADEEP
PONDICHERRY
STATES
U. T.

FIGURE-1

Table 4

State/Union Territory-wise Urban Literacy of Total and Scheduled Tribe Population of India as per 1991 Census*

Sl. No.	State	Total Urban Literacy		ST Urban Literacy	
		No. of Persons	Percentage	No. of Persons	No. Percentage
1.	Andhra Pradesh	10,049,306	66.35	97,312	37.48
2.	Arunachal Pradesh	64,552	71.59	1 7,952	71.68
3.	Assam	1,697,843	79.39	63,483	78.18
4	Bihar	6,357,468	67.89	199,505	52.28
5.	Goa	339,359	80.10	107	48.20
6	Gujarat	9,224,106	76.54	207,149	50.32
7.	** Haryana	2,474,086	73.66	...	...
8.	Himachal Pradesh	327,200	84.17	3,835	80.72
9.	Jammu & Kashmir	...	...	...	...
10.	Karnataka	8,762,573	74.20	130,936	55.08
11.	Kerala	6,203,553	92.25	6,840	71.16
12.	Madhya Pradesh	8,962,354	70.81	266,868	44.68
13.	Maharashtra	20,460,597	79.20	487,879	64.58
14.	Manipur	300,735	70.53	34,701	77.07
15.	Meghalaya	223,270	81.74	135,434	81.53
16.	Mizoram	245,063	93.45	228,345	94.26
17.	Nagaland	142,170	83.10	86,171	84.52
18.	Orissa	2,591,539	71.99	120,903	40.85
19.	** Punjab	3,633,473	72.08	...	...
20.	Rajasthan	5,370,395	65.33	90,342	44.50
21.	Sikkim	25,845	80.89	5,362	81.79
22.	Tamil Nadu	13,024,074	77.99	27,323	47.29
23.	Tripura	303,345	83.09	10,618	86.27
24.	Uttar Pradesh	13,739,707	6 1 .00	9,136	64.34
25.	West Bengal	12,370,562	75.27	69,517	42.53
	UNION TERRITORIES				
1.	Andaman & Nicobar Islands	52,633	81.69	408	90.67
2.	**Chandigarh	393,107	79.87	...	...
3.	Dadra & Nagar Haveli	7,732	78.44	1 ,507	52.13
4.	Daman and Diu	33,687	81.61	1,149	54.64
5.	** Delhi	5,380,149	76.18	...	...
6.	Lakshadweep	20,148	83.99	17,954	82.67
7.	**Pondicherry	359,696	79.88	...	...
***	INDIA	133,140,330	73.01	2,320,736	56.60

Source : Primary Census (1991) Abstract General and Scheduled Tribe Population, Series -I of 1992 & 1993, Govt. of India, New Delhi.

* Excludes population in the age-group of 0-6 years,

** Has no Scheduled Tribe

*** Figures of Jammu & Kashmir not included as Census was not conducted there in 1991.

According to "1991 census 25.73 per cent of the total population of India live in urban areas. Among the highly urbanised states come Mizoram (46.10), Goa (41,01), Maharashtra (38.69), Gujarat (34.49), Tamil Nadu (34.15). Karnataka (30.92), Punjab (29.55) etc. Similarly, the least urbanised states are Himachal Pradesh (8.69), Sikkim (9.10). Assam (11.10). Arunachal Pradesh (12.80) etc. Except Dadra & Nagar Haveli and Andaman & Nicobar Islands who account for 8.47 and 26.71 percentages of urban population respectively, all other union territories are highly urbanised. While Delhi has 89.93 per cent of urban population, Chandigarh with 89.69 per cent of urban population comes next. Likewise, Pondicherry, Lakshadweep and Daman & Diu account for 64.0 per cent, 56.31 per cent and 46.80 per cent of urban population respectively."[17] The total urban population of the country as per 1991 census is 213,283,817 excluding the figure of Jammu & Kashmir where Census was not conducted in 1991. Taking the projected figure of Jammu & Kashmir, the total population of the country for 1991 is 217,611,012. Orissa has a total urban population of 4,234,983 which constitutes 13.38 per cent of the state's total population.

As compared to the total population "Only 7.39 per cent of scheduled tribe population of India live in urban areas as compared to 25.73 per cent of total population and 18.72 per cent of the scheduled caste population living in urban areas. Thus, roughly 93 per cent of the scheduled tribe population in the country are rural based. Of the 15 major states, only 3 states, namely, Karnataka, Maharashtra and Tamil Nadu had more than 10 per cent of the scheduled tribe population living in the urban areas; the respective percentages being 14.94, 12.47 and 12.01. The percentages of scheduled tribe population living in urban areas in other major states are: Andhra Pradesh (7.6), Assam (3.4), Bihar (7.0), Gujarat (8.1), Kerala (3.5), Madhya Pradesh (4.8), Orissa (5.1), Rajasthan (4.6), Uttar Pradesh (5.9) and West Bengal (5.2)."[18] The total urban scheduled tribes of India constitute 2.32 per cent of the total population of the country. Out of the total 5,007,354 urban scheduled tribe population of the country as many as 361,708 live in the towns and cities of Orissa and constitute 5.14 per cent of the total urban population of the state and 8.54 per cent of the total population of the state.

So far as scheduled tribe population is concerned, Goa and Mizoram are the highly urbanised states of India with 76.33 and 45.21 percentages respectively of such people in these states having been recorded as urban. Among the union territories Lakshadweep with 55.41 per cent and Daman & Diu with 21.60 per cent of their ST population living in urban areas account for highly scheduled tribes urbanised union territories. Among all the states and union territories of India, Goa alone holds the record of having not only a higher but much higher percentage of scheduled tribe urbanites, than the percentage of urbanites of the country.

Out of the total 133,140,330 urban literates of the country 2,320,736 belong to the scheduled tribes. While the urban literacy rate for India as per 1991 census is 73.01 per cent, the corresponding percentage for scheduled tribes is 56.60. In Orissa out of the total 2,591,539 urban literates 120,903 persons belog to scheduled tribes. While the total urban literacy rate is 71.99 per cent, it is 40.85 per cent for the urban scheduled tribes of the state. For computing literacy rates the population in the age group of 0-6 years has not been included.

Table 5

Districtwise Total Population and Scheduled Tribe Population living in Urban areas of Orissa as per 1991 Census

Sl. No.	*District*	*Total Urban Population*	*Scheduled Tribe Urban population*	*% of ST Urban Population to Total Urban Population*
1.	Cuttack	485,861	8,253	1.698
2.	Jagatsinghpur	76,092	2,299	3.021

3. Jajpur	53,431	3,350	6.269
4. Kendrapara	63,235	297	0.469
5. Balasore	154,152	13,401	8.693
6. Bhadrak	109,841	2,702	2.459
7. Puri	163,479	674	0.412
8. Nayagarh	26,244	250	0.952
9. Khurda	516,281	18,492	3.581
10. Mayurbhanj	116,249	21,314	18.33
11. Sundargarh	525,005	106,281	20.24
12. Sambalpur	205,458	25,115	12.22
13. Bargarh	80,547	5,370	6.666
14. Deogarh	17,275	3,823	22.13
15. Jharsuguda	159,328	26,085	16.37
16. Bolangir	129,420	7,157	5.530
17. Sonepur	34,830	1,242	3.565
18. Keonjhar	166,874	40,551	24.30
19. Dhenkanal	78,112	4,298	5.502
20. Angul	110,123	7,059	6.410
21. Ganjam	423,753	2,619	0.618
22. Gajapati	46,769	666	1.424
23. Kalahandi	78,163	5,147	6.584
24. Nuapada	25,765	1,788	6.939
25. Koraput	171,705	28.098	16.36
26. Rayagada	89,326	11,300	12.65
27. Malkanagiri	34,428	4,490	13.04
28. Nawarangpur	42,1 17	4,916	11.67
29. Phulbani	35,662	4,462	12.51
30. Boudh	15,458	209	1.352
ORISSA	4,234,983	361,708	8.540

Source : Department of Welfare, Govt. of Orissa, Bhubaneswar.

In Orissa 4,234,983 persons live in urban areas. Heavy concentration of urban population in the state is seen in the coastal belt. Around 50 per cent of the total urhanites of the state live in only four undivided districts such as Balasore, Cuttack, Puri and Ganjam. The proportion of urban population to total population in the state has increased from 8.41 per cent in 1971 to 1 1.82 per cent in 1981 and 13.38 in 1991. The Scheduled Tribes had 4.61 per cent and 5.14 per cent of their population in the urban areas of the state in the respective censuses.

Table 6

Scheduled Tribe Households and Scheduled Tribe Population in Urban Areas of India and Orissa as Per 1991 Census

	Total Urban	No. of households with ST Members	Total ST Population		
			Persons	Males	Females
INDIA*	Total	12,787,720	67,758,380	34,363,271	33,395,109
	Urban	1,009,449	5,007,354	2,607,341	2,400,013
ORISSA	Total	1,475,596	7,032,214	3,512,891	3,519,323
	Urban	82,458	361,708	187,449	174,259

Source : Union Primary Census (1991) Abstract for Scheduled Castes and Scheduled Tribes, Series - 1(Paper - 1 of 1993), Govt of India, New Delhi.

* Figures of Jammu & Kashmir not included as Census was not conducted there in 1991.

Table - 7

Total Literates and Urban Literates Among Scheduled Tribes of India and Orissa As per 1991 Census

		Persons	Males	Females
INDIA*	Total literates	16,008,547	11,166,843	4,841,707
	Urban literates	2,320,736	1,428,911	891,825
ORISSA	Total literates	1,272,863	981,118	291,745
	Urban literates	1 20,903	81,61 0	39,293

Source: Union Primary Census (1991) Abstract for Scheduled Castes and Scheduled Tribes , Series- 1 (Paper - 1 of 1993), Govt. of India, New Delhi.

* Figures of Jammu & Kashmir not included as Census was not conducted there in 1991.

5,007,354 persons including 2,607,341 males and 2,400,013 females belonging to Scheduled Tribes live in 1,009,499 scheduled tribe households in urban areas of India. Compared to it, Orissa has 82,458 scheduled tribe households in urban areas accommodating 3,61,708 Scheduled Tribe persons including 1,87,449 males and 1,74,259 females. 2,320,736 Scheduled Tribe persons in urban India including 1,428,911 males and 891,825 females are literate as per 1991 census. In Orissa 120,903 urbanites belonging to the Scheduled Tribes including 81,610 males and 39,293 females are literate.

As to work participation of scheduled tribes in urban areas of India and Orissa, a comparative picture can be given as below. In India there are 1,65,182 main workers including 1,212,198 males and 4,22,984 females while in Orissa it is 121,467 persons including 93,417 males and 28,050 females. In India there are 170,529 cultivators including 120,982 males and 49,547 females while in Orissa the figures are respectively 13,601, 12,088 and 1,513. In the country there are 310,207 agricultural labourers including 183,033 males and 127,174 females while a total of 28,722 agricultural labourers are there in Orissa who include 18,462 males and 10,260 females. In livestock, forestry, fishing, hunting and plantations, orchards and allied activities there are 48,783 persons engaged in the country including 39,022 males and 9,761 females; the corresponding figures for Orissa being 2,717, 2230 and 487. In mining and quarrying 59, 733 persons including 50,034 males and 9,699 females are engaged at all India level while for Orissa the respective numbers are 7,001, 5,409 and 1,592. In the field of manufacturing, processing, servicing and repairing in household industry, 40,874 persons including 24,071 males and 16,803 females are engaged in India while 2,094 persons including 1080 males and 1014 females are engaged in the same field in Orissa. In the same work but in other than household industry a total member of 209,552 persons including 177,292 males and 32,260 females are engaged in India while in Orissa the corresponding numbers are 18,568, 15,914 and 2,654.

In constructions, 100,926 persons with 80,814 males and 20,112 females are engaged in all India level while in Orissa 6,549 persons including 4,881 males and 1668 females are employed in the same field. In trade and commerce 150,977 persons including 114,416 males and 36,561 females are engaged in India while 5,978 persons with 5,007 males and 971 females are engaged in the same work in Orissa. Regarding transport, storage and communication, the work participation at all India level is 118,377 persons with 113,240 males and 5,137 females and in Orissa the respective figures are 8,084, 7,448 and 636. In other services 425,224 persons with 309,294 males and 115,930 females are engaged in the country while in the same work in Orissa 28,153 persons including 20,898 males and 7,255 females are engaged. The total number of marginal workers in the country is 92,367 with 21,675 males and 70,692 females; the corresponding figures for Orissa being 6,214 with 1463 males and 4,751 females. The non-workers in the country are 3,279,805 persons including 1,373,468 males and 1,906,337 females. In Orissa the non-workers number 234,077 persons with 92,569 males and 141,458 females.

Quite a "sizable agglomeration of tribal population in Orissa has moved to mining, industrial and urban areas for earning a secured living through wage labour. During the past three decades the process of industrial urbanisation into the tribal belt of Orissa has been accelerated through the operation of mines and establishment of industries. Mostly, persons from advanced tribal communities such as Santal, Munda, Ho, Oraon, Kisan, Gond etc. have taken to this economic pursuit in order to relieve pressure from their limited land and other resources... In some instances industrialisation and mining operations have led to uprooting of tribal villages, and the displaced became industrial nomads. They lost their traditional occupation, agricultural land, houses and other immovable assets. They became unemployed and faced unfair competition with others in the labour market. Their aspiration gradually escalated although they invariably failed to acquire what they aspired for. Thus, the net result was frustration. Occasionally their disappointment has been reflected in unrest and agitation."[19]

Table - 8

Categorywise Total workers and Urban workers among the Scheduled Tribes in India and Orissa as per 1991 census

Sl. No.	Work category	Total (T) Urban (U)	India			Orissa		
			Persons	Males	Females	Persons	Males	Females
1	Main workers	T	28,475,765	18,460,004	10,01,576	2,829,688	2,020,152	809,536
		U	1,635,182	1,212,198	422,984	121,467	93,417	28,050
2	Cultivators	T	15,520,576	10,808,945	4,711,631	1,437,919	1,184,837	253,82
		U	170,529	120,982	49,547	13,601	12,088	1,513
3	Agricultural Labourers	T	9,308,705	4,873,771	4,434,934	1,082,907	610,377	472,534
		U	310,207	183,033	127,174	28,722	18,462	10,260
4	Livestock, Forestry, Fishing, Hunting and Plantations, Orchards & Allied Activities	T	574,642	400,100	174,542	24,533	18,772	5,761
		U	48,783	39,022	9,761	2,717	2,230	487
5.	Mining and Quarrying	T	230,754	183,513	47,241	43,418	30,312	13,106
		U	59,733	50,034	9,699	7,001	5,409	1,592
6	Manufacturing, Processing, Servicing and Repairs in Household Industry	T	297,098	167,693	129,405	46,990	23,037	23,953
		U	40,874	24,071	16,803	2,094	1,080	1,014
7.	Manufacturing, Processing, Servicing And Repairs in other than Household Industry	T	564,956	440,259	124,694	47,459	36,600	10,559
		U	209,552	177.292	32,260	18,568	15,914	2,654
8.	Constructions	T	237,456	197,098	40,358	13,791	10,445	3,346
		U	100,926	80,814	20,112	6,549	4,881	1,668

Table 8 Contd...

9	Trade and Commerce	T	339,301	260.392	78,909	24,012	18,229	5,783
		U	150,977	114,416	36,561	5,978	5,007	971
10.	Transport, Storage and	T	243,766	234,642	9,124	17,471	16,163	1,308
	Communication	U	118,377	113,240	5,137	8,084	7,448	636
11	Other services	T	1,158,511	893,591	264,920	91,118	71,384	19,804
		U	425,224	309,294	115,930	28,153	20,898	7,255
12.	Marginal Workers	T	4,931,573	350,001	4,581,572	641,662	50,199	591,463
		U	92,367	21,675	70,692	6,214	1,463	4,751
13	Non-Workers	T	34,351,042	15,553,266	18,797,776	3,560,864	1,442.540	2,118,324
		U	3,279,805	1,373,468	1,906,337	234,027	92,569	141,458

Source: Union primary Census (1991) Abstract for Total and Scheduled Tribe Population, Series-1 of 1992 & 1993, Govt. of India, New Delhi.

* Figures of Jammu & Kashmir not included as Census was not conducted there in 1991.

Democratic Decentralisation and the Urban Government

Democratic decentralisation in any political society justifies the very essence of popular sovereignty, the concept which mainly thrives on people's power or power of the masses. "Democratic decentralisation is intended to be an important medium for people's participation in the work of government at lower levels. It differs from administrative decentralisation as it involves devolution of authority. 'Administrative decentralisation'implies the right to the freedom of implementing a project which includes the necessary right to do associated with planning from the operative standpoint. Democratic decentralisation, however, implies people's right to initiate their own projects for local well-being and the power to execute and operate them in an autonomous manner. Again, the idea of democratic decentralisation is not to be confused with delegation or deconcentration. Delegation or deconcentration consists in the grant of authority from a superior to subordinate authority, to be enjoyed by him not in his own right but as a derived concession and that also to be exercised at the pleasure of the superior."[20]

In fact, "most of the modern states comprise vast areas and have huge population. This factor and the vastly increased scope of state activity have led to great centralisation of authority. Centralisation or concentration of authority at the centre is an important characteristic of almost all the large states. In order to offset the evils of centralisation, decentralisation has been considered as an essential remedy. 'Decentralisation', the reverse of centralisation, means spreading from the centre, thinning the centre, or lightening the centre. The word 'Decentralisation', implies different senses to different groups of people. To an economist it means dispersal of industries; to advocates of local authority it implies initiative, responsibility and discretion to local bodies; and to an administrator it means delegation of authority to regional and local officers. Political decentralisation with which we are concerned, means dispersal of all institutions performing administrative functions and housing political power. Decentralisation and deconcentration mean almost the same thing, i.e., devolution of power from above. Decentralisation in any large organisation is essential."[21]

As to the demerits of centralisation two major points may he mentioned such as "(i) remoteness of control resulting from loss of contact with local centres, and (ii) top-heavy management, or overload of work at the centre. The arguments put forward in favour of decentralisation may he summed up as : (I) It facilitates the extension of popular control over a large number of functions which may be delegated to the authorities at lower levels. It permits the adjustment of national policies to local physical and economic peculiarities. (3) It helps in avoiding delay and red-tape (which are the chief evils of centralised bureaucracy) by doing away with the requirement of frequent reference to central authorities before action can be taken in the field. (4) It helps in improving the morale of the people, who are enabled to participate more actively in administration, because through decentralisation many administrative operations are brought closer to the people served. It also develops in them initiative, responsibility and resourcefulness."[22]

About the ingredients of democratic decentralisation Iqbal Narain writes : "(1) as the word democratic indicates, the object postulated here implies a larger and closer association of the people with their own government. (2) There is devolution or dispersion of authority from the higher levels of the government to the lower levels. (3) This dispersion of authority assumes the form of autonomy to the people at lower levels to take political decisions with regard to policy formulation and work programme, to devise ways and means to execute it, to manage and control the finances required for it and ultimately to guide and control its administration. (4) The authority, thus decentralised, should be managed by the people directly or indirectly through their representatives and thus, the institutional machinery of democratic decentralisation should necessarily be elective."[23]

To highlight the need and justification of local Government Laski puts it more logically that, " the case indeed, for a strong system of local government in any state is clear almost beyond the needs of discussion. We can not realise the full benefit of democratic government unless we begin by the admission that all problems are not central problems, and that the results of problems not central in their incidence require decision at the place, and by the persons, where and by whom the incidence is most deeply felt. Among the inhabitants of some given area, that is to say, there is a consciousness of common purposes and common needs by which they are differentiated from the inhabitants of other areas."[24]

He further adds, "there are, moreover, other reasons why strong local government is an advantage. If a service is exclusively applied to the benefit of a particular district, it is obviously only fair that the inhabitants of the district should pay for it; and to raise from them the funds for payment means the certainty that they will demand control of service, and the probability that they will manage it efficientlv in order to keep their bills of costs as low as possible. Clearly, further, we can not make an average man realise his citizenship in any creative way if his only relation to government is obtained by voting once every four or five years in a national election. Its relevance to him must be brought more directly home, otherwise his interest in the political process will wane to vanishing process; and it is elementary that the more inert the citizen-body, the more likely is there to be corruption and sinister privilege in the state. A man who realises that his street is badly paved because a body of persons directly under his view and influence are inefficient begins to have a sense of the network of interest in which he is involved. Local government, in other words, is educative in perhaps a higher degree, at least contingently, than any other part of government. And it must be remembered that there is no other way of bringing the mass of citizens into intimate contact with the persons responsible for decisions. It is clear that any great degree of centralisation must mean, and can only mean, a bureaucratic system. No legislative assembly in the world will be able, however greedy of power, to make decisions upon more than the largest outlines of local problems. The application of their details will be left to the departments. Appointed officials will therefore dominate them, and they will never be genuinely accessible to public opinion. For complaint against them can only be investigated in general terms; and it will only produce a revised decision, again in general terms, which the same officials will proceed again to apply, with, doubtless, the same results."[25]

But he cautions that, "there are of course, dangers in the conference of power upon local territorial groups. Uniformity is usually cheaper, because it is almost always easier to make single solution to apply it wholesale than to make a variety of solutions and have them applied piecemeal. It involves, also, some sacrifice of the greater knowledge and greater capacity that are almost bound to be at the command of a central, compared with a local, authority. Localism, also, lends itself a little easily to the sinister influence of powerful persons or bodies within a given neighbourhood."[26]

About the nature and functions of the local government he writes, "area that is to say, must correspond to function, while, at the same time, we provide the opportunity for maintaining the special interest of each group of neighbours in the needs and possibilities of their special environment. That clearly involves two things. It means, first of all, that the persons responsible for the general principles upon which the different local circumstances are administered must be elected by the body of citizens and not appointed; and it means, secondly, that those so elected must oversee the general complex of services which relate to each local area. That will enable the same body of men to sit on bodies which deal with any given function by which their electorate is served. They will probably, for instance, completely control such services as paving and cleaning the streets, or providing public baths, where the area of provision can be small and yet efficient and economical; they will, probably, only partly control such services as lighting, university education, and provision of facilities for recreation and town-planning where the function needs to be organised over an area which transcends the principle of neighbourhood. But the interest of the elector in the person chosen will be protected by the fact that his nominee will sit on whatever body deals with the subject involved; and he will, accordingly, have the means directly at his disposal for the expression of his opinion. Cities could then be divided into electoral districts of a size small enough to permit adequate contact between the elector and his representative, and yet not so small as to make the governing municipal body too large for the efficient conduct of business".[27]

On the nature of membership he argues, "what is involved in such a scheme? Firstly, I think, elected service in local government will become exactly like service in the modern representative assembly, full-time and paid work. For any member who desires seriously to grasp the issues which come before him for judgement, many of them technical and all of them intricate, can not adequately do so if he is merely to deal with them in the intervals of his business. They require a fresh mind and a full mind. If we maintain the principle of unpaid work, we shall always find the membership of these local bodies will be predominantly representative of the richer classes in the community; and the standards of their performance will accordingly be set, not by the needs of the area, but by the desire of those classes to make local government as cheap as possible. They will provide excellent drainage but inadequate education, good roads but poor libraries. They will not grasp the psychological issues by which, for instance, the mind of the poor is moved. And the local government based on the unpaid member has, the world over, somehow seemed to accrete to itself a variety of persons—small contractors, publicans, shopkeepers and the like—whose disinterested zeal for the public welfare has been less apparent in the quality of work done than in their pronouncement of intention... The elected member, secondly, will have what may be called magnicompetence; he will oversee the administration of a general range of functions rather than be chosen, generally speaking, to attend to a special subject. The case for magnicompetence against socialism is, I think, a clear one. Functions dovetail into one another. Education and health, transport and housing, cannot, without the danger of Lilliputian administration be viewed separately."[28]

He adds, "the persons chosen to sit upon these magnicompetent bodies should, thirdly, be directly and not indirectly elected. This principle is as much a matter of solid experience as of abstract theory. The only way in which we can secure anything approaching a continuous democratic control of policy-making bodies is by preserving direct contact between the elector and his representative; for, otherwise, an inevitable remoteness supervenes, and public interest in the meaning of policy declines through that remoteness. The result, that is to say, is a diminution in the educative value of a representative system. People are less likely to be informed of the significance of what is being done because their access to its achievement is not straightforward. They miss the simplicity of being able immediately to affix responsibility for what they dislike. There are, moreover, two further dangers in an indirectly elected body. Almost inevitably it seems to tend to bureaucracy. Because it is not checked by public opinion, it fails to appreciate the importance of public opinion. Because it is removed from public control, it tends to be impatient of public control. It is, further, clear that an indirect system will exaggerate all the weaknesses of majority rule. It will reflect not the total opinion of the bodies from which it is chosen, but merely the dominant opinion."[29]

On the nature of control he writes, "it is obvious that the central government must retain a power generally to control the work of local authorities. How far is that power to extend ? It is clear, first of all, that these are many subjects in which at least a uniform standard of minimum attainment must be enforced. In education, in health, in housing, whatever the local will, it is impossible for the state to allow their standards to fall below a level consistent with the fulfilment of the rights of citizens. Such standards, therefore, require to be defined by the legislative assembly; and though their administration may he organised in concert with local bodies the power to inspect, and, if need be to control, cannot be surrendered to them. It is clear, also, that changes in social need involve continuous alteration both in the sources from which power is exercised and the area over which powers extend; and it is necessary to make the legislative assembly the ultimate reserve authority for the enactment of necessary changes. There are, thirdly, certain subjects over which local bodies ought not to exercise any control at all."[30]

The system of Urban Government anywhere in the world must owe its origin to the city states of the Greeks. Barker writes, "the Greek City-State is still of importance, and a living part of the living past, because it has left us a theory, expressed in the writings of Plato and Aristotle, which still lives in our minds, and colours out thoughts".[31]

It is an astonishing fact that the "Ancient India which was famous for its 'village republics' was also a land of big and well administered cities and towns. The excavations of Harappa and Mohanjodaro have brought out the remains of well-run cities. Kautilya, in his treatise on public administration, *Arthashastra*, has given a graphic description of the city of Pataliputra, the capital of the great Mauryas, and its administration Megasthenes, the Greek ambassador to the court of Chandragupta Maurya, has also left a description of the city of pataliputra. The cities continued to flourish under the Muslim rule and reached the peak of their glory under the mughals whose emperor Shah Jahan built a planned city called Shahjahanabad (modern old Delhi) which attracted tourists from all over the civilised world. The Britishers also developed cities like Bombay, Calcutta and Madras. The trend towards growing urbanisation has continued unabated since 1947."[32]

About the city of Pataliputra (modern Patna) Megasthenes wrote in his travel account 'Indika' thus: "those who have change of the city are divided into six bodies of five each. The members of the first look after everything relating to the industrial arts. Those of the second attend to the entertainment of foreigners. To these they assign lodgings, and they keep watch over their modes of life by means of these persons whom they give to them for assistance. They escort them on the way when they leave the country, or in the event of their dying forward their property to their relatives. They take care of them when they are sick, and if they die bury them. The third body consists of those who inquire when and how births and deaths occur, with the view not only of levying a tax, but also in order that births and deaths among both high and low may not escape the cognizance of government. The fourth class superintends trade and commerce. Its members have charge of weights and measures, and see that the products in their season are sold by public notice. No one is allowed to deal in more than one kind of commodity unless he pays a double tax. The fifth class supervises manufactured articles, which they sell by public notice. What is new is sold separately from what is old, and there is a fine for mixing the two together. The sixth and last class consists of those who collect the tenths of the price of the articles sold."[33]

In the second half of the twentieth century there has been "a marked shift of population from rural to urban areas. The accelerated growth of rate in Urban population is the natural consequence of modernisation and industrialisation to which we are committed. Search for security of life and property, greater employment opportunities, better amenities of life and just glamour are the main factors responsible for this exodus from rural to urban areas."[34]

In India " the municipal institutions were the first to be created by the rule of East India Company by the orders of the court of Directors. The first municipal corporation created in India was that of Madras set up in 1788. The presidency towns of Calcutta and Bombay had their own Corporations in 1772 and 1793 respectively. Other such local bodies were created after 1842. In 1871 and 1874 new municipal Acts were passed providing for elective municipal bodies. But the most important step was yet to come. In 1882 Lord Ripon issued his famous resolution of Local Self-Government which continued to be the basis of local self- government till 1947. That is why Ripon is regarded as the father of Local self-government in India."[35]

After independence, "the new constitution enforced on January 26, 1950 gave constitutional importance to Local Self-government but it abstained from giving constitutional status to it. Local bodies are just creatures of state legislatures and have no independent and separate status of their own. Entry five in the seventh schedule includes 'Local government, that is to say, the constitution of Municipal Corporations, improvement trusts, district boards, mining settlement authorities and other local authorities for the purpose of local self-government or village administration."[36]

In India, the Local Self-government is broadly divided into two categories—the Rural Local Self-governing bodies and the Urban Local Self-governing bodies. The Rural local bodies such as the Gram Panchayats, Panchayat Samities and the District Advisory Councils or of Similar names as they function in different states are collectively known as the 'Panchayatiraj institutions.'

The Urban administration comprehends within its fold Urban local bodies of various types and sizes. These units stand on their own, without any link between one local body and another... It is noteworthy that there is no uniformity in the types of local bodies found in different states. While municipal councils exist in all states, there is variation about other types. Thus, while Rajasthan has only one type of Urban local body, viz.. the municipal council, Uttar Pradesh has all types.. Of course, cantonment boards exist in all military areas throughout the country. It should be noted that the terms corporation, municipality, town area and notified area are mere territorial concepts. It is the council which as a body enjoys the corporate status and acts in that capacity."[37]

Table - 9 shows that while Municipal Corporations, Municipal Councils and Cantonment Boards have either remained static or have a very slow and insignificant growth in their number over the years from 1968 to 1990. The Notified Area Committees have sizably increased their number during the said period implying partially the steady growth of new towns in the country. However, the Town Area Committees have been reduced by their number during such period because in most of the states this name has been changed to Notified Area Council.

Table 9

Local Bodies in Urban India

Sl. No.	*Form of Urban local government*	*No. in 1968*	*No. in 1971*	*No. in 1987*	*No. in 1990*
1.	Municipal Corporations	30	34	73	73
2.	Municipal Councils	1,473	1,493	1,745	1770
3.	Notified Area Committees	1 15	202	-	717
4.	Town Area Committees	385	385	-	229
5.	Cantonment Boards	59	58	62	62

Source : S.R.Maheshwari, Local Government in India, Lakshmi Narain Agarwal, Agra, 1992-93, P. 172.

Municipal Corporations

When India attained her independence "in 1947, there were only three corporations in the metropolitan cities of Bombay, Calcutta and Madras. By 1975 the number rose to 34 and upto 1986 the number had risen to 68. There are some states where corporations are not found. There is a great variation in the area, population, status and the political, commercial and industrial importance of corporations. However, they have, more or less, a common administrative set up. It is interesting to note that the demand for converting municipal councils into corporations has been on the increase in recent years as this institution 'carries a larger degree of prestige, pride, power and autonomy'. Corporations are set up by Acts of the concerned state legislature and for the union territory by the parliament. There may be a separate Act for every corporation or there may be one common Act for all corporations like Act of 1956 passed in Madhya Pradesh."[38]

The corporations found in big cities "are headed by elected mayors. The administration of the city vests in an elected council and the powers of the corporation are exercised by three authorities : General Council, Standing Commitee and the Municipal/Chief executive Officer. The councillors are elected directly by the people usually for a term of four years. The councillors elect a certain number of aldermen, who enjoy the same powers and functions as the councillors but have a longer term and enjoy a little more dignity. The council, including councillors and aldermen, elect each year a president and a vice-president known as the Mayor and the Deputy Mayor. The Mayor is primarily an ornamental figure and a formal head of the corporation. His only active function is to preside over the meetings of the council. The council is the deliberative organ of the corporation. It makes bye-laws, passes the budget, appoints committees and most of the officers and exercises a general supervision over the working of the corporation. The standing committees are elected by the council and carry out most of the work of administration including taxation, finance and preparation of budget, engineering works, health and education services. The executive powers of the corporation are vested in the Municipal Commissioner who is appointed by the state government and is usually a senior member of the Indian Administrative Service. This officer stands at the head of the administrative organisation, prescribes the duties of various officers and supervises their work. The power of sanctioning estimates and contracts vests in the three authorities upto specified amounts. The functions of the municipal corporation include public safety, health, education and other conveniences of the citizens as well as construction and maintenance of waterworks and sewerage, streets and bridges, parks and recreation grounds, markets and shopping centres and so on. To perform their multifarious functions, corporations have been vested with authority to raise taxes. 'Here are certain taxes which the corporation must impose, for example, the Delhi Corporation must levy property tax, a tax on vehicles and animals, a theatre tax, a tax on advertisements with some limitations, a duty on the transfer of property and a tax on buildings. In addition, it may levy an education cess, a tax on professions, trades, callings, and employments, a betterment tax on the increase in Urban land values, a tax on boats, tolls, a local rate on land revenues and a tax on the sale and consumption of electricity. The other major source of revenue is the various types of grants given by the government concerned. Another source of income for the corporation is profits earned by municipal enterprises such as, the Delhi Electricity Supply Undertaking, the Delhi Transport Undertaking and the Delhi Water Supply and Sewerage Undertaking. Then there are miscellaneous items of revenue like rents, income from property, fines, donations etc." [39]

Municipal Councils or Municipalities

Next to Corporations, "all other towns and cities have municipalities established under the Acts of state legislature and in the case of union territories by the Union Parliament. Two Points deserve notice in this connection. First, municipal councils are known by different names in different parts of the country, e.g., city municipality, municipal committee, municipal board, borough municipality, municipality etc. Secondly, there is a general similarity in the organisation of these bodies all over the country. A municipal council differs from a municipal corporation not only in having a smaller area under its jurisdiction and fewer functions and financial powers but also in an important organisational matter. Unlike the corporation, the separations of the deliberative or legislative and executive or implementing wings has not been fully carried out in the cases of municipal councils. In many cases legislative wing takes decisions on administrative matters as well."[40]

Like the corporations the "Municipalities too have three authorities ; the council and its committees, Chairman/President and the Chief Executive Officer/ Chief Municipal Officer. The council consists of members specified in the Act or bye-laws made under the Act. This number differs from one municipality to the other depending upon its area and population. In the case of Madhya Pradesh municipalities have been grouped into four cases— A, B, C and D and in Andhra Pradesh into five categories on the basis of income. The same is true of Rajasthan where there exist six categories. The members of the council are elected by the voters directly on the basis of adult franchise. The tenure of these councils differs from state to state ranging between three to five years. The council decides all questions of policy and important details of administration. The powers of passing the budget, imposing taxes, voting expenditure and making rules and regulations vest in this body. The Municipal council, however, mostly functions through committees which exercise delegated powers or make recommendations to the council. The head of the municipality, known as the president/chairman is elected by the council. In Maharashtra, however, a system of direct election of president by the people was introduced in 1974. A similar system was tried in Madhya Pradesh and Uttar Pradesh for sometime and then given up. The Chairman/President enjoys a tenure coterminous with that of the council except in Karnataka where his term is only two years. He has the usual powers and discharges the usual functions of a presiding officer. But in many states he is also vested with executive powers like making of appointments to certain categories of posts, executing contracts and exercising supervision and control. The day-to-day work of the municipality is carried on by an executive officer, drawn sometimes from state civil service or a statewide cadre of municipal officers. In many states, however, the municipal councils continue to appoint their own executive officers and other officials. A municipality performs two types of functions, compulsory or obligatory and discretionary or optional. The council has to undertake and make reasonable provision for matters coming under obligatory duties. Matters included in this list are the usual civic functions which can be grouped under the four heads of public safety, public convenience, public health and public instruction. The Madhya Pradesh Municipalities Act of 1961 includes 22 items under this category. Discretionary functions are those which municipalities may undertake in their option. The Madhya Pradesh Act includes 35 items in this list like provision of parks, gardens, Libraries, Museums, Hospitals, Dispensaries, Secondary and higher education, reclaiming unhealthy localities, setting up to dairies, undertaking municipal enterprises, establishing and running lodging houses, restaurants, Canteens, constructing houses, etc. In addition, the state government may require its help and assistance in certain matters in times of distress and crisis. The council also manages its property and institutions. Each municipal council has a municipal fund placed to its credit. This fund is constituted of the income derived from various sources. The first and major source of revenue is the income from lax levied by it like house tax, tax on professions, trades, animals and vehicles, pilgrim tax, terminal tax, octroi on goods and animals brought within the municipality for use, sale or consumption, rates like water rate and lighting rate, tolls on roads and ferries and fees from cattle registration, markets and for carrying certain trades. Of all these taxes, property tax and octroi constitute the most important sources of income. Another important source of income is grant-in-aid by the state government. Such grants may be in the nature of block grants or specific grants. Municipal bodies are also authorised to borrow money. They can also run their own enterprises."[41]

Notified Area Councils/Committees

Further, "if in the opinion of the state government, improved arrangements are required within a specified local area which is not expedient to constitute as a municipality, it may, by notification, declare such local area to be a 'notified area'. Since it is created by a notification, it is called notified area. Such areas may also be created for newly developing towns or areas where industries have been or are being established. The state Government also constitutes a committee (council) called Notified Area Committee (Council) to administer such area. The committee exercises the powers of the municipal council."[42]

Town Area Committees

Town area committee "is a semi- municipal authority which is constituted for small towns. Such committees are governed by a separate Act of the state legislature, the members of the committee are partly elected and partly nominated; they can also be wholly elected or wholly nominated. The ambit of their activity is limited to few subjects like conservancy, street lighting, drainage and roads."[43]

Cantoment Boards

Besides, the "urban areas where troops are stationed are known as cantonments. Cantonment Boards have seen set up in such areas to provide civic amenities and welfare services to the people living there. These are autonomous bodies subject to supervision and control by the general officer commanding in charge of the command and the central government (Defence Department). The number of elected and nominated members is kept equal in these boards varying from 1 to 7 although according to statutory provisions the number of nominated members may exceed the elected members by one. These boards have the power of taxation which is their main source of revenue. The budget estimates prepared by the boards are scrutinised and sanctioned by the General Officer Commanding in charge of the command. The tenure of these boards is three years. The executive officer is the executive head of the board. He is appointed by the central government and belongs to the central cadre set up for the purpose."[44]

Supervision and Control

Supervisory control over local bodies by the state government is necessary and is seen in all countries, may be different in forms and degrees. Reasons for such control are : (i) Local authorities are legal creations of the state; (ii) They govern only a tiny part of the state and in the interest of the uniform development of all the areas, coordination by the state government becomes essential; (iii) the local authorities cannot command so much technical skill as the state or the union government and have only limited experience. The government, on the other hand, has in its employment a permanent body of professional experts who can bring upon the notice of the local authorities improved methods doing things successfully tried elsewhere; and (iv) financial assistance in whatever form it may be, implies control. Local bodies of all kinds depend a lot on the grants of the government which obviously must have power to ensure that the money so granted is properly and usefully utilised."[45]

Therefore, the purpose "of state supervision and control is to increase the efficiency of local government units. While supervision and control must secure the proper performance of the duties entrusted to local authorities, it must, at the same time concern itself with educational and technical support and training service to their staff. In other words, it should not acquire a negative content so as to restrict the initiative, discretion or assumption of responsibility on the part of local bodies but should be given a positive content helping the local authorities to avoid pitfalls and mistakes, strengthening their self-confidence and enabling them to assume growing responsibilities... State control as exercised over local bodies in India in the widest sense assumes three forms—legislative., Judicial and administrative. The State legislature controls them by making, amending and repealing the laws concerning them. The judiciary controls them by interpreting laws and judging their validity. Both types of control play their part occasionally, the former when a local authority is to be created or powers granted to it and the latter when a local authority commits an *ultra vires* act. It is the administrative control which is exercised at every step. The nature of administrative supervision and control exercised by the state departments connected with local government affairs in various states includes steps which are indirect and less rigorous, such as, advice and information, giving directions, obtaining of periodical reports and returns, review of local action, conditional grant-in-aid, etc., and also direct steps which are more binding in effect. These include prior approval of any local action taken, inspection, audit, suspension and annulment of decisions, removal of chairmen and councillors, supersession and dissolution of councils and taking over administration in case of default. The more extreme forms of control should, however, be exercised rarely, for their long term effect can be damaging to public confidence in local authorities which is essential to their success."[46]

Political Sub-Centres in Urban Orissa

On 1st April 1936 Orissa became a separate province and at that time "there were eight Municipalities in the six districts of Balasore, Cuttack, Ganjam, Koraput, Puri and Sambalpur. (The Berhampur Municipality was the oldest municipality of Orissa which was constituted in 1855. The other Municipalities were Kendrapara and Jajpur (1869), Cuttack (1876), Balasore (1877), Puri (1881), Sambalpur (1883) and Paralakhemundi (1886). The percentage of population and area of these Municipalities to the total population and area of Orissa were 1.83 and 9.19 respectively.) At that time two kinds of Municipal laws were in vogue in different areas, namely, Bihar and Orissa Municipal Act 1922, in Balasore, Cuttack, Puri and Sambalpur and Madras District Municipal Act, 1920, in Ganjam and Koraput districts. From 1936 to 1950 the Municipalities of portions of Orissa transferred from Bihar and Orissa were governed by Bihar Municipal Act 1922 as amended in 1930, 1931, 1932, 1935, 1936, 1940, 1943, 1949 and the Municipalities of the districts which were transferred from Madras were governed by the Municipalities Act, 1920 as amended in 1946 and 1949."[47]

The Bihar-Orissa Local Self-Government (Amendment) Act, 1922 initiated and engineered by the Local self-government minister of Bihar-Orissa Government, Mr. Madhusudan Das was the first liberal and progressive Act in India. "As minister it was probably his (Mr. Das's) greatest creditable achievement to have caused the passage of the Bihar-Orissa Local Government (Amendment) Act. The most important provision of the

Act was the system of recalling an elected representative if he loses the confidence of the constituency he represents. Sir Ganesh Dutta Sing, a bitter critic of Madhusudan in the Bihar-Orissa Legislative Council had admitted his calibre and contribution towards qualitative improvement of Local Self-Administration. He had written—Both the Municipal and Local Self Government Acts are monuments of his work in the council and of his ideas of the liberty of the people. They were the first liberal Acts passed in India in the Reformed Council. I have had as a minister to deal with both the Acts for a number of years. No doubt, there are defects and sometimes considerable difficulty is felt in dealing with local bodies which do not observe the provision of law, still I must admit that the liberal spirit of Mr. Das is noticed everywhere."[48]

As the elected persons to local bodies were serving honorarily, Madhusudan Das being the minister himself of the concerned subject argued for a honorary minister for the Department. "Madhusudan's proposal that he himself would work as a minister without salary and at the same time practise law in order to meet his expenses was not accepted by the Lieutenant Governor on the ground of lack of precedent. On the other hand his ministerial colleague Mr. Fakhruddin betrayed him and accepted the proposal of a reduced pay. To save his friend's face he accepted the proposal too though he was strongly against it. But as a matter of principle he resigned the ministership on 9th March, 1923 and became the first Indian minister to resign in the legislative history of the country."[49]

It is noteworthy to mention here that "in 1948, all the princely states merged with the state of Orissa except Mayurbhanj which merged with it in 1949. In these princely states the Municipal Governments were constituted by their own regulations e.g., Baripada since 1905, Deogarh since 1912 and Sonepur since 1913. (9 Municipalities and 2 Notified Area Councils were functioning in. these areas)... But enforcement of such regulations continued even after the merger. Despite the fact that there were several laws for the governance of the municipalities, they had very limited powers and there was also limited franchise for election to those local bodies. Hence, the first task of the state Government was to frame a common legislation to bring all the local bodies under one Act. As a result, the Orissa Municipal Act, 1950 was passed to consolidate and amend the laws relating to municipalities in the state of Orissa. The Act came into force since 16 April 1951 and subsequently 19 municipalities were constituted in the state. (The Orissa Act 23 of 1950 received the assent of the Governor on 11.11.1 950 and published in the Orissa Gazette Extraordinary of the even date and it came into force since 16th April 1951 vide Notification No. 3001-LSG dated 16th April, 1951 and published in the Orissa Gazette Extraordinary of the even date. The Act came into force in Cuttack, Jajpur, Bhawanipatna, Puri, Berhampur, Talcher, Balasore, Paralakhemundi, Dhenkanal, Sambalpur, Baripada, Keonjhar, Kendrapara, Bolangir,Deogarh, Sonepur and Sundargarh. The Act came into force in Bargarh and Jeypore on 28th August, 1951 vide Notification No. 5117-LSG, dated 28th August 1951 and published in the Orissa Gazette, pt. 111, 1094)..The Act provided for the election of councillors to Municipal councils on the basis of adult suffrage. For the first time in the history of Orissa, Municipal elections were held in 1951-52. The Municipal Act 1950 was subsequently amended without any significant change except that of Act XIX of 1951."[50]

In the original Municipal Act of 1950 no provision was there for administration of Semi-Urban Areas and as such "there were large scale demands from different parts of the state for the formation of NACs (Notified Area Councils) with either a new Act or under the existing Municipal Act. Hence, the Government proposed to establish NACs in some selected areas through an amendment (the Act XIX of 1951) to the existing Municipal Act, and a separate Chapter XXX-A was added to the original Act of 1950 for the governance of Notified Areas. As such in Orissa even now there is no separate Act for the governance of the Notified Areas. In 1951 two NAC areas were constituted in Titilagarh and Kantabanji. But with regard to the Notified Area councils, the chairman and Councillors were nominated by the Government, the Chairman being invariably Sub-divisional officers of the concerned NACs."[51]

From 26th January, 1961 Panchayatiraj was introduced in Orissa by the state government as per the recommendation of Mehta Committee. "As a consequence, there were large scale demands by the public for further decentralisation in the Urban local bodies to the same extent as has been attempted in case of panchayat Samities. The main reason advanced for such a change was that the Orissa Municipal Act, 1950 which regulated the working of Urban Local Bodies in Orissa had ceased to be progressive in matters touching municipal administration in the state... In response to these demands, the Government of Orissa set up an Administrative Enquiry Committee in 1961 under the chairmanship of Biswanath Das, one of the former Chief Ministers of Orissa to enquire and make extensive study of the problems about the financial conditions and administration of Urban Local Bodies and to make recommendations to improve them. The committee gave its report in July 1962. The committee made recommendations for decentralisation of power and function of Local Bodies by releasing it from unnecessary restrictions and inadvisable controls imposed and exercised by the state Government. Out of 16 recommendations only 7 were implemented which were insignificant in nature... It is to be noted that, though on the line of the Das Committee Report the Government amended the Municipal Act, 1950 and added a new clause 393(A) for the appointment of Director and Deputy Director (of Municipal Administration), the actual implementation of the provision by appointing a Director took place only in the year 1968. The Director works in the secretariat and is also given concurrent secretarial responsibilities."[52]

Conceding to the public demands, the state government framed the Orissa Notified Area Councils (Elected Chairman and members) Rules, 1969 for making these bodies elective in nature.

Till 1994 the Municipal Act (Act XXIII) of 1950 was amended by the Act XIX of 1951, Act XXX of 1951, Act XII of 1953, Act III of 1954, Act I of 1956, Act XVI of 1957, Act-XX of 1958, Act XVI of 1968, Act XX of 1968, Act XXIII of 1972, Act IV of 1974, Act XXII of 1978, Act XXI of 1979, Act VIII of 1984, Act XX of 1986, Act V of 1988, Act V of 1990, Act II of 1992, Act XXIII of 1992 and Act XI (11) of 1994.

The last mentioned Act i.e. Act ll of 1994 which came into force with effect from 31.5.1994 amended several provisions of the original Act of 1950 as existed before such amendment and brought about major changes in the structuring and functioning of the urban local bodies of the state. This was done in conformity with the guidelines of the 74th Constitution Amendment Act of 1992 popularly known as Nagarpalika Act which aimed at giving the Urban local self-Government in the country a constitutional status and an uniform national pattern. The Act inserted into the constitution, a new part i.e., part IXA as well as 18 new sub- Articles of Artcle 243 such as 243P, 243Q, 243R,243S, 243T,243U, 243V, 243W, 243X, 243 Y, 243Z, 243ZA, 243ZB, 243ZC, 243ZD, 243ZE, 243ZF and 243ZG. Besides, the Act also added a new schedule i.e. the twelfth schedule to the constitution which enumerates 18 categories of functions to which the powers, authority and responsibilities of the Municipalities shall apply.

Of late, the Orissa Legislative Assembly passed on 22.9.1997 the Orissa Municipal (Amendment) Bill, 1997 to give permanent legal sanction to the Governor's ordinance of 15.5.1997. The Bill provides that the ceiling amount of election expenses of a councillor shall be Rs. 25,000. Besides, the Bill amended section 73 of the Municipal Act and provided that the Urban bodies of the state cannot make any appointment of staff without the prior consent of the state government. However, in case of emergency they could do so only upto a maximum period of 44 days.[53]

The Structure in Orissa

In pursuance of Article 243P of the constitution of India Sub clause 17(b) of section 3 under Orissa Municipal Act 1950 as amended by Orissa Act 11 of 1 994 explains that the word 'Municipality' means a Notified Area Council (NAC) or a Municipal Council or a Municipal Corporation. Thus, there is no need of separate Acts and provisions for different types of Urban bodies in the state. For this purpose Chapter-XXX-A in the Act dealing with Notified Areas has been Omitted by Act 11 of 1994. Sub-clause 17 (b) of Section 3 explains 'Municipal area' to be the territorial area of a Municipality.Section 4 under Chapter 2 of the Act explains that the state Government shall constitute (a) a Notified Area Council (NAC) for every transitional area having a population of not less than 10,000, (b) a Municipal Council (popularly known as Municipality) for every smaller Urban area having a population of not less than 25,000 and (c) a Municipal corporation for every larger urban area having a population of not less than 3,00,000. The Governor of the state has the power to notify, under clause(2) of Article 243Q of the constitution, an area as 'a transitional area, 'a smaller Urban area, or 'a larger Urban area' having regard to the population of the area, the density of the population therein, the revenue generated for local administration, the percentage of employment in non-agricultural activities, the economic importance or such other factors as he may deem fit.

Table 10

In relation to powers, Authority and responsibilities of Municipalities

Twelfth Schedule* (Article 243W)

1. Urban planning including town planning.
2. Regulation of land-use and construction of buildings.
3. Planning for economic and social development.
4. Roads and bridges.
5. Water supply for domestic, industrial and commercial purposes.
6. Public health, sanitation conservancy and solid waste management.
7. Fire services.
8. Urban forestry, protection of the environment and promotion ot ecological aspects.
9. Safeguarding the interests of weaker sections of society, including the handicapped and mentally retarded.
10. Slum improvement and upgradation.
11. Urban poverty alleviation.
12. Provision of urban amenities and facilities such as parks, gardens, playgrounds.
13. Promotion of cultural, educational and aesthetic aspects.
14. Burials and burial grounds, cremations, cremation grounds and electric crematoriums.
15. Cattle pounds, prevention of cruelty to animals.
16. Vital statistics including registration of births and deaths.
17. Public amenities including street lighting, parking lots, bus stops and public conveniences.
18. Regulation of Slaughter houses and tanneries.

* The twelfth schedule 'added by the Constitution (74th Amendment) Act, 1992.

Table 11

Li st of Urban Local Bodies in Scheduled (Tribal) Areas of Orissa

Sl. No.	*Name of the Urban Body in Scheduled Area.*
1.	Baripada Municipality
2.	Rairangpur N A C.
3.	Udala N A.C.
4.	Karanjia N.AC.
5.	Keonjhargarh Municipality.
6.	Barbil Municipality.
7.	Joda Municipality.
8.	Sundargarh Municipality.
9.	Rajgangpur Municipality.
10.	Biramitrapur Municipality.
11.	Rourkela Municipality.
12.	Phulbani N.A.C.
13	G.Udayagiri N.A.C.

14.	Jeypore Municipality
15.	Koraput N.A.C.
16.	Kotpad N.A.C.
17.	Rayagada Municipality
18.	Gunupur N.A.C.
19.	Gudari N.A.C.
20	Nabrangpur Municipality
21.	Umerkote N.A.C.
22.	Malkanagiri N A.C.
23.	Sorada N A.C.
24	KuchindaN.A.C.
25.	Sunabeda N.A.C.
26.	Balimela N.A.C.

Source: Housing and Urban Development Department, Govt. of Orissa, Bhubaneswar.

At present there are 102 Urban Local Bodies in Orissa including 2 Municipal Corporations, 30 Municipalities and 70 Notified Area Councils. Out of these 26 are in Scheduled (Tribal) Areas.

In pursuance of Article 243R of the constitution, Section 8 under Chapter 2 of the Act mentions about composition of Municipality in the manner that one councillor be elected directly from every ward within the Municipal area and a person having special knowledge or experience in Municipal administration may be nominated by the state Government provided that such nominated member shall have the right to attend meetings of the Municipality without having the right to vote. For delimitation of wards section 12 of the Act specifies that on the basis of equitable distribution of population and compactness of area, each Urban body of the state shall be divided into several wards whose number shall not be less than 11 and more than 40.

Conforming to Article 243T of the constitution, Section 11 of the Act provides reservation of seats by the state Government for scheduled castes, Scheduled Tribes, women and backward class of citizens in every Urban Body. The number of seats reserved for the scheduled castes (SC), the scheduled tribes (ST) or the Backward class of citizens (BCC) in a Municipal area shall bear, as nearly as may be, the same proportion to the total number of seats to be filled by direct election as to total population of every such group in the concerned Municipal area bears to the total population of that area and such seats shall be allotted by rotation to different wards in a Municipal area. Thus, in other words, each of the reserved categories viz., the scheduled castes, the scheduled tribes and the Backward class of citizens shall have, as nearly as may be, the same percentage of seats in each Municipal area as the percentage of its population to the total population of such Municipal area, provided that where the population of the scheduled castes or, as the case may be, the scheduled tribes in a Municipal area is not sufficient for reservation of any seat, one seat for the scheduled castes or as the case may be, one seat for the scheduled tribes shall he reserved in that municipal area.

As nearly as may be, one-third of the total seats reserved for scheduled tribes shall be reserved for scheduled tribe women. If only two seats are reserved for scheduled tribes in a municipal area one seat shall be reserved for scheduled tribe women. The same reservation formula which applies to the scheduled tribe women shall also apply to the scheduled caste women. However, as nearly as may be, but not less than one-third (including the number of seats reserved for women belonging to the scheduled castes and the scheduled tribes) of the total number of seats to be filled by direct election in every municipal area shall be reserved for women and such seats shall be allotted by rotation to different wards in a municipal area.

As per section 41 of the Act framed in concurrence to Article 243 of the constitution the councillors shall hold office for a period of five years from the date appointed for the first meeting of the municipality.They shall not receive any remuneration according to section 40 of the Act.

At the first meeting of the Municipality held after elections to it, the councillors shall elect one from among them as the chairperson and in a subsequent meeting another from among them as vice-chairperson as per section 47 of the Act. According to section 53 of the Act the Government can remove a Chairperson/Vice-Chairperson from office for his/her incapacity or wilful omission or refusal to carry out the provision of the Act. Similarly, under section 17 of the Act a councillor who incurs disqualification may be removed by the state Government. If the office of the Chairperson of a Municipality is not reserved for women or where a Chairperson elected under the Act is not a woman, the office of the vice-chairperson shall be reserved for women. The percentage of offices of chairpersons of all the Municipalities of the state reserved for each of the categories viz., scheduled castes, scheduled tribes or the backward class of citizens shall, as nearly as may be, the same as the percentage of population of such category in the stale to the total population of the state. As nearly as may be, one-third of the total number of seats reserved for scheduled castes or, as the case may be, the scheduled tribes shall be reserved for women of the said category. As nearly as may be, one-third (including the number of offices reserved for women belonging to the scheduled castes and the scheduled tribes) of the total number of offices of chairperson in the Municipalities shall be reserved for women. Reservation of offices of chairperson shall be made by the state Government by rotation among different Municipalities in the prescribed manner.

In pursuance of the 74th Constitution Amendment Act, 1992, the state Government has promulgated Orissa Municipal (delimitation of wards. Reservation of seats and Election conduct) Rules, 1994. Out of the total 1664 wards belonging to 102 Urban Bodies including 2 Municipal Corporations, 30 Municipalities and 70 Notified Area Councils, the number of seats reserved for scheduled castes is 155, for scheduled castes (women) 98, scheduled tribes 119, scheduled tribes (women) 49, for backward class citizens 231 and for backward class

Table 12

Abstract of Reservation of Wards for Scheduled Castes (SC), Scheduled Tribes (ST), Backward Class Citizens (BCC) and Women (W) in Urban Local Bodies (ULBS) of Orissa

Sl. No.	*Type of Urban Body*	*Total No. of ULBS*	*Total No. of wards*	*Wards Reserved for*							
				SC	*SC(W)*	*ST*	*ST*	*BCC (W)*	*BCC (W)*	*W*	*UR*
(1)	(2)	(3)	(4)	(5)	(6)	(7)	(8)	(9)	(10)	(11)	(12)
1.	Municipal Corporation	02	65	05	02	02	01	12	06	13	24
2.	Municipal Council	30	600	46	32	44	24	70	37	113	234
3.	Notified Area Council (NAC) or Nagar Palika	70	999	104	64	73	24	149	70	187	328
	Total	102	1664	155	98	119	49	231	113	313	586

Source: Housing and Urban Development Department, Government of Orissa, Bhubaneswar.

citizens (women) 113, Women 313 and 586 are unreserved. Similarly, the break up of reservation for the 102 offices of the chairperson is 9 for scheduled castes, 5 for scheduled castes (women), 5 for scheduled Tribes, 3 for scheduled tribe women, 14 for Backward class citizens, 7 for Backward class citizens (women), 19 for women and the rest 40 are unreserved.

Conduct of Business

The councillors of the Municipality shall meet at least once in every month and shall meet as often as may be intimated by the chairperson or the vice-chairperson, as the case may be. One-third of the total councillors or five, whichever is greater, shall constitute the quorum of an ordinary meeting in which the chairperson or in his/ her absence the vice-chairperson shall preside. In the absence of both, a councillor elected at the meeting shall preside. A special meeting can be called by the chairperson or in his/her absence by the vice-chairperson within ten days if at least one-third of total councillors requisition such a meeting. The Municipality has the power to make regulations as to business and affairs subject to the control and approval of state Government. It has also the power to make its own establishment including appointment of its own staff subject to approval of the state Government.

A Municipality has to function through committees. In regard to all or any of the following subjects the Municipality may appoint committees to assist them in discharge of the duties.

(a) Finance.
(b) Public health, hospital and dispensaries.
(c) Public works.
(d) Education.
(e) Water works (Where there is piped water supply).
(f) Any other special subject.

In every Municipal Area having a population of three lakhs or more, a ward committee for every ward may be constituted there.

The Executive Officer appointed by the state Government is the chief executive or Administrative officer of the Municipality and remains in charge and control of all assets, funds and records of the Municipality.He/she also executes, supervises and controls the different functions and programmes conducted by it. Besides, he/she also acts as the secretary to the council and records the minutes of the Municipal meetings.

Table 13

Details of Reservation of Wards alongwith the Office of Chairperson in individual Urban Local Bodies of Orissa (1997)

Sl. No.	Name of the ULB	Total No. of wards	Assignment of wards SC	SC(W)	ST	ST(W)	BCC	BCC(W)	Women	UR	Chair-person
1	2	3	4	5	6	7	8	9	10	11	12
	CORPORATIONS										
1.	Bhubaneswar	30	2	1	1	1	6	3	5	11	UR
2.	Cuttack	35	3	1	1	0	6	3	8	13	BCC
	MUNICIPAL COUNCILS										
1.	Talcher	21	2	2	1	0	4	2	3	7	BCC
2.	Bolangir	17	1	1	1	0	3	2	3	6	UR
3.	Balasore	31	2	1	1	1	6	3	6	11	BCC
4.	Bargarh	17	1	2	1	0	3	2	2	6	UR
5.	Bhadrak	27	1	1	1	0	5	2	6	11	UR
6.	Choudwar	17	1	1	1	0	3	2	3	6	UR
7.	Deogarh	11	1	1	1	1	2	1	1	3	BCC
8.	Dhenkanal	21	2	1	1	0	4	2	4	7	BCC
9.	Paralakhe-mundi	16	1	1	0	1	3	2	2	6	BCC (W)
10.	Berhampur	27	2	1	1	0	5	3	5	10	BCC
11.	Jajpur Road	25	2	2	2	1	5	2	4	7	UR
12.	Jajpur	15	2	1	0	0	3	2	2	5	UR
13.	Brajarajnagar	17	3	1	1	1	3	2	2	4	BCC
14.	Jharsuguda	24	3	1	3	2	5	2	3	5	UR
15.	Bhawani-patna	15	1	1	1	0	3	1	3	5	UR
16.	Kendrapara	20	1	1	1	0	4	2	4	7	UR
17.	Barbil	14	1	1	3	1	0	0	3	5	ST
18.	Joda	13	1	1	3	1	0	0	2	5	ST (W)
19.	Keonjhar	17	1	1	3	1	0	0	4	7	UR
20.	Jeypore	25	2	1	2	1	0	0	6	13	W
21.	Baripada	25	2	1	2	1	0	0	7	12	UR
22.	Nabarangpur	16	1	1	1	1	0	0	3	9	W

23. Puri	30	2	1	1	0	5	3	6	12	UR
24. Rayagada	18	1	1	2	1	0	0	4	9	UR
25. Sambalpur	29	3	1	2	1	5	3	5	9	UR
26. Sonepur	14	2	1	0	0	3	1	3	4	UR
27. Biramitrapur	11	1	1	2	2	0	0	1	4	ST (W)
28. Rajgangpur	19	1	0	2	3	0	0	4	9	UR
29. Rourkela	32	1	1	2	2	0	0	8	18	UR
30. Sundargarh	16	1	1	2	2	0	0	3	7	UR
NOTIFIED AREA COUNCILS										
1. Angul	19	2	1	1	0	4	2	4	5	UR
2. Athamallik	11	1	1	1	0	2	1	2	3	UR
3. Kantabanji	12	1	1	0	0	2	1	2	5	UR
4. Patnagarh	13	1	1	1	0	3	1	3	3	W
5. Titilagarh	15	1	1	1	0	3	1	3	5	BCC
6. Jaleswar	17	0	1	1	1	3	2	2	7	BCC (W)
7. Nilagiri	13	1	1	2	1	2	2	1	3	UR
8. Soro	19	2	1	1	0	4	2	4	5	W
9. Barapali	11	1	1	1	1	1	0	2	4	SC
10. Padmapur	11	0	1	1	1	2	1	0	5	UR
11. Basudevpur	17	2	1	0	0	3	2	3	6	UR
12. Boudh	14	2	1	0	0	4	0	4	3	SC
13. Athagarh	14	2	1	1	0	3	1	3	3	UR
14. Banki	17	2	1	1	0	3	2	3	5	BCC
15. Bhuban	15	1	1	1	0	3	1	1	5	UR
16. Kamakshya-Nagar	12	1	1	1	0	2	1	2	4	UR
17. Kashinagar	13	2	1	0	1	3	1	2	3	SC
18. Aska	18	2	1	1	0	3	2	3	6	UR
19. Belaguntha	12	1	0	1	0	3	1	3	3	BCC (W)
20. Bhanjanagar	15	2	1	1	0	3	2	2	4	W
21. Buguda	11	1	0	1	0	2	1	3	3	W
22. Chhatrapur	12	1	0	1	0	3	1	3	3	BCC (W)
23. Chikiti	12	1	0	1	0	3	1	3	3	UR
24. Digapahandi	11	1	1	1	0	2	1	2	3	W
25. Ganjam	12	2	1	1	0	3	1	2	2	SC
26. Gopalpur	11	1	0	1	0	2	1	3	3	BCC (W)
27. Hinjililcut	21	2	1	1	0	4	2	3	8	W
28. Kabisurya-nagar	16	1	1	1	0	3	2	3	5	BCC
29. Khallikote	12	1	0	1	0	3	1	3	3	UR
30. Kodala	13	1	0	1	0	3	1	4	3	BCC
31. Polasara	13	1	1	1	0	3	1	3	3	W
32. Purusot-tampur	14	1	1	1	0	3	1	3	4	BCC (W)
33 Rambha	13	2	2	1	0	3	1	2	2	SC (W)

34. Sorada	11	2	1	1	0	2	1	2	2	SC
35. Jagatsingh-pur	20	3	1	1	0	3	2	4	6	UR
36. Junagarh	12	0	1	0	1	3	1	1	5	W
37. Kesinga	12	1	1	1	0	3	1	2	3	W
38. G.Udayagiri	13	1	1	2	1	0	0	3	5	W
39. Phulbani	13	1	2	1	0	0	0	3	6	UR
40. Pattamundei	20	4	2	1	0	4	2	3	4	SC (W)
41. Anandpur	16	2	1	1	0	3	2	2	5	BCC
42. Balugaon	11	2	1	1	0	2	1	2	2	SC
43. Banapur	15	1	1	1	0	3	1	3	5	W
44. Jatani	21	2	1	0	1	4	2	3	8	UR
45. Khurda	22	2	1	0	1	4	2	3	9	UR
46. Koraput	15	1	1	2	1	0	0	3	7	UR
47. Kotpad	13	1	1	2	1	0	0	2	6	W
48. Malkanagiri	15	3	1	2	1	0	0	3	5	SC
49. Karanjia	15	1	1	2	2	0	0	2	7	ST
50. Rairangpur	15	1	0	1	1	0	0	4	8	UR
51. Udala	12	1	0	2	1	0	0	3	5	ST
52. Umerkote	13	3	2	1	1	0	0	2	4	SC (W)
53. Khandapada	13	1	0	1	0	2	2	3	4	UR
54. Nayagarh	13	1	0	1	0	2	2	3	4	BCC
55. Khariar Road	17	2	1	1	0	3	2	3	5	W
56. Khariar	13	2	1	1	0	3	1	2	3	BCC (W)
57. Konark	13	2	1	1	0	3	1	2	3	SC
58. Nimapara	11	1	1	1	0	2	1	2	3	BCC
59. Pipili	16	2	1	1	0	3	1	3	5	W
60. Gudari	11	1	1	1	0	0	0	2	6	W
61. Gunupur	15	2	1	1	0	0	0	4	7	W
62. Hirakud	17	2	1	1	1	3	2	2	5	UR
63. Kuchinda	11	1	0	2	2	0	0	2	4	ST
64. Binika	12	2	1	1	0	2	1	2	3	SC (W)
65. Tarava	12	1	1	0	0	2	1	2	5	W
66. Paradeep	15	1	0	1	0	0	0	5	8	UR
67. Belpahar	16	1	1	2	2	0	0	3	7	ST (W)
68. Balimela	12	2	2	1	0	0	0	2	5	SC (W)
69. Sunabeda	24	3	2	3	2	0	0	4	10	ST
70. Burla	15	2	2	1	0	0	0	3	7	SC

Source: Housing and Urban Development Department, Govt. of Orissa, Bhubaneswar.

* List of Reservation of Offices of Chairpersons of the Municipalities of the State for various categories of persons was published in the Orissa Gazette Extraordinary No. 21, dated the 8th January, 1997.

Functions

The Municipal fund may be spent, besides for other approved purposes, for the following functions as per section 117 of the Act :

(i) the construction, diversion, maintenance and improvement of roads, tramways, bridges, parks, squares, gardens, tanks, ghats, wells, channels, latrines and urinals;

(ii) the watering and cleaning of roads;

(iii) the lighting of public roads and provision, purchase, exploitation and maintenance of electric, gas or other undertakings for lighting public and private roads, places and buildings;

(iv) water-supply;

(v) conservancy and drainage, including outfall works and sewage disposal;

(vi) disposal of night-soil by the conversion of the same into compost manure;

(vii) the acquiring, keeping and equipping of open space for purposes of ventilation or for the promotion of physical exercise and public recreation;

(viii) the planting and preservation of trees on roads and public places;

(ix) the construction, maintenance and improvement of offices and other buildings under the control of the municipal council or required for municipal purposes;

(x) the construction and maintenance of model dwelling houses for the working classes and for poorer classes and encouragement as cooperative building societies by loans;

(xi) construction and maintenance of homes for disabled and homeless paupers;

(xii) maintenance of public monuments;

(xiii) the construction, establishment,

maintenance and improvement of schools and hostels to be used in connection with schools either wholly or by means of grants-in-aid;

(xiv) the training of teachers and the establishment of scholarships;

(xv) the construction, establishment, maintenance and improvement of hospitals, dispensaries, sanatoria, leprosy asylums, lunatic asylums, orphanages, rescue houses, maternity houses, child welfare centres, sarais, poor-houses and *dharmasalas* either wholly or by means of grants-in-aid;

(xvi) the employment of vaccinators and the promotion of vaccination;

(xvii) the training and employment of health officers, sanitary inspectors, medical practitioners, compounders, nurses, health visitors, matrons, *dhais* and midwives;

(xviii) the prevention of the spread of dangerous diseases;

(xix) regulating and abating offensive or dangerous trades and removing noxious vegetation;

(xx) the registration of births, deaths and marriages;

(xxi) the payment of the expenses of indigent inhabitants of the municipality for journeys to and from any hospital, established in any part of India, for the treatment of special diseases, and of the subsistence and proper clothing thereat according to such scale as may be fixed by the municipality;

(xxii) payment of contribution for the treatment at recognised sanatorium for the municipal employees suffering from leprosy or tuberculosis;

(xxiii) the improvement of the breed of cattle;

(xxiv) the payment of rewards for the destruction of noxious animals or diseased or unclaimed dogs;

(xxv) all acts and things which are necessary for carrying out the purposes of cruelty to animals;

(xxvi) the construction, establishment, maintenance and improvement of municipal markets or cart stands or slaughter houses or the taking of markets or slaughter houses on lease;

(xxvii) the construction, establishment, maintenance and improvement of municipal dairy farms, grazing grounds and milk depots and all acts and things that may be necessary for the increase and improvement of the supply of milk and milk-products;

(xxviii) the establishment and maintenance of public places for the disposal of the dead;

(xxix) the provision and maintenance of and assistance to public libraries, reading rooms, art galleries, gymnasia or other institutions connected with the diffusion of mental and physical culture or technical instruction;

(xxx) the establishment and maintenance of a fire brigade;

(xxxi) the holding of fairs and industrial sanitary and health exhibitions and cattle shows;

(xxxii) the takings of a census for the purposes of the municipal area;

(xxxiii) the survey of buildings and lands and the preparation and maintenance from time to time of survey maps and plans and of other land records relating to survey and survey marks;

(xxxiv) the giving of relief and the establishment of relief works in time of famine, scarcity, or any natural calamity;

(xxxv) the disposal of unclaimed corpses and the burial or cremation of paupers, and the payment of contributions to charitable institutions for assisting in such disposal, burial or cremation;

(xxxvi) provision and regulation of standard weights, scales and measures and public weighing places;

(xxxvii) the re-excavation and repair of private tanks, wells and other sources of water-supply on such terms and conditions as the council may deem proper;

(xxxviii) contributions to the union of municipal councils;

(xxxix) the payment of expenses of the chairperson, vice-chairperson, councillor or any officer or servant of the municipality to attend any conference or meeting or for any other purpose in the interest of local authorities concerned; and

(xxxx) all acts and things which are likely to promote the safety, health, welfare or convenience of the inhabitants of municipal area, expenditure whereon may be declared by the municipality to be an appropriate charge on the municipal fund.

Provided that where any such act or thing involves an expenditure of more than five thousand rupees, the municipality shall obtain the sanction of the state Government before making a declaration under this clause.

Municipal Fund

Section 114 of the Municipal Act provides For a Municipal Fund which includes all the taxes, fees, fines, all other sums received by the Municipality including loans and the balance and unspent amount running down from previous years and it shall be deposited in the local or nearby Government Treasury. Under section 131 of the Act, the Municipality has the power to impose within the limit of the municipal area the following taxes and fees or any of them:

(a) a tax on holding situated within the municipality assessed on their annual value;
(b) a latrine tax on the annual value of holdings;
(c) a water tax on the annual value of holdings;
(d) lighting tax on the annual value of the holdings;
(e) a drainage tax on the annual value of holdings;
(f) a tax on carriages, carts, horses and other animals named in the Third Schedule;
(g) a tax on profession, art and callings as may be prescribed;
(h) a pool tax subject to such maximum and minimum rates, as may be prescribed, on animal carts and carriages other than motor vehicles carrying goods or passengers and entering the municipality where a festival or fair is held and notified by the municipality for the purpose;
(i) a fee on registration of dogs;
(j) a fee on vessels moored within the limits of the municipal area at ghats or landing places constructed and maintained by the municipality;
(k) any other tax which the municipality is empowered to impose under any law for the time being in force;
(l) an octroi on goods brought within the limits of a municipal area for consumption, use, or safe therein, provided the municipality has obtained prior sanction of the state government in this regard;
(m) any other fee for services rendered by the municipality under the Act for the health, safety and convenience of residents.

Table - 14 (Schedule -III)
Tax on Carriages, Carts, Horses and other Animals [See Section 131 (I) (f) and 176]

SI No	Item	Rate per year
(1)	(2)	(3)
1	For every four wheeled carriage drawn by horses or other animals.	Rs. 20.00
2.	For every two wheeled vehicle including a cart, Jhatka and Tanga excluding bi-cycle.	Rs. 20.00
3.	For every bi-cycle	Rs. 8.00
4.	For every rickshaw	Rs. 4.00
5.	For every cycle rickshaw including trolly rickshaw	Rs. 15.00
6.	For every horse other than pony.	Rs. 8.00
7.	For every pony, mule, donkey or ass	Rs. 4.00
8.	For every elephant	Rs. 24.00
9.	For every hullock or bull	Rs. 2.00
10.	For every camel	Rs. 12.00
11.	For every buffalo and she-buffalo	Rs. 8.00

Source : Orissa Municipal Manual, S C Lal, The Law, Cuttack, 1995.

Supervision and Control

Under the Orissa Municipal Act, 1950 as stands amended till date, the government has the power and option to supervise and control the Municipal Bodies in the following ways :–

(a) Under section 393 of the Municipal Act, every Municipal body shall have to submit before the state government an annual consolidated report of administration of the municipality prepared by the chairperson relating to the latest expired financial year.

(b) The state government has the power to appoint Director and Deputy Director of Municipal Administration for direct control and administration of Municipal Bodies as per the provision of section 393 A of the Act.

(c) The state Government has the power under Section 394 of the Act to appoint officers for the purpose of inspecting and superintending the operation of all or any of the Municipalities of the state. Under Sections 395 and 396, the officers so authorised shall have the right to inspect any record, document, property of the Municipality or work undertaken by it. They can also enter into institutions established and maintained by the Municipality. The employees and servants of the Municipality are bound to cooperate them in this work.

(d) Under Section 398 of the Act the state Government may suspend or cancel any resolution of the Municipality passed, order issued or licence or permission granted or prohibit the doing of any act which is about to be done or is being done provided that such acts have not been legally passed or are done in excess of the powers of the Municipality.

(e) Under Section 399 of the Act the District Magistrate has been empowered with extraordinary powers to direct Municipality or its chairperson or executive officer to execute an act with immediate effect.

(f) Under Section 401 of the Act the state Government has the power of dissolution and reconstitution of a Municipality if in their opinion it is incompetent to perform or persistently makes default in performing the duties imposed on it by law or exceeds or abuses its powers. However, this action can be taken after the charge levelled against such Municipality has been duly informed to it, the show cause notice has been served and explanations and objections of the Municipality have been considered.

In the state of "Orissa, the state Government's Supervision and control over local bodies are almost absolute and mostly negative in character. Despite the considerable improvements in the Act over the years the obnoxious system of supersession still continues. The control and supervision becomes more real when the two opposite parties hold office in a municipality and the state Government respectively. Thus, when the same political party is in power both at the state and the Municipality, the Municipal authority may tend to have the appearance of autonomy, but when the groups at the two levels are opposite, the appearance of autonomy tends to evaporate and the predominance of vertical authority and influence becomes clear. In these circumstances the state level actors play the notorious part of influencing the outcome in the Municipal area by frequent intervention....In Orissa almost all Municipal Bodies were superseded. Cuttack Municipality alone was under supersession for more than 18 years within the first 27 years of Indian Independence. Between 1978 and 1981, the Municipalities of Cuttack, Berhampur and Puri were supervised by the Government, where the chairpersons were from the opposition."[54]

The urban politics is also influenced by "the relationship between the chairman, the popular representative and the Executive Officer appointed by the Government of Orissa under the framework of Orissa Municipal Act, 1950. The chairman is the focal point of urban local set up and as such, he is expected to be the people's voice within the decentralised sector of administration. But in Orissa, the chairmen either try to impose themselves on the administration or neatly surrender to it thereby tilting the balance of local administration in either case. Sometimes the chairman becomes over ambitious or enthusiastic and in the process tries to dominate officers in the council; sometimes also by-pass the popular representatives and impose themselves on the administration. Thus, in either case begins the hitch between the chairman and the executive officer leading to the administrative disruption which becomes a good excuse for the supersession of the council....Further, the frequent intrusion of party politics in local administration has posed serious problems in the smooth functioning of these urban democratic structures. A large section of the public does not favour political parties getting themselves involved in the activities of the local governments. As these bodies have to deal with strictly local problems, the infusion of party politics has no relevance and can only hamper local activities. The necessity of party activities arises only at state and national levels where policy making decisions

Table 15 (Schedule - IV)
Ordinary Penalties (See Section 383)

Section or rule	*Sub section or clause*	*Subject*	*Fine which may be imposed*
1	2	3	4
143	...	Failure of owner or occupier to furnish return of rent.	one hundred rupees
148	...	Failure to give notice of transfer of title or to produce documents.	Fifty rupees
177	...	Failure to furnish statement of carriages, carts,horses and other animals liable to taxation or furnishing incorrect statement .	Ten rupees
[179]	(3)	Failure to affix municipal number plate to cart or carriage.	Ditto
181	...	Keeping carriages, carts, horses and other animals without licence.	Ditto
194	...	Failure of owner or occupier to obey requisition to furnish list of persons carrying on profession, cart.	One hundred rupees
195	...	Failure of employer or head of an office, firm or company to obey requisition to furnish list of persons in his employment.	Ditto
199	...	Trespassing on premises connected with the water suppply.	Fifty rupees
202	...	failure to maintain house connection in conformity with byelaws and regulations.	Ditto
203	(2)	Failure to obey requisition to make house connection.	Ditto
211	...	Failure to maintain house-drains in conformity with byelaws and regulations	Ditto
212	(2) and (3)	Failure to obey requisition as to home drainage.	Ditto
213	(1) (b)	Failure to obey direction as to limited use of drain or notice requiring construction of distinct drain.	Fifty rupees
215	...	Unlawful construction of building over public drain.	One Hundred rupees
216	...	Failure to obey requisition regarding culverts, or to keep them free from obstruction.	Fifty rupees

Contd...

Table 15 Contd...

1	2	3	4
217	...	Failure to obey requisition to maintain troughs and pipes for catching water from roof or other part of building.	Ditto
219	...	Making connection with mains without permission.	Two hundred rupees
223	...	Improper disposal of carcases, rubbish and filth.	Ten rupees
224	...	Allowing rubbish or filth to accumulate on premises for more than twenty four hours.	Twenty rupees
225	...	Allowing filth to flow in roads.	Ten rupees
226	...	Using cart without cover in removal of filth.	Twenty rupees
227	...	Throwing rubbish or filth into drains.	Ditto
229	...	Construction of latrine or urinal near road, tank and water course.	Five hundred rupees
230	...	Failure to obey requisition to provide latrine or to remove latrine to another site and failure to keep latrines clean and in proper order.	One hundred rupees
231	...	Failure to provide latrines for premises used by large numbers of people or to keep them clean in proper order.	Ditto
232	...	Failure to obey requisition to provide latrines for market, cattle stand or cart-stand or to keep them clean and in proper order.	One hundred rupees
233	...	Failure to construct Utilities so as to screen persons using them from view.	Twenty rupees
239	...	Building within regular lines of road.	One hundred rupees
240	(1)	Failure to obey orders to set back buildings.	Five hundred rupees
245	...	Unlawful displacement of pavement or fences, posts and other materials of public road.	Fifty rupees
247	...	Failure to provide roads on building-sites prior to disposal.	Two hundred rupees
248	(5)	Unlawful making or lying of new private roads.	Five hundred rupees

Contd...

Table 15 Contd...

1	2	3	4
250	...	Failure to obey requisition to metal private roads.	One hundred rupees
252	...	Building wall or erecting fence in a public road.	Ditto
253	...	Allowing doors, ground-floor windows to open outwards without licence or contrary to notice.	Twenty rupees
254	...	Failure to remove permanent encroachment.	Two hundred rupees
255	...	Failure to remove temporary encroachment.	Fifty rupees
257	...	Unlawful removal of bar or shoring timber or removal or extinction of light.	Ditto
258	(5)	Unlawful making of hole or placing of obstruction in roads.	Ditto
259	...	Construction of building without licence where road or footway is likely to be obstructed.	Ditto
		Failure to fence such building while under repair or failure to remove obstruction.	Ditto
260	...	Failure to remove obstruction caused in road by fall of trees within 12 hours of fall.	Ditto
261	(3)	Unlawful destruction of name of road.	Twenty rupees
269	(2)	Unlawful destruction of number of buildings.	Five rupees
	(3)	Failure to replace number when required to do so.	Twenty rupees
275	(1)	Failure to obey requisition to take down, repair or secure dangerous structure.	Five hundred rupees
	(3)	Failure to obey requisition to secure , lop or cut down dangerous trees.	Fifty rupees
	(5)	Failure to obey requisition to repair tank or other place dangerous to passers-by or persons living in neighbourhood.	Ditto
276	...	Failure to obey requisition to stop dangerous quarrying.	One hundred rupees
277	...	Failure to obey notice regarding precautions against fire.	Ditto

Contd...

Table 15 Contd...

1	2	3	4
278	(1)	Constructing well without permission.	Fifty rupees
	(3)	Failure to obey notice to fill up or demolish well.	Ditto
279	...	Failure to obey requisition to fill up tank or well or drain off water.	Fifty rupees
280	...	Failure to obey requisition to cleanse or close tank, well or other source of water used for drinking.	Ditto
282	...	Unlawful washing and fishing in river after prohibition or contrary to regulations.	Ditto
283	...	Defiling water of tanks.	Ditto
284	...	Failure to obey requisition to enclose, clear or cleanse untenanted prmises.	Ditto
285	...	Failure to obey requisition to clear or cleanse building or land in filthy state or overgrown with noxious vegetation.	Fifty rupees
286	...	Using or allowing the use of building unfit for human habitation after prohibition.	Twenty rupees for each day
287	...	Unlawful keeping of animals so as to be a nuisance or dangerous.	Ten rupees
290	(1)	Using a place for any of the purposes specified in Section 290 (1) without licence or contrary to licence.	One hundred rupees
291	...	Unlawful erection of factory, workshop.	One thousand rupees
292	...	Disobedience of order regarding abatement of nuisance.	One hundred rupees
296	...	Sale or exposure for sale in public market of animal or article without licence or contrary to licence.	Twenty rupees
297	...	Opening or keeping open private market without licence or contrary to licence.	Five hundred rupees
299	...	Sale or exposure for sale of animal or article in unlicensed private market.	Twenty rupees

Contd...

Table 15 Contd...

1	2	3	4
300	...	Failure to obey direction to contract approaches, drains to private markets or to pave them.	Five rupees
301	(2)	Opening or keeping open private market after suspension or refusal of licence for default to carry out works.	Twenty rupees for each
302	...	Nuisances in private markets.	Twenty rupees
307	...	Sale or exposure for sale of animal or article in public road.	Ten rupees
310	...	Using a public place or the sites of a public road or public landing place.	Two hundred rupees
312	...	Opening or keeping open a new private cart-stand without licence or contrary to licence.	Ditto
314	...	Slaughter of cattle in places other than public slaughter-house.	Ditto
316	...	Carrying on milk trade without licence or contrary to licence.	Fifty rupees
320	...	Burying or burning corpses in unregistered ground.	One hundred rupees
337	(5)	Failure to produce licence on request.	Five rupees
379	...	Removal of notice exhibited by or under order of the council.	Fifty rupees
380	...	Failure to obey summons.	Ditto

Source : Orissa Municipal Manual, S. C. Lal, The Law, Cuttack, 1995.

Table 16 (Schedule - V)
Penalties for continuing Breaches (See Section 383)

Section or rule	*Sub-section or Clause*	*Subject*	*Daily fine which may be imposed*
1	2	3	4
202	...	Failure to maintain house connection in conformity with bye-laws and regulations.	five rupees
203	(2)	Failure to obey requisition to make house-connection.	Ditto
211	...	Failure to maintain house-drains, in conformity with bye-laws and regulations.	Ten rupees
212	(2) and (3)	Failure to obey requisition as to house drainage.	Ditto
217	...	Failure to obey requisition to maintain troughs and pipes for catching water from roof or other part of building.	Ditto
230	...	Failure to obey requisition to provide latrine or to remove latrine to another site and failure to keep latrines clean and in proper order.	Ditto
231	...	Failure to provide latrines for premises used by large numbers of people or to keep them clean and in proper order.	Twenty rupees
232	...	Failure to obey requisition to provide latrines for market, cattle-stand or cart stand or to keep them clean and in proper order.	Ditto
239	...	Building within regular lines of road	One hundred rupees
254	...	Failure to remove permanent encroachment.	Ten rupees
255	...	Failure to remove temporary encroachment.	Five rupees
258	...	Unlawful making of hole or placing of obstruction in road.	Ten rupees
259	...	Construction of building without licence where street or foot-way is likely to be obstructed.	Ten rupees
275	...	Failure to obey requisition to repair tank or other place dangerous to passers-by or persons living in neighbourhood.	Ditto

Contd...

Table 16 Contd...

1	2	3	4
276	...	Failure to obey requisition to stop dangerous quarrying.	Ditto
277	...	Failure to obey notice regarding precautions against fire.	Ditto
279	...	Failure to obey requisition to fill up tank or well or drain off water.	Ditto
280	...	Failure to obey requisition to cleanse or close tank, well, other source of water used for drinking.	Ditto
284	...	Failure to obey requisition to enclose, clear or cleanse untenanted premises.	Ditto
285	...	Failure to obey requisition to clear or cleanse building or land in filthy state or overgrown with noxious vegetation.	Ditto
287	...	Unlawful keeping of animal so as to be a nuisance or dangerous.	Five rupees
290	(1)	Using a place for any of the purposes specified in Sec. 290 (1) without licence or contrary to licence.	Twenty rupees
291	...	Unlawful erection of factory, workshop.	One hundred rupees
292	...	Disobedience of order regarding abatement of nuisance.	Ditto
297	...	Opening or keeping open private market without licence or contrary to licence.	Ditto
299	...	Sale or exposure for sale of animal or article in unlicenced private market.	Twenty rupees
313	...	Using a public place or the sites of a public road as a public landing place.	Ditto
312	...	Opening or keeping open a new private cart-stand without licence or contrary to licence.	Twenty rupees
316	...	Carry on milk trade without licence or contrary to licence.	Five rupees

Source: Orissa Municipal Manual, S. C. Lal, The Law, Cuttack, 1995.

Table 17
Orissa Municipal Elections, 1997
Position of Different Political Parties in Individual Urban Bodies

Sl. No.	Name of Urban bodies	Total no. of Councillors elected	Congress (I)	Janata Dal	BJP	CPI	CPI(M)	Others	Independents
1	2	3	4	5	6	7	8	9	10
1.	Angul NAC	19	14	2	1	...	...	...	2
2.	Athamallik NAC	11	7	4	...	...	...	...	...
3.	Talcher Municipality	(21-2)19	13	1	3	...	...	2	...
4.	Bolangir Municipality	17	9	6	2	...	...	...	...
5.	Kantabanji N.A C	12	1	...	3	...	...	...	8
6.	Patanagarh N A C	13	I	...	9	...	...	...	3
7.	Titlagarh N.A.C	...	Election not held		...	...	...	...	
8.	Balasore Municipality	31	11	2	6	...	...	...	12
9.	Jaleswar N. A.C.	17	11	...	1	...	1	...	4
10.	Nilgiri N.A.C	13	8	2	...	...	...	...	3
11.	Soro N.A.C	19	13	...	5	...	...	...	1
12.	Bargarh Municipality	17	11	1	...	...	...	...	5
13.	Barpali N.A.C	11	11	...	...	...	...	...	...
14.	Padmapur N.A.C	11	5	...	5	...	...	...	1
15.	Basudevpur N.A.C	17	15	1	...	...	1	...	...
16.	Bhadrak Municipality	27	22	1	...	...	1	...	3
17.	Boudh N A C	14	5	5	4	...	...	...	1
18.	Athagarh N.A..C	14	14	...	...	...	...	...	...

Contd...

Table 17 Contd...

1	2	3	4	5	6	7	8	9	10
19.	Banki N.A.C	(17-1)16	10	6	...	...	...	...	...
20.	Choudwar Municipality	17	8	6	1	...	...	...	2
21.	Cuttack Corporation	35	20	7	7	...	...	...	1
22.	Deogarh Municipality	11	5	1	3	...	...	...	2
23.	Bhuban N A.C	15	7	...	1	5	...	...	2
24.	Dhenkanal Municipality	21	7	...	8	...	...	...	6
25.	Kamakshyanagar N.A.C	12	5	...	4	...	...	...	3
26.	Kashinagar N.A.C	(13-1)12	4	1	1	...	...	...	6
27.	Paralakhemundi Municipality	16	9	3	...	...	1	...	3
28.	Aska N.A.C	18	13	1	2	...	...	...	2
29.	Belaguntha N.A.C	12	2	8	2	...	...	...	...
30.	Berhampur Municipality	27	14	2	2	...	1	...	.8
31.	Bhanjanagara N.A.C	15	8	5	...	...	...	...	2
32.	Buguda N.A.C	11	4	4	...	...	...	...	3
33.	Chhatrapur N.A.C	12	9	1	...	...	...	...	2
34.	Chikiti N.A.C	12	4	8	...	...	...	...	...
35.	Digapahandi N.A.C	11	6	2	1	2	...	...	...
36.	Ganjam N.A.C	(12-1)11	5	...	...	2	...	...	4
37.	Gopalpur N.A.C	(11-1)10	7	...	...	...	...	...	3
38.	Hinjilicut N.A.C	(21-1)20	6	9	2	...	...	...	3
39.	Kabisuryanagar N.A.C	16	14	...	...	...	1	...	1
40.	Khallikote N.A.C	(12-1)11	5	4	...	...	...	...	2
41.	Kodala N.A.C	(13-1)12	...	...	11	...	...	...	1
42.	Polasara N.A.C	13	3	10	...	...	...	...	...
43.	Puroshottampur N.A.C	(14-1)13	2	3	...	...	...	...	8

Contd...

Table 17 Contd...

1	2	3	4	5	6	7	8	9	10
44.	Rambha N.AC.	13	3	2	2	1	...	...	5
45.	Sorada N.A.C	11	4	...	...	...	...	...	7
46.	Jagatsinghpur N.A.C	20	18	1	...	...	...	...	1
47.	Jajpur Road Municipality	25	13	4	1	1	1	...	5
48.	Jajpur Municipality	25	3	12	...	...	...	...	...
49.	Brajrajanagar Municipality	17	9	2	2	...	...	...	4
50.	Jharsuguda Municipality	24	8	11	2	...	...	...	3
51.	Bhawanipatna Municipality	15	4	3	3	...	...	3	2
52.	Junagarh N.A.C	12	1	...	3	...	...	7	1
53.	Kesinga N.A.C	12	1	2	3	...	...	5	1
54.	G.Udayagiri N.A.C	13	9	1	...	...	...	...	3
55.	Phulbani N.A.C	13	8	...	2	...	...	...	3
56.	Kendrapada Municipality	20	11	2	6	...	...	...	1
57.	Pattamundei N.A.C	(20-1)19	10	9	...	...	...	...	...
58.	Anandapur N.A.C	16	5	1	8	...	...	...	2
59.	Barbil Municipality	14	2	6	5	...	...	...	1
60.	Joda Municipality	13	12	...	...	...	...	...	1
61.	Keonjhargarh Municipality	17	10	5	...	...	...	...	2
62.	Balugaon N.A.C	(11-1)10	9	...	1	...	...	...	...
63.	Banapur N.A.C	(15-1)14	7	...	5	...	...	...	2
64.	Bhubaneswar Corporation	30	8	5	7	...	1	...	9
65.	Jatani N.A.C	21	8	4	5	...	...	...	4
66.	Khurda N.A.C	22	18	...	2	...	...	...	2
67.	Jeypore NAC	25	9	7	1	...	...	...	8
68.	Koraput NAC	15	10	2	1	...	...	...	2

Contd...

Table 17 Contd...

1	2	3	4	5	6	7	8	9	10
69.	Kotpad NAC	13	7	3	1	...	...	...	2
70.	Malkanagiri NAC	15	6	4	3	...	...	...	2
71.	Baripada Municipality	25	8	2	1	...	...	...	14
72.	Karanjia NAC	15	4	...	9	...	...	...	2
73.	Rairangpur NAC	15	2	...	9	...	...	...	4
74.	Udala NAC	12	4	...	2	...	...	...	6
75.	Nawrangpur Municipality	16	12	...	...	...	...	...	4
76.	Umerkote NAC	13	6	6	1	...	...	...	...
77.	Khandapada NAC	13	6	3	1	...	...	...	3
78.	Nayagarh NAC	13	6	3	...	...	...	...	4
79.	Khariar Road NAC	17	8	3	5	...	...	...	1
80.	Khariar NAC	13	6	1	3	...	...	1	2
81.	Konark NAC	(13-1)12	5	6	...	...	...	...	1
82.	Nimapara NAC	11	8	...	1	...	...	...	2
83.	Pipili NAC	16	13	3	...	...	...	...	...
84.	Puri Municipality	30	11	11	7	...	...	...	1
85.	Gudari NAC	11	6	...	...	...	...	...	5
86.	Gunupur NAC	15	6	...	1	...	...	...	8
87.	Rayagada Municipality	18	8	9	1	...	...	...	...
88.	Hirakud NAC	17	7	...	8	...	...	...	2
89.	Kuchinda NAC	11	4	...	4	...	...	...	3
90.	Sambalpur Municipality	29	13	...	13	...	...	...	3
91.	Binika N.A.C	12	5	3	...	...	...	...	4
92.	Sonepur Municipality	14	4	3	3	...	...	...	4
93.	Tarava N.A.C.	12	1	...	1	...	...	...	10

Contd...

Table 17 Contd...

1	2	3	4	5	6	7	8	9	10
94.	Biramitrapur Municipality	11	6	1	2	...	...	2	...
95.	Rajgangpur Municipality	19	4	1	5	...	...	3	6
96.	Rourkela Municipality	32	15	11	3	...	...	...	3
97.	Sundargarh Municipality	16	9	1	3	...	...	1	2
	TOTAL :-	1553	750	259	230	11	08	24	271

Soucre: State Election Commission, Orissa, Bhubaneswar.

are being taken. Local functions are so simple and basic that there is hardly any scope for different opinions to prevail. As such the main interest of these parties in capturing seats in the Urban local bodies, is to advance their party interests in the local areas and use them as spring boards to jump to the state and national level politics."[55]

The very peculiar thing is that, "probably the Government of Orissa is equating effectiveness with the increase in the number of Urban local bodies. But growth of development, though it contributes partially to the effectiveness of the process, can not be equated either with efficiency or effectiveness of the process. To make the Urban bodies more effective, the state Government should pay adequate attention to solve some of the important problems that have remained hitherto unattended. First, the power of supersession of Urban local bodies should be rarely used and that too only in extreme cases of delinquency and default, after giving essential instruction and reasonable period of notice. The aim should be to reform and improve the council from within by infusing greater enthusiasm for self-government and civic responsibility among the inhabitants of the civic community rather than to pronounce capital punishment on them."[56]

1997 Municipal Elections - A Review

Nearly two years after having been kept under supersession, 94 local bodies of the state went to polls on 11.07.1997 and a little later another body, i.e., Sambalpur Municipality availed the opportunity on 4th and 10th August. The delay in election to Sambalpur Municipality was due to some technical defects in reservation of wards and torrential rains. The state election commission having been empowered under Article 243ZA of the constitution conducted the Municipal Elections. Elections to 5 local bodies such as Paradeep N.A.C, Belpahad N.A.C, Balimela N.A.C,

Sunabeda N.A.C and Burla N.A.C were not needed as elections were held there in 1995. Elections to Kabisuryanagar N.A.C. were not needed as all the 16 wards there were uncontested. Elections to Titlagarh N.A.C. could not be held as no candidate filed nomination in any of the 15 wards in protest against Government policies and apathy towards the area.

Thus, excluding Titlagarh N.A.C, the rest 96 Municipal Bodies went to polls in July-August, 1997. Out of the total 1567 wards assigned to these 96 Municipal bodies, elections to 14 wards could not be held due to various reasons including death of candidates in some wards. From the rest 1553 wards, even number of councillors were elected.Out of them, 750 belong to Congress(I), 259 to Janata Dal, 230 to BJP, 11 to CPI, 8 to CPI(M) and 24 to others. But the independent candidates occupied as many as 271 seats. In terms of percentages of seats of councillors, Congress(I) has occupied a lion's share of 48.29 per cent of seats, Janata Dal has captured 16.68 per cent seats, BJP has a share of 14.81 per cent of scats, while the independent candidates have a strength of 17.45 per cent of the seats. CPI, CPI(M) and others account for 0.71 per cent, 0.52 per cent and 1.55 per cent of the seats respectively. Thus, the congress(I) has been returned with a dominant voice in the Urban politics of the state including the two Urban bodies of Phulbani district.

Table 18

Partywise Position of Chairpersons and Vice-Chairpersons in 1997 Municipal Elections of Orissa

	Congress(I)	*Janata Dal*	*B.J.P.*	*Samata party*	*Independ-tents*	*Total*
Chairpersons	64	15	06	03	07	95
Vice-Chairpersons	51	13	13	02	16	95

Source: State Election Commission, Orissa, Bhubaneswar.

For elections to the offices of chairpersons, vice-chairpersons of Municipal Bodies of the state 95 out of 97 Bodies have been taken into account. Elections for these posts were not held in Joda Municipality and Titilagarh N.A.C. Out of 95 seats of chairpersons,Congress(I) captured 64 seats which constitutes 67.37 per cent of the total scats. Janata Dal with 15 seats had a share of 15.79 per cent of the total scats. B.J.P, Samata Party and independents captured respectively 6, 3 and 7 seats constituting 6.32 per cent, 3.16 per cent and 7.37 per cent of the seats respectively. For the offices of vice-chairpersons, Congress(I) got 51 seats having claimed 53.68 per cent of the total seats. Janata Dal, B.J.P, Samata party and Independents got 13, 13, 2, and 16 scats respectively. The respective percentages of seats occupied by them are 13.68, 13.68, 2.11 and 16.84. Thus, Congress(l) has claimed the majority of both the categories of seats in the state including all such seats in both the N.A.Cs of Phulbani districts.

References

1. W. S. Thompson; in *Encyclopaedia of the Social Science,* The MacMillan Company, Newyork, 1953, pp. 189-190.
2. A. B. Gallion, and S.Eisner; *The Urban pattern,* Affiliated East West Press Pvt. Ltd., New Delhi, 1969, p.3
3. *Ibid.*
4. *Ibid.*
5. K. Marx, and F. Engels ; *Manifesto of the Communist Party,* Progress Publishers, Moscow, 1977, p.40.
6. K. Davis, *Human Society,* Surjeet Publications, Delhi, 1981, pp.121-322.
7. J.L. Nehru, *Glimpses of World History,* Oxford University press, New Delhi, 1989, pp. 204-205.
8 A. B. Gallion, and S. Eisner ; *op. cit,* pp. 119-120.
9. *Ibid.* p. 167.
10. N. Anderson, *The Urban Community,* Routledlge & Kegan Paul Ltd., London, 1960, pp. 1-2.
11. K. Mannheim, *Freedom, Power and Democratic Planning,* Oxford University Press, Newyork, 1950, p. 62.
12. R. M. MacIver, and C. H. Page; *Society - An Introductory Analysis,* Macmillan India Limited, Madras, 1990, p. 321.
13. K. Davis, *op.cit,* pp. 317-318.
14. B. R. Chauhan, *Towns in the Tribal Setting,* National Publishing House, Delhi, 1970, p. 148.
15. N. V. Sovani, *Urbanisation and Urban India,* Asia publishing House, Bombay, 1965, p. 33.
16. S. R. Maheshwari, ; *Local Government in India.* Lakshmi Narain Agarwal, Agra, 1992-93, pp. 170-171.
17. *Union Primary Census (1991) Abstract for Scheduled Castes and Scheduled Tribes, Series- 1 (Paper -1 of 1993),* Govt. of India, New Delhi.

18. *Ibid.*
19. N. K. Behura, ; in *Tribes of Orissa,* Triibal and Harijan Welfare Department, Orissa, Bhubaneswar, 1990. p. 15.
20. P. Sharan, ; *Comparative Government and Politics,* Meenakshi Prakashan, Meerut, 1981, p. 433.
21. *Ibid,* p. 416.
22. *Ibid,* p. 418–419.
23. I. Narain, ; in *Indian Journal of Public Administration,* Vol IX. No. I, New Delhi, pp 10-11.
24. H. J. Laski, ; *A Grammar of Politics,* S Chand & Company Ltd, New Delhi, p. 411.
25. *Ibid.,* pp. 412-413.
26. *Ibid.*
27. *Ibid.,* p. 415.
28. *Ibid.,* pp. 416-419.
29. *Ibid.*
30. *Ibid.*
31. E. Barker, ; *Principles of Social & Political Theory,* Oxford University Press, Calcutta, 1983, p. 5.
32. A. Avasthi, ; *in The Gazetteer of India (Vol.IV) - Administration and Public Welfare,* Ministry of Education and Social Welfare, New Delhi, 1978, pp 251 - 252.
33. As quoted in *The Imperial Gazetteer of India,* Vol. IV, Oxford, Clarendon Press, 1909, p.282.
34. A. Avasthi, ; *Municipal Administration in India,* Lakshmi Narain Agarwal, Agra, 1972, p. 519.
35. A. Avasthi, and A. P. Avasthi, *Indian Administration,* Lakshmi Narain Agarwal, Agra, pp. 520-521.
36. *Ibid.*
37. *Ibid.,* p. 533.
38. *Ibid.*
39. *Ibid.,* pp. 533-534.
40. *Ibid.,* pp. 534-535.
41. *Ibid.,* pp. 535-536.
42. *Ibid.,* p. 536.
43. *Ibid.*
44. *Ibid.,* pp. 536-537.
45. *Ibid.,* pp. 537-538.
46. *Ibid.,* p. 538.
47. L. K. Patnaik, ; in *Government and Politics in Orissa (ed.),* B. B. Jena & J.K. Baral, Print House (India), Lucknow, 1988, p.367.
48. G. C. Nayak, (Self) ; *Indian Political Tradition,* Kalyani Publishers, New Delhi, 2nd Edn. 1995, p.219.
49. *Ibid.,* p. 220
50. K. K. Patnaik, ; *op cit* pp.367-369
51. *Ibid.*
52. *Ibid.*
53. *The Samaj,* Cuttack, dated 24.9.7 1997.
54. L. K. Patnaik, ; *op. cit.,* pp.376-379
55. *Ibid.*
56. *Ibid.*

3
The Political Elite

Conceptual and Theoretical Perspectives

The wheels of political change in any modern society are no doubt propelled by the socio-political dynamics like political parties, political participation, public opinion, modernisation, broad-based education, secularism etc. with which the mass power is involved in unorganised and unsophisticated sense. The political elite either through political parties or of their own convert the mass power into the power of the Elite and thus, convert the 'popular sovereignty' into supremacy of the elite. The authoritative allocations in the given political society are initiated, controlled, and guided, in one form or the other, by the society's well-organised microscopic minority—the political elite which metamorphosises the concept of Government by the people and of the people into Government by the elite and of the elite. Conforming to the norms of political pluralism, the political elites not only function at the top power circles but also control power and authority at political sub-centres—the local bodies.

To define, "an elite, as the dictionary says, is choice, a chosen element in the population. An elite, unlike an oligarchy or an aristocracy owes its peculiar position to the recognition and esteem accorded to it by the masses. The term 'elite' implies that although men may consider themselves equal in the sense that they are citizens and not subjects, some are considered to possess superior qualities. As already pointed out, it also means that the position of the elite depends on recognition—formal or informal by the vast majority, not forming part of the elite. The concept of the 'elite' is classificatory and descriptive, designating the holders of high positions in a given society. There are as many elites as there are values".[1]

To put it "typically, an adjective precedes the word 'elite' clarifying its aim (oligarchic elite, modernising elite), or its style (innovating elite, brokerage elite), or its institutional domain (legislative elite, bureaucratic elite), or its resources base (media elite, financial elite), or the decisional stage it dominates (planning elite, implementing elite), or its eligibility grounds (birth elite, credentialed elite)".[2]

As to the nature of Elites, "two quite different traditions of inquiry persist. In the older tradition, elites are treated as examplars; fulfilling some historic mission, meeting a crucial need, possessing superior talents, or otherwise demonstrating qualities which set them apart. Whether they stabilise the old order or transform it into a new one, they are seen as pattern setters. In the newer approach, elites are routinely understood to be incumbents: those who are collectively the influential figures in the governance of any sector of society, any institutional structure, any geographic locality or translocal community. Idiomatically, elites are roughly the same as leaders, decision-makers or influential, and not too different from spokesmen, dignitaries, or central figures. This second use is more matter-of-fact, less normative in tone... Still elites are seen by many as selfish people in power, bent upon protecting their vested interests, contemptuous of the restraints on constitutional order, callous about the needs of larger public, ready to manipulate opinion, to rig elections, to use force, if necessary, to retain power. A conspiratorial variant worries those who fear revolutionary subversive elites; fanatical, selfless, disciplined, competent, and devoted to their cause, equally contemptuous of political democracy, constitutional order, or mass contentment, willing to exploit hatred and misery, to misrepresent beliefs and facts, and to face personal degradation and social obloquy. Whether to preserve old patterns of life or to exemplify new one, elites are those who set the styles".[3]

About the position of authority, "Mosca and Pareto (see Meisel, 1965) both presumed that a ruling class effectively monopolised the command posts of a society. Michels insisted that his 'iron law of oligarchy' was inevitable; in any organisation an inner circle of participants would take over and run it for their selfish purposes. By contrast, Lasswell's formulation in the 1930s was radically pluralistic. Elites are those who get the most of what there is to get in any institutionalised sector of society and not only in the governing institutions and ancillary process of organised political life. At every functional stage of any decision process—indeed, in any relevant arena—some participants will be found who have sequestered disproportionate shares of those values, whether money, esteem, power or some other condition of life which people seek and struggle for. They are the elite at the stage and in that context. The social formations—classes, communities, movements—from which elites derive are not fixed, either. Elites are usually studied by asking which communities they represent or dominate, which classes they are exponents or products of, which interests they reflect or foreshadow, which personality types they are prone to recruit or to shunt aside, which circumstances of time and place (periods of crisis, tranquillity, or transitions) seem to provide missions and challenges for them."[4]

Elite character is subject to change. "Specialised Elites—engineers, soldiers, priests—have often served as second tier elites recruited in the service of a ruling class that continues to set a governing style but whose numbers lack the skills to cope with new and pressing problems. Some scholars hold that a true elite emerges when those who perform the historic mission—whether to bring change, adapt to change, or resist to the end-become convinced that only they can carry out the mission properly, self-consciously, they come to think of themselves as superior by nature—for example, able to think like scientists or soldiers, willing to take risks like capitalists or revolutionaries."[5]

In other words, "viewed as incumbents, those who hold key positions in the governing institutions of a community are, collectively the elite. They are the custodians of the machinery for making policy... In the modern World, when elites are seen as housed within conventionally recognised establishments such as military, diplomatic, legislative, or party organisational structures, mid-cities and cadres are linked hierarchically to top elites and specialised to implement the specific public and system goals of their domains."[6]

Suzanne Keller observes— "The concept of elites is used to describe certain fundamental features of organised social life. All societies—simple and complex, agricultural and industrial—need authorities within and spokesmen and agents without who are also symbols of the common life and embodiments of the values that maintain it. Inequalities in performance and reward support this arrangement, and the inequality in the distribution of deference acknowledges the differences in authority, achievement, and reward. Elites are those minorities which are set apart from the rest of society by their pre-eminence in one or more of these various distributions."[7]

Tracing back to its history one will find that, "the word 'elite' first originated in the seventeenth century and was used to refer to commodities of excellence. It is only later that the term came into vogue to describe superior social groups in the society. But it did not enter the vocabulary of political science in Europe until the nineteenth century, and the use of this term in Great Britain and U.S.A. began only in the thirties. Two Italian Sociologists Vilfred Pareto (1848-1923) and Gaetano Mosca (1858-1941) were the first to develop the Elite Theory."[8]

Vilfred Pareto observes that some individuals are superior in their attributes while others possess inferior abilities. The former class of superior ability constitutes the *elite*, which again falls into two classes: "*non governing elite*, comprising individuals who directly or indirectly play some considerable part in government and a *non-governing elite*, comprising the rest".[9] Thus, Pareto divides the society into two classes: the elite and the non-elite and further he divides the elite into the governing elite and non-governing elite.

Pareto stated that the elites possess 'lion' and /or 'fox' qualities 'Lion' qualities include strength and courage while 'fox' qualities comprise intelligence, shrewdness and cunningness. He believes that elites cannot be constant or static and they tend to decay. To him, "History is a graveyard of aristocracies", because there is 'circulation of elites', the concept which he used in two senses. First, it is a process in which the individuals circulate between the Elite and the non-elite strata. Second, it is a process in which one elite is replaced by another elite. Referring to the first type he observes that 'the governing class is restored not only in numbers but— and that is the more important thing— in quality, by families rising from the lower classes." Exemplifying the second type he states that "a slowing down of this circulation (of individuals) may result in a considerable increase of the degenerate elements in the classes which still hold power, and on the other hand, in an increase of elements of superior quality in the subject classes. In such a case, the social equilibrium becomes unstable... and the slightest shock will destroy it. A conquest or a revolution produces an upheaval, brings a new elite to power, and establishes a new equilibrium."[10]

Pareto's theory was further developed by Mosca who believed that irrespective of its outer form every Government is essentially ruled by a minority which he calls 'the ruling class'. This springs out from his conviction that it is only a few in any society who are of superior intellect and are well organised while the majority are unorganised and are persons of no conspicuous calibre. He explains that "in all societies—

from societies that are very meagrely developed and have barely attained the dawnings of civilisation down to the most advanced and powerful societies—two classes of people appear—a class that rules and a class that is ruled. The first class, always the less numerous, performs all political functions, monopolises power and enjoys the advantages that power brings. Whereas the second, the more numerous class, is directed and controlled by the first, in a manner that is now more or less legal, now more or less arbitrary and violent..."[11]

Robert Michaels (1876-1936), an Italian Political Scientist made significant contribution to the Elite theory through his 'Iron Law of Oligarchy'. He viewed that democracy, which is projected to be the rule of the masses or the majority is not conceivable without organisation. In any complex society the common mass cannot voice their demands effectively without an organisation. As the issues are complex and demand specialist knowledge which the rank and fiile members do not ordinarily possess, they only form organisations by joining hands together. Decisions are therefore, left to the executive committees and smaller groups. Thus, the organisations are antithetical to democracy as they invariably produce oligarchy and this is termed as *the iron law of oligarchy* by Michaels.

Conforming to Michaels' 'Iron Law of Oligarchy' even V.I. Lenin (1870-1924) believed that scientific socialism or communism which stood for dictatorship of the proletariat and a classless society ultimately, could not be possible without an elite—the organised minority in the form of communist party. "The socialist philosophy of Marx and Engels, Lenin argued, was as a matter of historical fact created by representatives of the bourgeois intelligentsia and it was introduced into Russia by a similar group. A trade union movement is incapable of developing a revolutionary ideology for itself. Hence, the choice for a revolutionary party lies between allowing the trade unions to fall a prey to the ideology of the middle class or indoctrinating it with the ideology of socialist intellectuals". [12]

However, Bottomore viewed that the elite theory was originally conceived by bourgeois intellectuals to oppose the Marxist idea of social classes. He observed — "The elitists also oppose socialist doctrines in a more general way, by substituting for notion of class which rules by virtue of economic and military power, the notion of an elite which rules because of the superior qualities of its members."[13]

C. Wright Mills, an American Sociologist advocated his theory of 'Power Elites' in a quite different way. He did not agree that the members of the elite necessarily possess superior traits. Rather the structure of the institutions in a society is such that those occupying top positions in the institutional hierarchy are of key significance, and those who are holding positions of command in them hold the levers of power in the society. He believed that in U.S.A. the corporations, the military and the federal government being three separate elites known as 'power elites'.

Lasswell observes that the elite profoundly affect its fate by the ways in which it manipulates the environment whether by the use of violence, goods, symbols or practices. To him, "an elite defends and asserts itself in the name of symbols of the common destiny. Such symbols are the 'ideology' of the established order and the 'utopia' of counter-elites. By the use of sanctioned words and gestures the elite elicits blood, work, taxes and applause' from the masses."[14]

Dahl believes that "a small stratum of individuals is much more involved in political thought, discussion and action than the rest of the population. Such leaders have direct influence on decisions in the sense that they can initiate proposals for policies, or successfully veto the proposals of others."[15]

The identification of "political elite in a particular society is fundamental to understanding the actual workings of politics. But the concept of an elite must be used in its broadest sense so that no significant elements are overlooked. The elite first of all includes those who are holding high political office at a given time. Also important are those who have held office and who are considered to be supporters of the current leaders and thus might be able to influence their decisions. Those, whose future leadership seems likely are also to be considered. Active opposition leaders whose views may have to be taken into account are another part of the elite, as well as influential leaders of political parties, interest groups, and so on. In other words, in the broadest sense, a political elite includes those who, over a span of time, of perhaps a generation can have a marked effect on decision-making."[16]

Within the nations which are growing, "the character of their leadership to a large extent determines the goals and path of modernisation. Countries under colonial domination were generally ruled by an elite of colonial administrators, who governed directly or indirectly with traditional leaders and economic elites. In the newly independent states, during the periods when independence was being achieved, nationalist elites, often gathered around a charismatic leader, held power. But in those states traditional elites are again entering the political process, in combination with newer elements of leadership. The power of tradition elites is based on custom, religion, land, family, and other established cultural patterns. However, in modern times the power of religious elites has generally weakened on the national level as society has become more secular and differentiated. But religion still influences some political parties."[17]

The peculiarity of "all elite societies is that the 'more equal few' have an advantage over the many. Such societies differ from one another particularly in the type of people who comprise the few. In most societies until recent times the men (What Lipson in "The great issues of Polities' calls the unfair sex) have had an advantage over the women. One of the earliest exponents of the so called elitism was Plato, whose guardians were men who possessed a proper religious sense, military glory and above all an intellectual capacity of the highest order. In practice, as government has grown more complex and the ruling classes more heterogeneous, entry into the elite has become more open although a personal capacity is becoming necessary for admission to the 'power elite'."[18]

The definition given by Marx on the "elite (or rather 'dominant class' because he did not use the term) is the one most of us know best. He argued that the aristocracy has given way to the bourgeoisie, and he described the ruling class primarily in economic terms. The ownership of the means of production distinguished the bourgeoisie from the others. It is true that in most liberal democracies 'capitalists' still have an influence and prestige, which seem in some ways inconsistent with the principles these countries profess".[19]

Varney is of the opinion that, "one way in which elite theories challenge the notion that politics depends on general participation by the whole people is by showing, or at least implying that such a notion takes inadequate account of certain important features of the political system. The concentration on the electoral process is thought to be too narrow an approach to the problem of government. The general argument in favour of elite theory is, therefore, that it accurately describes the extent of political life, even in the so called liberal democracies. The people may think that they fully participate in the political process but in reality their influence is largely confined to elections. At the centre of power there is in being a social elite which wields considerable influence. Another argument is that government depends on expert knowledge which makes it impossible for its members to be truly representative of the people generally. This is most clearly seen in the composition of the higher civil services and in the senior ranks of the armed forces."[20]

Broad Profiles and Functional Syndrome

To Gandhi, "A leader is only a reflection of the people he

leads."[21]Similarly, Toynbee in his study of history has described leaders as creative minorities. As he says, "all growth originates with creative individuals or small minorities of individuals and their task is two-fold: first the achievement of their inspiration or discovery, whatever it may be, and second by the conversion of the society, to which they belong, to this new way of life."[22]

C.J.Friedrich writes, "Many attempts have been made to discover the traits of the leader, to discover an abstract, general pattern of qualities or characteristics which constitute 'leadership'. Indeed, many foundations, colleges, and other groups seeking to select the future 'Leader' cheerfully take it for granted that these qualities are known. Yet, actually, the greatest diversity of opinion prevails as to what constitutes even 'executive ability', let alone leadership ability. A survey of the various inquiries, as well as our general knowledge, leads to the conclusion that these qualities depend very largely upon the conditions under which leadership operates. The nature of the group and of the task will make much difference. An American President needs different qualities from a British Prime Minister, and his qualities today need to be different from what they were a hundred years ago. Take only the single instance of Radio appeal; we do not know for sure, but indications are that elections are being vitally affected by that intangible quality. No man can hope to be a success as Prime Minister in Britain who lacks the capacity of handling himself effectively in the give and take of parliamentary debate; the American President does not need that ability. This functional approach to the problem of leadership becomes even more essential when we go farther afield. A religious leader differs markedly from a business leader, and both contrast sharply with a military leader...we are not at present in a position to 'explain' leadership, and we may never be. When we consider a great religious or spiritual leader like Luther or Jean Jacques Rousseau, we are apt to admit that we are facing the ultimate creative force in human society working through such a leader. The same would be true of the scientific and artistic leader. When we come to political and social leaders, to the shapers of organisations and governments, we are obliged to be more skeptical. Many students of history would see a clear analogy between a work of art and a 'state'; indeed to Machiavelli the state appeared the greatest work of art of all. But recent history has shown or at least suggested that many, if not all, men can participate in the building and maintaining of a government; that a constitutional system is never the work of one great leader. Once law is placed in the centre of attention, it is evident that many minds and many, many hands have gathered and are gathering the detailed insights, devising the particular solutions to particular problems, and that no one can know enough to devise a 'state'. The 'state' concept as such was an outgrowth of the opposite view—a view constructed to justify and rationalise the despotic powers of monarchical rulers in the seventeenth century."[23]

He adds, "It is possible, however, to spell out, so to speak, certain functional aspects of a leader. One such functional aspect is the leader's representatives. We all know that an Irishman is more likely to get Irish votes than a Yankee. Likewise a man wanting to reform a church would have to be a member of that church. Again, no one who was not a member of a given profession or craft would be apt to succeed in 'reforming' such a profession, no matter how sound his views might be. Representativeness is compounded of likeness of behavior, of outlook and of general qualities of that sort. Another functional aspect of leadership is a capacity to find solutions to commonly recognised problems. Here the creative aspect is most apparent. The solution of problems presupposes intelligence; without intelligence these cannot be leadership—that much is certain. But intelligence unrelated to problems recognised by the group is unproductive of leadership. Intelligence is a matter of degree. Leadership, therefore, is likely to be a matter of degree also. A governmental system always presents many concrete problems; some are very small and specific, others vast and comprehensive. The man who gets a convincing solution acquires leadership as others follow his lead...A third functional aspect, related to the preceding, but distinct, is the capacity to foresee problems that are not yet generally recognised, to bring them into clear view and to dramatize their urgency. Again it is a matter of intelligence, but of analytical insight rather than inventiveness, plus the ability to generate and radiate emotion. All the progressive movements, particularly of recent times, abound with leaders of this type. They show, at the same time, how easily this capacity is stultified by unexpected developments.

Thus, Marx's analysis, while a brilliant anticipation of the rising labour class problem, overlooked the importance of the managerial class in an expanding industrialism by indiscriminately lumping it together with capital owners as the capitalist class. His expectation of an inevitable labour majority has therefore remained unfulfilled, and the policies of the socialist parties built upon that expectation have foundered. If the leader functions well as an anticipator and solver of group problems, he will naturally seem superior to his fellows."[24]

Further he writes, "Whether physical process distinguishes the leader, as it did Achilles, or whether a Kin Wit enables him to succeed where others fail, prestige will invariably be associated with his position. Prestige is not a separate result of leadership; it is part and parcel of it. Napoleon, the winner of battles can afford to be a ruffian; a successful leader commands a margin of freedom from communal restraints. This fact is universally recognised. It is not limited to despotic regimes; everyone knows that there is such a margin in the most democratic constitutionalism, and when the British Constitution to this day maintains that 'the King can do no wrong,' it gives symbolic recognition to that fact. Here we can see once again the root of constitutional restraints: they are designed to prevent the erstwhile leader from becoming a despot which he might otherwise do by utilising this margin of freedom for the systematic destruction of his opponents."[25]

David Easton views, "Of course, in describing and explaining the patterns of rule-making in a society, we must consider the importance of individual leadership and of the cultural environment. As in the consideration of the performance of the other political functions, discussion of the emergence and functioning of particular political structures involves the roles of individuals who may utilise their skills, resources, and energy to shape the direction of political events. It is all too easy to forget the relative fluidity and impermanence of many political structures and performance patterns, and their dependence upon the particular coherence and direction given by the leadership of a single individual. Moreover, the patterns of political culture in the society, or among the leaders in particular, may shape and perhaps limit the sorts of rules and decisions which are made. A traditional or ideologically-oriented set of attitudes will tend to close off certain alternatives of political decision making. Secularization, on the other hand, will increase the range of means available to solve political problems and to promote the rational and pragmatic evaluation of these means. But even in a highly secularised system, an accepted pattern of policy making tends to acquire considerable inertia to become traditional in its own right, so to speak."[26]

In broad profiles and in practice, the elites are the same as leaders. In determining the attributes of an effective leader Bailey observes: "The effective leader is said to be 'group-oriented', fulfills 'group needs' and oils the wheels of human interaction. But that is only one style of leadership: it is egalitarian in its assumptions, manipulative at its strongest, and sometimes no more than the hypothetical claim of a leader to be only the mouthpiece for his followers. There are also leaders who do not read a consensus, but impose it: remote majestic men and women, objects of fear and reverence. Followers can be bought, but the purchaser is not a leader, he is an employer. Domination can also be achieved by force. That can be one element in effective leadership; but not that alone, if only because the required concentration of sustained force is an impossibility. The right to dominate is voluntarily given to one who has the 'gift of leadership; what Max Weber called 'Charisma'. Weber saw Charisma as one among other styles of domination but in fact all effective leaders command some measure of devotion. In one way or another a leader must seem to be superhuman...Sometimes leaders are officially declared gods, as with all Roman Emperors from Augustus onwards. Sometimes the deification is a matter of image and metaphor, as when NKrumah was called the 'Redeemer'. Sometimes it is no more than human attributes expanded beyond the normal: courage, perseverance, endurance and the like. One essential capacity combines ideas of effectiveness with flair, intuition or luck; an ability to come to the right decision in a manner that transcends rationality. In case after case, leaders, even those not overtly anti-intellectual, make clear that reason has its limits, that leadership is an art (not a science), and is a talent which some people have and others do not. Since leaders in fact cannot work miracles, the study of leadership becomes the examination of strategies (including institutional arrangements) (1) for maintaining in the followers the illusion of a unique talent in the leader and (2) for solving problems which the real world presents, or, failing solutions, for imposing on the situation a definition which leaves unhurt the image of the leader's effectiveness."[27]

Bhupinder Singh mentions, "the important principles which need to be considered for classification (of leadership in a tribal society) are (1) level of socio-cultural integration (2) nature of social system in terms of egalitarianism, ranking and stratification (3) mode of succession and (4) socio-political situations."[28] To him, "Leadership in single egalitarian societies rests upon authority and lacks connotation of power...In a rank society, leaders have the capacity to lead but the followers may not act according to the wishes of the leaders. The leaders may give commands but the followers may not pay heed to such commands."[29] Leadership in crisis was seen "...when the tribesmen failed in their open revolts against oppressing landlords, middlemen, moneylenders, police or forest officials or princely chiefs, charismatic leaders arose to pull their brethren out of crisis. In most of the cases the authority of the charismatic leaders transcended the bounds of single tribes."[30]

Hemphill[31] and his colleagues postulated nine *a priori* dimensions of leader behavior such as (1) Initiation (2) Membership (3) Representation (4) Integration (5) Organisation (6) Domination (7) Communication (8) Recognition (9) Production.

Singh further writes, "Though hard to single out anyone, it appears that of all the dimensions, the dimension 'communication' is the most important because it affects leadership and its performance in groups vitally. Communication is the process by which one person influences another and is, therefore, basic to leadership...It has been the experience among the workers in the tribal areas that in the virtual absence of mass-media, information regarding development gets disseminated by word of mouth and, in this task, the leaders act as key communicators...People go to different leaders for different purposes. Categorising leaders on this basis, some leaders may be monomorphic, i.e., one leader for one field of service, and others polymorphic, i.e., one leader advising or helping in several fields. It is believed that in traditional societies leadership is more polymorphic than monomorphic.[32]

Trends of Reality

Paul Kennedy observes that, "the man and woman in the street know that their world is changing and worry about it. Above all, unease about present or impending changes is behind the widespread disenchantment with political leaderships whether in advanced industrial nations like America, France, and Japan, in existing or recently dissolved Marxist regimes, in large parts of Latin America and Africa, in the Asian giants of India and China, or, for the matter, in the Muslim World, where discontented youths turn to fundamentalist prescriptions. Much of this is suppressed in authoritarian states, but in both the older and the newer democracies the demand for political responses to the new challenges is immense. Such responses can often be reactionary. Protectionism, anti-immigrant policies blocking new technologies, and finding new enemies to replace cold war foes are common reactions at a time of 'jolts and jars and smashes in the social life of humanity.' Clearly, a society which desires to be better prepared for the twenty-first century will pay a price to achieve that transition; it will need to retool its national skills and infrastructure, challenge vested interests, alter many old habits, and perhaps amend its governmental structures. But this assumes long-term vision at a time when most politicians—in both rich and poor countries—can hardly deal with even short-term problems; and it means political risk, since many of the reforms proposed would be unpopular among the vested interests."[33]

Change is inevitable in the life of any given society and the world as a whole. "The human mind seeks order and revolts against uncertainty, irrationality and chaos. It attempts to bring some order into the chaotic facts and experiences. Man is not merely a tool-maker, he is also a pattern-maker. He looks at the world and finds that things supersede one another in perpetual succession. All things are subject to the domination of time. The greatest works of art, the greatest civilisations are not exempt from change."[34]

But even within the currents of change what men desire always is 'peace and happiness' and to secure them this, must he the fervent and ultimate goal of their leaders, in spite of the fact that happiness not only varies in kind but also in degree. The pursuit of happiness is admirable as a social goal. But the notion of happiness lacks philosophical exactitude; there is agreement neither on its substance not its source. We know that it is "a profound instinctive union with the stream of life."[35]

In every society, more particularly in developing and underdeveloped ones, the political leadership is looked upon for economic security-increased production, better and more or less equitable distribution of goods. "The desire for economic security was long considered the great enemy of increased production. This attitude was firmly grounded in the belief that the insecurity of the competitive model was essential for efficiency. Alongwith the carrot of pecuniary reward must go the stick of personal economic disaster. Both were essential. To remove the stick, which must be the consequence of increasing economic security, would be to remove half the incentives by which men were inspired."[36] But "the ancient preoccupations of economic life—with equality, security and productivity—have now narrowed down to a preoccupation with productivity and production. Production has become the solvent of the tensions once associated with inequality, and it has become the indispensable remedy for the comforts, anxieties and privations associated with economic insecurity...Production has become the centre of a concern that had hitherto been shared with equality and security."[37]

On Indian context Morris-Jones writes, "The language of modern politics is undoubtedly important in India—more so than perhaps in most other parts of Asia. This is less on account of the long period of British rule in itself than because of one of its consequences—the existence of nearly a hundred years of an Indian Elite steeped in its grammar and masters of its accents. Members of this elite were not only the agents of much of the administrative and economic development of the country; they also provided the leadership of some of the more important movements of social reform and of the nationalist movement itself. It is true that an important change came over the nationalist movement with the impact of Gandhi's leadership after 1917, but it would be a mistake to imagine that Gandhi did not employ the modern idiom; he combined it with another, but by no means abandoned it or prevented its continuous development. This language is so widespread in India that it has seemed possible to give comprehensive accounts of Indian Political life without removing outside its terms. 'This modern language of politics is the language of the Indian constitution and the courts; of Parliamentary debate; of the higher administration; of the upper levels of all the main political parties; of the entire English Press and much of the Indian language press. It is a language which speaks of policies and interests, programmes and plans. It expresses itself in arguments and representations, discussions and demonstrations, deliberations and decisions."[38]

Paradoxically, the British Rule which was an antithesis of Indian Independence, was either directly or indirectly responsible for national solidarity and political new birth of India. "British Rule nonetheless brought India benefits of considerable magnitude, *Pax Britannica* and reasonable facsimiles of Britain's own legal, administrative and educational institutions. Above all, it gave India the magnificent gift which was to become the common bond of its diverse peoples and the conduit of their revolutionary aspirations, the English Language.[39]

After independence, "the Indian government's attempts to bring about social and economic change were consolidated as a political programme based on organised planning within the machinery of government.

Continuing the British tradition of making conscientious surveys of social and economic conditions, the planning commission generated ancillary bodies empowered to investigate and make recommendations on almost every aspect of Indian Life... India was the first country in South Asia and for long time the only one, to follow this practice."[40] But unfortunately, "corruption and nepotism among politicians and officials are freely discussed (in India) and are generally assumed to be on the increase. The Central Government has admitted the existence of corruption in the administration on a fairly large scale."[41]

Palkhivala observes that in India "today the situation remains unchanged—only the number of files has increased a thousandfold. Millions of man-hours are wasted every day in coping with inane bureaucratic regulations, a torrential spate of amendments."[42] To exemplify he writes, "In several parts of Africa when the rains do not come, the tribal chief conducts a ritual dance watched by the anxious members of the tribe. The dance does not bring rains, but it consoles and satisfies the people who feel that their chief is doing something to alleviate their misery. Our feverish changes in the law are intended to serve the same purpose as the tribal chief's rain dance."[43] He regrets that, "the greatest problem of India is that its finest men— men of calibre and vision, knowledge and character—are not in politics and stand little chance of getting elected having regard to the murky atmosphere of our political life. Caste is the football in the political game which our men in public life play".[44]

Further, "the tragedy of the Indian situation is that people are more religious than communal, while leadership is more communal than religious. Rise of Hindu chauvinism, Muslim fundamentalism, regionalism, casteism, separatism, terrorism etc., are now pushing serious danger to our country... Corruption in all walks of life has posed a serious problem to common men. It has diluted moral and ethical standards over the years and has hampered the economic development of the country."[45]

However, in India, "largely as a result of the operation of adult franchise, considerable shifts have occurred in the social base of politics. Sections of the people who had been hitherto denied access to political power and who had considered politics to be the legitimate concern of the material and the learned classes have been exposed to new ideology, have realised the power of numbers, and have started organising themselves through their own associations and leaders. This is the rise of the "newly enfranchised" in politics. As a result of both political competition and the impact of programmes of development and welfare on the leaders of society, there has arisen a mutual awareness between party politicians and community leaders anxious to have greater say in the allocation of economic and political resources."[46]

Verrier Elwin observes that, "earlier the backward and unprivileged sections of the society were denied this facility. As for example, the tribal people were not adequately represented in the legislatures and on local bodies. There were only 24 tribal representatives in the Provincial Legislative Assemblies under the Government of India Act, 1935 against a total of 1535 members".[47]

The Scene from Tribal Orissa

In Orissa, among the tribes, "there was organised political life with spatial delimitation. There are both secular and religious functionaries to administer and arbiter on various issues. A *Shaman,* a sorcerer, a witch doctor have their hold on tribals both on sacred and profane ambits. A leader either elected or selected worked in the interest of the community. A *gamang* of the Soars or a *saonta* of the Kandhas or a sardar of the Juangs and the Bhuiyans has his authority over the tribesmen till he does not deviate from the traditional prescriptions. No doubt sometimes some of the leaders transform themselves as arbitrary rulers. But there is always a check on the growth of such propensity... On the other hand the elected system based on adult franchise introduced in almost all the tribal areas produced new leaders on a totally different perspective... If Panchayat elections gave this dismal picture, Assembly or Parliamentary elections did not indicate anything better. The electorate hardly understood party affiliations or higher policies enunciated by the candidates. The percentage of polling is usually low. This apathy is noticed in reserved constituencies for Scheduled Tribes. Hence, elected representatives are neither leaders, nor their words carry much weight in deciding tribal issues. Interestingly, the elected persons have little contact with tribals. More often advanced societies of tribals occupy all the important positions. Most of the tribals are, therefore, in a transitional phase, where the traditional leadership has lost its hold and the elected leadership is yet to establish itself."[48]

In the state, "the socio-cultural structure of each tribe is unique. With slight variations, the tribes have a highly egalitarian society, with high status for women, dignity of labour and love for freedom as basic planks of their ethos... The traditional leadership pattern based on the erstwhile city states of Greek model of direct democracy continues to operate despite emergence of new political structures including the Panchayatiraj institutions and representative legislatures. The tribals do not find a place in the elitist and coast-biased history of the state in more than one way. The Khond and Santal rebellions of the pre-independence era are cases in the point. The frequent defections and withdrawals of support by the tribal M.L.As, after 1947 are mere manifestations of these revolts and disapproval of the system that is antithetic to their social system and socio-cultural values. The conflict situation is bound to continue unless serious efforts are made to understand and appreciate the world from which the tribal views the outside... Consequently after independence, a new pattern of leadership emerged in the Tribal areas and the traditional socio-political leaders in large measure withdrew from the scene. In this leadership pattern a band of town-bred half-educated elites came forward who were in search of new dilemmas. The opening of all the tribal areas to modern communications facilitated free exchange of ideas and helped the tribal elites to play their role effectively. But, the hangover of the traditional value system was so strong that these elites instead of playing their role as catalysts for change and modernisation responded in a queer manner. Having failed to internalise the new political system to their advantage, they responded to the system in such a manner that could be termed as tangential and peripheral These responses were in the shape of defections and withdrawals of the tribal representatives from the established Governments creating instability in the functioning of the Government... Unless a systematic political education is attempted and a real role perspective closer to the Tribal world view is brought home to the tribes of this state, the situation is likely to bring about further instability in the political future of the state."[49]

The socio-political organisation and leadership pattern among the Dongria Kondhs of the state shows that, "the leaders not only enjoy status and high prestige in the society, but they also exercise considerable authority in getting things done in the most correct manner. Their opinion in settling quarrels and conflicts is decisive... The leaders shoulder all responsibilities, participate in all social activities and effectively influence the life of their fellowmen. In this process this becomes an institution and office turn to hereditary normally. The traditional leadership is based on hereditary status and position. The status is ascribed rather than achieved. This rests upon the formal arrangement of the society. In contrast to the traditional leadership, modern leadership is achieved. The functions of modern leaders are diverse. They are more oriented towards development activities. They are progressive and make liaison between government agencies and the people. They held elective posts under the statutory panchayat system. Modern leaders are amophorous and unstable."[50]

N.K.Behura writes, "the traditional political organisation of any tribe has three components, namely (i) norms, customary laws and social sanctions, (ii) functionaries and (iii) territoriality. Norms, customary laws and social sanctions are culture specific, and hence their similarity among the tribes of Orissa can be obtained at a level of obstruction. Functionaries and territorial organisation, also show considerable amount of uniformity among the tribes of Orissa.... Norms governing proper conduct, customary laws relating to social, economic, religious and political organisations, and soical sanctions relating to regulations of sex, community natural resources and social solidarity do not show much difference from one tribe to another in Orissa. However, the traditional political organisation of the Orissan tribes, in spite of the broad similarity, can be divided into three sub-types, namely (i) northern, (ii) southern, and (iii) north-western. Each of these is coterminous with the local revenue administrative units of the area. The northern type is known as *Pirha*, the southern type as *Mutha* and the north-western type as *Pargana*".[51]

He adds, "tribes in Orissa mainly inhabit the Eastern-Ghat hill range which runs in the north-south direction. Most of the areas in which various tribal communities traditionally lived were parts of different feudatory states of Orissa. And the traditional political organisation of the tribes was influenced by the revenue administrative organisation of the concerned state. For instance the political organisation of the Santal, Munda, Ho, Bhumij, Bathudi etc., who lived in the state of Mayurbhanj was influenced by the revenue territorial organisation of the state. Thus, among these tribes the hierarchical order of the political organisation, from bottom to top, runs as, (i) family, (ii) lineage, (iii) village, (iv) pargana and (v) the king symbolising the state. This is the hierarchical order of the traditional political organisation of other tribes of Orissa too, but among north Orissan tribes such as Bhuiyan and Juang, and among the south Orissan tribes, such as, the Kandha, Saora, Gadaba, Koya, Didayi, Jhadia, etc., the inter-village political organisation is called *Pirha* and *Mutha* respectively. But in reality situation the lineage and the village are effective political machineries among the tribal communities, and indeed these are the guardians and custodians of tribal customs, norms and customary laws. The inter-village political organisation, that is, the *Pargana* or *Pirha* or *Mutha* as the case may be, used to be periodically called into action or as and when it became absolutely necessary. The Jurisdiction, powers and functions of each level of the political organisation from the family to the king was specific and represented a stage in the socio-cultural life of the concerned tribe. The traditional political organisation up to the village level is still in existence and is influential. After the introduction of statutory Panchayatiraj system the traditional tribal political organisations are gradually becoming feeble, yet they are considered as important socio-cultural institutions to regulate the socio-cultural life."[52]

He further observes that, "the roles of all the functionaries are important, but those of the lineage-heads and the village headmen are very crucial in the maintenance of social order. The role of village priest in the implementation of social control is supportive only. The traditional leadership among the tribes was corporate in nature. The joint authority system is still there. This means that the traditional leadership pattern continues to exist alongside the modern democratic leadership pattern. The traditional village level tribal panchayat is a corporate body of village elders, the priest and the Head-man. A messenger is nominated by the head-man from among the villagers to assist him in the discharge of his duties. Only, men constitute the panchayat as all the tribal societies of Orissa are patrilineal and patriarchal... The position of priest, village headman and the inter-village headman are hereditary. The village headman is invariably from original settlers' clan of the village, which is obviously dominant. Punishments or corrective measures are proportional to the gravity of the breach of set norms or crime, and the punishments range from simple oral admonition to other measures, such as corporal punishments, imposition of fines, payment of compensation, observance of prophylactic rites and excommunication from the community. Truth of an incident is determined by oath, ordeals and occult mechanism...Among all the tribes conformity to customs and norms and social integration continue to be achieved through their traditional political organisations. The tributary institutions of social control, such as family, kinship and public opinion continue to fulfill central social control functions. The relevance of tribal political organisation in the context of economic development and social change continues to be there undiminished. Modern elites in tribal societies elicit scant respect and have very little followings. And as the traditional leaders continue to wield influence over their fellow tribesmen, it is worthwhile to take them into confidence in the context of economic development and social change."[53]

L.P.Vidyarthi points out that, 'the rural-bred charismatic and traditional oriented leadership which worked for revitalising the tribals on the Hindu model was later greatly disturbed owing to the devoted work of the missionaries and their continuous efforts to uplift the tribals brought nbout new standards for choosing leadership."[54]

As far back as 1959, Bailey conducted a research in Bisipara, a tribal village situated 10 kilometres south-west of Phulbani town and lying within Phulbani district of Orissa and observed certain basic traits of leadership, more particularly the tribal leadership. He observed that "the voters, in fact, project their own code of morality and obligation upon all but a very few politicians and active political workers. The voters themselves feel no direct interest in the common weal; indeed few have any conception of the common weal. Consequently, they believe that anyone who offers himself as a candidate is out to make money for himself and they think that those who campaign actively for a candidate do make money. There is an ambivalent attitude towards this money: on the one hand no one in his senses would do the work unless he got some profit out of it; on the other hand the protestations of disinterestedness and regard for the public weal are tainted with insincerity. The few persons whose record, personality, or social background free them from the taint of hypocrisy and self-interest have a long start over the ordinary run-of-the will politician...It is, in short, almost an axiom that politicians—at least those at the lower level whom the villagers know—have dirty hands. But the villagers do not draw this conclusion solely from their experience of election campaigns but more from their own knowledge of the kind but more among themselves who enter politics."[55]

He added, "the politician wants power. Whether his intention is public service or private gain, or both, the first step is accession to a position of power, to be elected a member of the Legislative Assembly. To say that a politician has a 'mass contact', is in Orissa, to pay a high compliment. Such a man—and there are very few—has risen above the ordinary run of politicians who rely on cliques and factions for support. If a constituency consisted exclusively of the members of one caste and they all supported a candidate because he came from their caste, then, in the opinion of those with whom I discussed this question, it would be wrong to call this 'mass contact'. An essential part of this relationship seems to be that it should transcend traditional loyalties."[56]

On electoral game he commented, "a machine is fuelled, so to speak, not by moral fervour, but by calculations of profit and advantage. This distinction is an ideal one, and any group of people working to win an election will certainly show both the moral element and an element of calculation in their activities."[57]

However, Bailey hoped that, the "vote-banks of this kind will disappear quite rapidly as a new generation grows up, unless they are consolidated and fortified by other means. The old structure has gone and it no longer regulates power relations. Only sentiment remains."[58]

Emphasising on the structural and normative aspects of political activities, which he expected the elites and the voters to follow, he commented that "the 'Political' is that aspect of any act which concerns the distribution of power, providing that there is competition for this power and provided, secondly, that the competition takes place under a set of rules which the competitors observe and which ensure that the competition is orderly. In so far as there may be no competition, then the action ceases to be political and becomes merely administrative. If the competitors do not agree upon rules and institutions which make for orderly competition and resort to violence, then their actions are war like and not political."[59]

To improve upon this he suggested, "the more effectively representative institutions bring the elite into contact with the villages, the more must the elite too lose their 'parochial' qualities, cease to operate so much within the unspecialised highly personal relationships which they have with one another, and make more effective use of specialised impersonal political links with the mass."[60]

References

1. P. Sharan, ; *Comparative Government and Politics,* Meenakshi Prakashan, Meerut, 1981, p. 54.
2. D. Marvick, ; in *The Social Sciences Encyclopaedia,* Routledge & Kegan Paul, London, 1985, pp. 243-245.
3. *Ibid.*
4. *Ibid.*
5. *Ibid.*
6. *Ibid.*

7. S. Keller, ; in *International Encyclopaedia of the Social Sciences,* Vol. 5, p. 26.
8. S. R. Maheshwari, ; *Comparative Government and Politics,* Lakshmi Narain Agarwal, Agra, 1994, p. 142.
9. V. Pareto, ; *The Mind and Society,* Third Volume, Jonathan Cape, London, 1935, p. 1423.
10. *Ibid.* p. 30.
11. G. Mosca, ; *The Ruling Class,* McGraw-Hill, New York, 1939, p.50.
12. G. H. Sabine, & T. L. Thorson; *A History of Political Theory,* Oxford & I B H Publishing Co., New Delhi, 1973, p.731.
13. T. B. Bottomore, ; *Elites and Society,* Penguin, Middlesex, 1966, p.18.
14. H. D. Lasswell, ; *Politics : Who Gets What, When, How ?* Collected in the Political Writings of H.D. Lasswell, Free press, Illions, 1951, p. 311.
15. R. A. Dahl, ; *Who Governs ?.* Yale University Press, New Haven, 1961, pp. 90-102.
16. P. Sharan, *op. cit.*
17. *Ibid.* pp. 54-55.
18. *Ibid.* p. 56.
19. *Ibid.*
20. D. V. Verney, ; as quoted by P. Sharan, *op. cit.*
21. M. K. Gandhi, ; as quoted in *Freedom at Midnight,* L. Collins & D. Lapierre, Tarang Paperbacks, New Delhi, 1990, p.39.
22. A. Toynbee, ; as quoted in *Adibasi,* No.2, November, Bhubaneswar, 1963, p.5.
23. C. J. Friedrich, ; in *Comparative Government—A Reader,* (ed.) J. Blondel, MacMillan, London, 1985, pp. 178-180.
24. *Ibid.*
25. *Ibid.*
26. D. Easton, ; as quoted in *Comparative Politics : A Developmental Approach,* G. A. Almond & G. B.Powell, Jr., Oxford & IBH Publishing Co, New Delhi, 1972, pp. 1411-142.
27. F. G. Bailey, ; in *The Social Sciences Encyclopaedia, op. cit,* pp. 449-450.
28. B. Singh, ; *The Saora Highlander- Leadership and Development,* Somaiya Publications Pvt. Ltd., Bombay, 1984, p.74.
29. *Ibid.* pp. 59-60.
30. *Ibid.,* p. 61.
31. Hemphill ; As quoted by B. Singh, *op cit.,* p. 62-63.
32. *Ibid.,* pp. 63-67.
33. P. Kennedy, ; *Preparing for the Twenty-first Century,* Indus, New Delhi, 1994, pp.344-345.
34. S. Radhakrishnan, ; *Towards a New World,* Orient Paperbacks,

Delhi, 1980, P.144.

35. B. Russel, ; *The Conquest of Happiness,* Allen & Unwin, London, 1930, p. 248.
36. J. K. Galbraith, ; *The Affluent Society,* Pelican Books, Middlesex, 1984, p. 114.
37. *Ibid.,* p. 118.
38. W. H. Morris-Jones, ; *The Government and Politics of India,* B.I. Publications, New Delhi, 1979 pp. 53-54.
39. L. Collins, and D Lapierre, ; *op. cit.,* p. 12.
40. G. Myrdal, ; *Asian Drama -An Inquiry into the Poverty of Nations,* Vol. I, Pelican Books Middlesex, 1968, pp. 271-272.
41. *Ibid.,* p. 287.
42. N. A. Palkhivala, ; *We, the Nation - The Lost Decades,* UBS Publishers Distributors ltd, New Delhi, 1994, p. 6.
43. *Ibid.* p. 164.
44. *Ibid.,* pp. 10-11.
45. B. C. Rout, ; in *The Orissa Political Science Journal,* Vol. IX, Bhubaneswar, 1990-91. p. 5.
46. R. Kothari, ; *Politics in India,* Orient Longman, New Delhi, 1986, p. 128.
47. V. Elwin, ; *A New Deal for Tribal India (ed.),* Ministry of Home Affairs, New Delhi, 1962, p. 14.
48. N. Das, ; in *Tribal Situation in India (ed.),* Vol. 13, K. S. Singh, Indian Institute of Advanced Study, Shimla 1972, pp. 191-192.
49. R. K. Nayak, ; in *Government and Politics in Orissa, (ed.),* B. B. Jena and J. K. Baral, Print House (India), Lucknow, 1988, pp. 461-464.
50. N. Patnaik, and P.S. Das Patnaik; *The Kondh of Orissa,* Tribal and Harijan Research-cum-Training Institute, Bhubaneswar, 1982, p. 117.
51. N. K. Behura, ; in *Tribes of Orissa (ed.),* Harijan and Tribal Welfare Department of Orissa, Bhubaneswar, 1990, pp. 19-20.
52. *Ibid.*
53. *Ibid.*
54. L. P. Vidyarthi, ; in *Tribal Situation in India, (ed.),* Vol.13, *op.cit.,* No. 48, p.443.
55. F. G. Bailey, ; *Politics and Social Change: Orissa in 1959,* University of California Press, London, 1963, pp.35-36.
56. *Ibid.,* p. 107.
57. *Ibid.,* p. 141.
58. *Ibid.,* p. 120.
59. *Ibid.,* p. 223.
60. *Ibid.,* p. 234.

4

The Urban Political Elite in Tribal India-A Study of Two Towns

For the purpose of a sample study under this project, Phulbani District of Orissa was selected. There are only two urban bodies in the district, namely, Phulbani N.A.C and G.Udayagiri N.A.C. Before a primary study of the target group is made, it is but necessary that a mention should be made about the setting, history and features of these two towns and their local bodies.

Phulbani N.A.C. Town

The NAC town "Phulbani', situated in 20° 29´ N. and 84° 16´ E., at an elevation of about 1, 600 feet (487.68 metres) above the sea-level was the headquarters of the Khondmals sub-division which formed a part of the different former districts such as Angul and Boudh-khondmals. At present it is the headquarters of both the Kandhmal sub-division and the Phulbani district which has been renamed as Kandhmal district but is still popularly know as Phulbani district. Phulbani N.A.C town is on the east bank of the river Pila salki, which winds round its western and northern sides. On two sides, it is enclosed by hills, between which there are narrow outlets to the country beyond, but to the south-east and north-west the country is more open. The *kandha* name for Phulbani is *Damsingh*, the name of an adjoining *Mutha*, in which it was formerly included."[1] Etymologically the word Phulbani consists of two syllables - *Phul* (means flower) and *bani* (means message) - and it literally means the message of the flower. Practically speaking Phulbani is a town of flowers.

Regarding origin of the name 'Phulbani' there exists a view in some circles in the form of a love story. After the British occupation of Orissa, the officials of the Colonial Government gradually tried to penetrate deep into the interiors of the province and at the same time were in search of cool and ideal places for their outposts as well as habitats. In this process, one of their rank officials who first arrived in the place incidentally fell in love with a local tribal woman named 'Phulbani'. To commemorate her name, he named the place 'Phulbani' before leaving it.

One will find that, "the climate of Phulbani is dry. In the cold weather an unpleasant mist, blown in by westerly breezes from the river spreads over the town at night and hangs over it till late hours in the morning."[2]

No part of Phulbani district is connected with rail. Phulbani town is reached on road from Berhampur, its railhead to which it is connected with regular bus services.There are also bus services from here to all other important places of the district as well as to Bhubaneswar, Cuttack, Rourkela, Sambalpur and other importart places outside the district. It is situated 58 kilometres northwest of G. Udayagiri, the other N.A C. town of the district. Besides, it is 211 kms, away from Bhubaneswar, 240 kms. away from Cuttack and 165kms. away from Berhampur by road. It is one of the midpoints of State Highway No.1 connecting Khurda with Rampur and is one of the extreme points of State Highway No.7 connecting Berhampur with Phulbani.

Ghumsar Udayagiri N.A.C. Town

India Today observes, "travel brochures call it the 'Kashmir of Orissa', and with reason, Ghumsar Udayagiri is a picturesque little village (town), mostly of *Adivasis* and *Harijans*, tucked away in a remote, lush part of Orissa. But a pleasant climate and a profusion of green are not the only natural attractions of the village."[3]

Udayagiri, prefixed with a letter G. which is a sobriquet for Ghumsar was formerly a part of the Ghumsar kingdom ruled by the kings of Bhanja dynasty. Apparently for identifying this Udayagiri from some other important places of the state with identical name, the place takes such prefix and is officially and otherwise known in the like manner. Udayagiri near Lalitgiri in the district of Jajpur is historically famous as a Buddhist centre; Udayagiri near Khandagiri within the Municipal Area of Bhubaneswar corporation is also historically noted for Jain temple and caves. Similarly, Udayagiri near Ramagiri (therefore known as R.Udayagiri) is a small town in the Gajapati district.

Etymologically the word 'Udayagiri' consists of two syllables - 'Udaya' (means rising) and 'giri"' (means hill)- and thus, it literally means the place of rising hills. Interestingly enough, the place justifies its name as it actually depicts the same what the name connotes. The town appears to be a mesmerised applique dexterously interwoven with patches of concrete and flora, slinging down from the tops of decorated hills all around which seem to have been symmetrically erected as meditating pillars around an amphitheatre.

Till very recently this valley of flowers experienced only almost two seasons during the year - Rainy season from mid-March to mid-September and Winter season from mid-September to mid-March with all other seasons almost non-existent. Winter is biting but pleasant with a decline in thermometer beyond 0° Centigrade during peak winter in December-January with occasional snowfalls. Of course, in recent years due to ecological imbalance and global heat the place has started showing the symptoms of a mild and brief summer. Due to its pleasant climate, attractive scenario and typical culture, foreign tourists from different parts of the globe are seen here round the year.

Fig. 1. A View of Phulbani N.A.C. Town

Fig. 2. A view of G. Udayagiri N.A.C Town

Fig. 3. Phulbani N.A.C. Office

Fig. 4. G. Udayagiri N.A.C Office

Fig. 5. Councillors' Meeting in Progress at G. Udayagiri N.A.C., 1997

To add, "Ghumsar Udayagiri which is situated more than 2,500 feet above the sea level, has a very good climate which can favourably compare with any of the other hill stations of the country. Due to the excellent climate, the boys and girls here are quite attractive. When the area was conquered by the Maratha, soldiers and rulers were charmed by the beauty of the local girls and assaulted them sexually. This upset the local people and women, who felt that once their chastity was destroyed nobody would even look at them. They, therefore, decided to sacrifice their most valuable asset — their beauty — by disfiguring their faces with *tatoo* marks. Since then it has become a custom for the ladies of this area to tattoo their faces profusely so as to look ugly. Though with the passage of time some have given up this practice, in many areas it is still observed strictly."[4]

It may be mentioned here that, "the district was occupied by Britishers in 1865 and was one of their last strongholds. After the area came under British occupation, the missionaries entered and preached Christianity and attempted to 'civilise' the people. But when Government officials were posted in the area in the 1940's they were quick to exploit the ignorance and simplicity of the people and finally to demoralise the people of the area. They started calling it *Prem Nagar*, the town of love. Even in the post independence era, this trend continued. The poor innocent tribals and *harijans* were thoroughly exploited and their girls were used to satisfy the lust of government officials, businessmen and contractors,"

G.Udayagiri N.A.C. town is situated on State Highway No.7A connecting Kalinga with Balliguda and is 58 kilometres south-east of the district headquarters and the other N.A.C town of the district — Phulbani. It is well connected with bus services from important places of the district as well as of the state. It is 216 kilometres away from Bhubaneswar, 245 kilometers away from Cuttack and 123 kilometres away from Berhampur by road. The 10-kilometre long Kalinga Ghat filled with beautiful scenic spots serves as the gate way to this place.

N.A.C. : Formation and Structure

According to Orissa Gram Panchayat Act, 1948, a Grama Panchayat consisting of 34 villages was formed at Phulbani in 1951 and it continued till the 13th February, 1963. As per the Government Notification No. 9227-L.S.G., dated the 14th September, 1962 a portion of this Grama Panchayat consisting of 12 villages was converted into a Notified Area Council (N.A.C). The Phulbani Notified Area Council was constituted on the 14th February, 1963 with an area of 7.77 square kilometres (3 square miles). It consisted of 9 wards with 11 councillors in the first election held on the 20th October, 1963. Two wards were double-seated. Ward No. II was reserved for the scheduled castes and Ward No. VI was reserved for the scheduled tribe candidates. Its population in 1961 census was 4,031, in 1971 census it was 10,677, in 1981 census it was 18,326, and in 1991 census it was 27,154 including 14,737 males and 12,417 females. There are 2,595

Table 1
Area and Population

Name of NAC	*Geographical area in sq. km.*	*No. of households*	*No. of residential houses*	*Total Population*			*Scheduled Tribe population*			*% of ST Population to Total Population*
				Male	*Female*	*Total*	*Male*	*Female*	*Total*	
	1	2	3	4	5	6	7	8	9	10
Phulbani (NAC)	16.00	5,820	5,759	14,737	12,417	27,154	1444	1151	2595	9.56
G. Udayagiri (NAC)	13.24	1,799	1,790	4,257	4,251	8,508	883	984	1867	21.94

Source : District Statistical Handbook, Kandhamal, Directorate of Economics and Statistics, Government of Orissa, Bhubaneswar, 1993.

scheduled tribe persons with 1,444 males and 1,151 females. The Scheduled Tribes constitute 9.56 per cent of the total population of the town. At present the Phulbani N.A.C covers an area of 16 square kilometres with 5,820 number of households and 5,759 number of residential houses. The N.A.C is divided into 13 wards out of which 1 is reserved for scheduled castes, 2 for scheduled caste women, 1 for scheduled tribes and 3 for women.

G. Udayagiri was declared to have a Notified Area Council under State Government in Housing and Urban Development Department Notification No. 39519, dated the 27th December, 1979 and was constituted on 9th February, 1981 with an area of 13.24 square kilometers (1323.956 hectares) and covering six villages. There are 1,799 number of households and 1,790 number of residential houses in the town at present. In 1971 its population was 3,752, in 1981 census it was 6841, and in 1991 census it was 8,508 with 4,257 males and 4,251 females. According to 1991 census there are 1,867 scheduled tribe persons in the N.A.C town with 883 males and 984 females and they constitute 21.94 per cent of the total population of the town. At present the N.A.C. has 13 wards out of which 1 is reserved for scheduled castes, 1 for scheduled caste women and 3 for women.

Table 2
Literacy

	Total Literate persons			*% of literate persons**		
	Male	*Female*	*Total*	*Male*	*Female*	*Total*
	1	2	3	4	5	6
Phulbani NAC	11,212	6,692	17,904	88.56	63.93	77.41
G.Udayagiri NAC	3,132	2,330	5,462	87.53	64.90	76.20

Source: District Statistical Handbook, Kandhamal, Directorate of Economics and Statistics, Government of Orissa, Bhubaneswar, 1993.

* Excluding population in the age-group of 0-6 years.

In Phulbani NAC there are 17,904 literates including 11,212 males and 6,692 females. The literates (excluding the population in the age group of 0-6 years) of the town constitute 77.41 per cent of the total population of the town. In G. Udayagiri N.A.C, there are 5,462 literates including 3,132 males and 2,330 females. The literates of the town constitute 76.20 per cent of the total population of the town.

For education there were 15 primary schools, 7 middle schools, 3 secondary schools, 3 colleges within Phulbani N.A.C by 1992-93. By the same period there were 8 primary schools, 3 middle schools, 3 secondary schools and 1 college within G.Udayagiri N.A.C.

Table 3
Work Force

	PHULBANI NAC			*G. UDYAGIRI NAC*		
	Male	*Female*	*Total*	*Male*	*Female*	*Total*
	1	2	3	4	5	6
Total workers	6,810	1,380	8,190	1,916	556	2,472
Main workers	6,740	1,222	7,962	1,827	373	2,200
Marginal workers	70	158	228	89	183	272
Non-workers	7,927	11,037	18,964	2,341	3,695	6,036

Source: District Statistical Handbook, Kandhamal, Directorate of Economics and Statistics, Government of Orissa, Bhubaneswar, 1993.

The Phulbani N.A.C has 8,190 workers in total including 6,810 males and 1,380 females. Of the total workers of the town 7,962 persons including 6,740 males and 1,222 females are main workers. Out of the 228 marginal workers of the town 70 are males and 158 are females. 7,927 males and 11,037 females totalling 18,964 persons of the town are non-workers. It is found that only 30.16 per cent of the town population are workers while 69.84 per cent of the total population of the town are non-workers. This is definitely a negative trend towards economic progress of the town as majority of the town's population do not work. Almost same is the case with G. Udayagiri N.A.C where only 29.06 per cent of the town's population are engaged in work and the rest 70.94 per cent do not work. Numerically speaking, out of the 2,472 total workers, 1,916 are males and 556 are females for the G. Udayagiri N.A.C. town. There are 1,827 males and 373 females totalling 2,200 as main workers. Of the 272 persons as marginal workers, 89 are males and 183 are females. 2,341 males and 3,695 females together form the group of 6,036 persons as non-workers of the G.Udayagiri N.A.C town.

Table 4
Main Workers Classified

Category of workers	*Phulbani NAC in persons*	*G Udayagiri NAC in persons*
Cultivators	441	262
Agricultural labourers	717	360
Live-stock, forestry, fishing, hunting and plantation, orchards and allied activities	553	190
Mining and Quarrying	11	01
Manufacturing, — In household processing, industries servicing and - other than repairs	93	40
household industries	479	100
Constructions	292	28
Trade and commerce	1,365	430
Transport, storage and communications	430	89
other services	3,581	700
Total main workers	7,962	2,200

Source: District Statistical Handbook, Kandhamal, Directorate of Economics and Statistics, Government of Orissa, Bhubaneswar, 1993.

In Phulbani N.A.C 97.22 per cent of the total workers are main workers and in G. Udayagiri N.A.C the corresponding percentage is 89.0. Of the total workers in Phulbani N.A.C. 5.38 per cent are cultivators, 8.75 per cent are Agricultural labourers, 6.75 per cent are in livestock, forestry, fishing, hunting, plantation, orchards and allied activities; 0.13 per cent in mining and quarrying, 1.14 per cent are in household manufacturing, processing, servicing and repairs, 5.85 per cent are in other than household manufacturing, processing, servicing and repair works, 3.57 per cent are in constructions, 16.67 per cent are in trade and commerce, 5.25 per cent are in transport, storage and communication services and 43.72 per cent are in other services.

Table 5
Staff Pattern

Sl. No	Staff category	Phulbani NAC	G Udayagiri NAC
1	Executive officer	1	1
2	Municipal Engineer (Junior)	1	1
3	Head Assistant	1	Nil
4	Senior Assistant	1(Vacant)	Nil
5	Junior Assistant	4	2
6	Community Organiser	1	Nil
7	Sanitary inspector	1	1
8	Vital Statistician	1	1
9	Tax collector	2	2
10	Assistant Tax collector	1	Nil
11	Octroi Moharior	7	8
12	Jamadar	1	Nil
13	Pump Khalasi	1	Nil
14	Tank watcher	1	Nil
15	Octroi peon	7	7
16	Office peon	5	2
17	Sweeper	32	20
18	Night watchman	1	1
	Total	68	46

Source: Respective NAC Offices.

Of the total workers in G. Udayagiri N.A.C. 10.60 per cent are cultivators, 14.56 per cent are Agricultural labourers, 7.69 per cent are in livestock, forestry, fishing, hunting and plantation, orchards and allied activities, 0.04 per cent are in mining and quarrying, 1.62 per cent are in household manufacturing, processing, servicing and repairs, 4.05 per cent are in other than household manufacturing, processing, servicing and repairs, 1.13 per cent are in constructions, 17.39 per cent are in trade and commerce, 3.60 per cent are in transport, storage and communications, and 28.32 per cent are in other services.

Taking into consideration the percentage of

cultivators and agricultural labourers in both the towns, it is found that Phulbani is more divorced from Agriculture than G. Udayagiri is. Besides, the percentage of workers in other services than the selected main workers are sufficiently higher in Phulbani N.A.C (43.72) than they are in G.Udayagiri N.A.C (28.32).

The staff pattern in both the Notified Area Councils is not all comprehensive. The staff particularly in G. Udayagiri N.A.C. are not adequate.

Budget

The income sources for both the N.A.Cs. include octroi tax, taxes on houses and lands, lighting, water and conservancy rates, taxes on profession and trade, other rates and taxes, receipts from markets, slaughter houses and lands, other fees and revenue, grants from Government, other grants and income from miscellaneous sources. The income schedule shows that for the given period 1995-96 and 1996-97 Phulbani NAC has no income under other fees and revenue while G. Udayagiri NAC has earned nothing under the head receipts from markets, slaughter houses and lands. Phulbani N.A.C. has increased its income from Rs. 41,73,239 in 1995-96 to Rs. 46,90,187 in 1996-97, the increment percentage over the year being 12.39. But on the other hand G. Udayagiri N.A.C. increased its income from Rs. 10,28,670 in 1995-96 to Rs. 23,98,743 in 1996-97 with an income growth of 133.19 per cent over the same period. The income growth of G. Udayagiri N.A.C. for 1996-97 over 1995-96 is nearly 11 times of the income growth of Phulbani N.A.C. for the same period. This high growth rate of income for the G.Udayagiri N.A.C. was mainly due to increase of grant-in-aid from Government and other sources by 194.5 per cent and also increase of income from Octroi taxes by 119.05 per cent. It may be mentioned here that the collection of Octroi taxes which were imposed very recently in G.Udayagiri N.A.C. was geared up. From the income table

Table 6

Income Schedule (In Rupees)

SI. No.	Source of Income	Phulbani NAC		G. Udayagiri NAC	
		1995-96	1996-97	1995-96	1996-97
1	2	3	4	5	6
1.	Octroi taxes	13,23,087	14,45,369	1,47,493	3,23,090
2.	Taxes on houses and lands	1,13,236	53,361	1,41,923	1,14,590
3.	Lighting, Water and conservancy rates	1,93,305	88,648	45,381	39,593
4.	Taxes on profession and trade, other rates and taxes	88,350	79,807	58,062	69,668
5.	Receipts from markets, slaughter houses and lands	2,30,462	1,61,290	...	...
6.	Other fees and revenue	...	...	35,040	60,477
7.	Grants from government	13,79,712	15,73,974	5,46,000	12,20,000
8.	Other grants	2,62,783	2,81,653	50,000	5,35,000
9.	Miscellaneous	5,82,304	10,06,085	4,771	36,325
	Total	41,73,239	46,90,187	10,28,670	23,98,743

Source : Respective N.A.C Offices.

Table 7
Expenditure Schedule (in Rupees)

Sl. No.	*Head of Expenditure*	*Phulbani NAC*		*G. Udayagiri NAC*	
		1995-96	*1996-97*	*1995-96*	*1996-97*
1	2	3	4	5	6
1.	Public lighting & water supply	7,90,533	3,53,362	2,47,103	2,68,450
2.	Drainage, conservancies & Sanitation	9,37,376	9,40,553	94,993	1,22,400
3.	Miscellaneous	2,99,176	5,33,982	12,570	13,659
4.	Roads	2,63,592	1,72,245	Nil	1,92,672
5.	Others including buildings	11,06,097	7,18,609	33,212	3,80,903
6.	Repayment of Govt. loans	3,20,335	3,99,039	...	...
7.	Other expenditure including staff salary	17,18,977	17,83,689	4,20,641	5,13,924
	Total	54,36,086	49,01,479	8,08,519	14,92,008

Source : Respective NAC offices.

it is seen that for both the years grant-in-aid from Government and other sources constitutes the biggest source of income for both the Notified Area Councils. While for Phulbani N.A.C. such aid constitutes nearly 40 per cent for each year, it constitutes nearly 58 per cent for 1995-96 and above 73 per cent for 1996-97 for G.Udayagiri N.A.C. This is a clear evidence of the fact that these urban local bodies primary depend on the grant-in-aid from Government for their existence. This opportunity is easily misutiliscd by the Government to curb the independence and autonomy of such bodies by controlling and guiding them on their sweet will. However, the next other major sources of income for them are Octroi tax, taxes on houses and lands and lighting, water and conservancy rates. Inspite of these, the incomes do not seem to be adequate.

Taking a look at the expenditure schedule, it can be observed that Phulbani N.A.C. has a deficit budget for both the years 1995-96 and 1996-97 while G.Udayagiri N.A.C. has a surplus budget for both the years. This difference was primarily due to the fact that for 1995-96 the per head expenditure in Phulbani N.A.C. was about Rs. 200 while it was only Rs. 95 for G.Udayagiri N.A.C. in the same year. Thus, the development works for the G.Udayagiri N.A.C. for 1995-96 were very much limited.

The major head of expenditure for the Notified Area Councils for both the years 1995-96 and 1996-97 is the other expenditure which is mainly and primarily incurred for payment of Staff salary. The respective percentages of total expenditure for 1995-96 and 1996-97 for Phulbani N.A.C. under the head were 31.62 and 36.39 while percentages for G.Udayagiri were 52.02 and 34.45. This overshadows the developmental activities in these areas. The next major heads of expenditure for both the Notified Area Councils are public lighting and water supply, drainage, conservancies and sanitation, and other expenses including buildings etc.

Psephological Trends—A Sample Study of 1997 Elections

After its constitution in 1963, the Phulbani N.A.C. for the first time went to the polls in the same year. Subsequent elections to it were held in 1968, 1973, 1978, 1984, 1992 and 1997. In the election held on 11th July 1997, the total number of voters in the electoral rolls was 21,068 including 11,895 males and 9,173 females. A total of 11,695 voters including 6,481 males and 5,214 females exercised their franchise conducted in 24 polling stations. The percentage of polling was 55.51. Out of 70 nominations filed 1 was rejected and 6 were withdrawn and actually 63 candidates were in the fray. Out of the 13 councillors elected, 8 belonged to Congress(I), two belonged to BJP and three were independents. Sri Basanta Bihari Pradhan and Smt. Suryakanti Nayak (SC woman), both of Congress(I) were elected indirectly as chairperson and vice-chairperson respectively. Since its inception, the Phulbani Notified Area Council has been dominated most of the time by the Congress Party.

The first election to G.Udayagiri N.A.C., constituted in 1981, was held in 1992 and besides, a bye-election in 1993 for the post of chairperson, the latest election to it was held on 11th July, 1997. Out of 6,124 voters including 3,386 males and 2,738 females in the electoral rolls, actually 3,673 voters including 1,854 males and 1,819 females exercised their franchise in 12 polling stations. The percentage of polling was 65.96. Out of 42 nominations, 1 was rejected, 1 was withdrawn and 1 was elected without contest. As many as 39 contestants remained in the fray for the rest 12 posts of councillors. Of the total 13 councillors elected, 9 belonged to Congress(I), 1 belonged to Janata Dal and 3 were Independents. Smt. Bijayalaxmi Bhoi and Smt. Rekha Naik, both of Congress(I) were elected indirectly as chairperson and vice-chairperson respectively. In 1992 election, Janata Dal was in a dominant position while in 1997 election Congress (I) has stolen the show.

The Elite Profile in Urban Phulbani District

The core of this study "The Urban Political Elite in Tribal India" is the study of the Urban Political Elite - the councillors, both past and present, of the two Notified Area Councils of the Phulbani district such as Phulbani N.A.C. and G.Udayagiri N.A.C, a total of 54 Elite members - 31 from Phulbani and 23 from G.Udayagiri. This includes almost all the Councillors, past and present, of the respective Notified Area Councils, who are staying within such NAC areas. Several Councillors were elected for two or more number of terms but were interviewed as single Councillors. Termwise, 54 interviewees represent 64 Councillors including 5 Chairpersons and 6 Vice-Chairpersons both past and present, of both the NACs.

The Councillors were interviewed directly and separately by the author and the interviews proceeded only according as questionnaire as given in the Appendix. An elite member does not cease to be so only because he is not an elected representative now or at any point of time earlier. Thus, the selection of these members does not harm the desired goal, rather it helps the same in several other ways such as in giving a link of continuity, peculiarity of time and age etc. The questionnaire was divided into five parts— A, B, C, D, and E. Part A containing 8 main questions tried to find out the socio-economic status of the elite. Part B containing 2 major questions desired to assess the level of political awareness and communication of the elite. Part C with 10 queries aimed at finding out the type and level of political involvement and their leadership process of the elite. Part D having 15 questions intended to know their political ideals and aspirations. And finally part E with 9 main questions tried to assess their approach to development. While some questions were open, some others were closed having given selected choices as answers.

Table 8
Termwise (Election Year) Distribution of Councillors Interviewed

	1963	*1968*	*1973*	*1978*	*1984*	*1992*	*1997*	*Total*
Phulbani NAC	1	1	2	4	8	10	13	39
G. Udayagiri NAC	...	...	...	...	...	12	13	25
Phulbani District (Urban)	1	1	2	4	8	22	26	64*

* The number includes 5 chairpersons and 6 vice-chairpersons, past and present, of both the NACs.

Table 9
Age Composition of Elite*

Age group (in years)	*21-30*	*31-40*	*41-50*	*51 and above*	*Total*
Phulbani NAC	4(12.90)	8(25.81)	13(41.94)	6(19.35)	31
G. Udayagiri NAC	5(21.74)	11(47.83)	5(21.74)	2(8.69)	23
Urban Phulbani District	9(16.67)	19(35.19)	18(33.33)	8(14.81)	54

* Figures within the brackets indicate respective percentages.

The age composition of elite members shows that in Phulbani N.A.C. 12.90 per cent elite members are in the age group of 21 and 30, 25.81 per cent are in the age group of 31 and 40, 41.94 per cent are in the age group of 41 and 50 and 19.35 per cent are at the age of 51 or above. In G.Udayagiri N.A.C. 21.74 per cent of the elite members are in the age group of 21 and 30, 47.83 per cent are in the age group of 31 and 40, 21.74 per cent are in the age group of 41 and 50 and 8.69 per cent are at the age of 51 or above. The study shows heavy concentration of elite members in the age group of 31 and 40 in G.Udayagiri N.A.C. and in the age group of 41 and 50 in Phulbani N.A.C. In the consolidated form the urban political elites of Phulbani district constitute 16.67 per cent in the age group of 21 and 30, 35.19 per cent in the age group of 31 and 40, 33.33 per cent in the age group of 41 and 50, 14.81 per cent in the age group of 51 and above. The last group includes 5.55 per cent of elite members in the age group of 60 and 70 and 3.70

per cent above 70 years of age. The study reveals that the urban political elites of Phulbani district are more active and operative in the age group of 31 and 40. Thus, young blood is more active in elite role.

Table 10

Sex Composition of Elite*

	Male	*Female*	*Total*
Phulbani NAC	24(77.42)	7(22.58)	31
G Udayagiri NAC	14(60.87)	9(39.13)	23
Urban Phulbani District	38(70.37)	16(29.63)	54

* Figures within the brackets indicate respective percentages

The sex composition of the elite members points out that in Phulbani N.A.C. males are more numerous as urban political elite than the females. In G.Udayagiri N.A.C., the females as political elites are nearer or at least trying to be nearer to their male counterparts. To state it otherwise, among the elite members 77.42 per cent are males and 22.58 per cent are females in Phulbani N.A.C. and 60.87 per cent are males and 39.13 per cent are females in G.Udayagiri N.A.C. Among the urban political elites of Phulbani district 70.37 per cent are males and 29.63 per cent are females. The females have to take more interest and effort to be at par with or nearer to their male counterparts. Widening of the base of education, economic and socio-cultural activities will help bring the desired goal. Besides, the present statutory provision inserted into Orissa Municipal Act, 1950 by Act 11 of 1994 for reservation of one-third seats of councillors for women will improve the situation in future in a compulsive way.

Table 11

Marital Status of Elite*

	Married	*Unmarried*	*Total*
Phulbanj NAC	28(90.32)	03(9.68)	31
G .Udayagiri NAC	21(91.30)	02(8.70)	23
Urban Phulbani District.	49(90.74)	05(9.26)	54

* Figures within the brackets indicate respective percentages.

Among the elite members of Phulbani N.A.C. 90.32

per cent are married and 9.68 per cent are unmarried. The corresponding percentages for G. Udayagiri N.A.C. are 91.30 and 8.70. The urban political elites in Phulbani district are seen to be married by 90.74 per cent and unmarried by 9.26 per cent. Probably due to ripened age and married status the elite members get an advantage in public relation and political engineering.

Table 12

Native and Non-Native Composition of Elite*

	Native	*Non-native*	*Total*
Phulbani NAC	19(61.29)	12(38.71)	31
G. Udayagiri NAC	14(60.87)	09(39.13)	23
Urban Phulbani District	33(61.11)	21(38.89)	54

* Figures within the brackets indicate respective percentages.

The study revealed an interesting fact that 61.29 per cent of elite members in Phulbani N.A.C, 60.87 per cent of elite members in G. Udayagiri N.A.C. and 61.11 per cent of the urban political elites in Phulbani district are natives while 38.71 per cent in Phulbani N.A.C., 39.13 per cent in G.Udayagiri N.A.C. and 38.89 per cent in urban Phulbani district among the elites are non-natives. Among the natives 47.37 per cent in Phulbani N.A.C., 35.71 per cent in G.Udayagiri N.A.C. and 42.42 per cent in urban Phulbani district have settled down in the respective areas within last three or four generations. Further, among the non-native elites 58.33 per cent in Phulbani N.A.C., 55.56 per cent in G. Udayagiri N.A.C. and 57.14 per cent in urban Phulbani district have migrated from rural areas of the district while 41.67 per cent in Phulbani N.A.C., 44.44 per cent in G.Udayagiri N.A.C. and 42.86 per cent in urban Phulbani district from among the non-native elites have migrated from outside the district including some from outside the state. This shows a serious dislocation in boosting the real natives into elite structure and involving them more in solving their own local problems in the urban setting.

Table 13

Caste Composition of Elite*

	Scheduled Castes	*Scheduled Tribes*	*OBC*	*General*	*Total*
Phulbani NAC	9(29.03)	3(9.68)	3(9.68)	16(51.61)	31
G. Udayagiri NAC	4(17.39)	8(34.78)	5(21.74)	6(26.09)	23
Urban Phulbani District	13(24.07)	11(20.37)	8(14.82)	22(40.74)	54

* Figures within the brackets indicate respective percentages.

About nomenclature of castes among the elite members, 29.03 per cent in Phulbani N.A.C,. 17.39 per cent in G.Udayagiri N.A.C. and 24.07 per cent in urban Phulbani district are Scheduled Castes. The corresponding percentages for Scheduled Tribes are 9.68, 34.78 and 20.37. The corresponding percentages for other backward classes (O.B.C.) are 9.68, 21.74 and 14.82 and the corresponding percentages for General Castes are 51.61, 26.09 and 40.74. It may be pointed out here that in various elections to the two NACs, 6.45 per cent in Phulhani NAC, 17.39 per cent in G. Udayagiri NAC and 11.11 per cent in entire Phulbani district of the elected councillors were from the Scheduled tribe community who occupied the seats from unreserved wards. In Phulbani NAC the post of Chairperson in 1978 and the post of Vice -Chairperson in 1992 were occupied by Scheduled tribes. In G. Udayagiri NAC in 1993 bye-election the post of chairperson was occupied by a Scheduled Tribe person. Also in 1992 the post of Vice-Chairperson was occupied by a person of the same community. The significance of all these was that the Scheduled Tribe members occupied these posts through open contest and not through reservation. In 1997 election in G.Udayagiri NAC two councillors - one male and another female from the same community were elected in open contest from unreserved wards defeating their arch rivals with heavy margins. This shows the emerging dominant role of the tribal elites.

In composition of religion, the elites are mainly

Table 14
Occupational Structure of Elite*

	Business men	Cultivators	Agricultural laboures	Contractors	Advocates	House-wives	Journalists	Others	Total
Phulbani NAC	8(25.81)	4(12.90)	...	5(16.13)	6(19.35)	7(22.58)	...	1(3.23)	31
G. Udayagiri NAC	6(26.09)	4(17.39)	2(8.69)	...	1(4.35)	6(26.09)	1(4.35)	3(13.04)	23
Urban Phulbani District	14(25.93)	8(14.82)	2(3.70)	5(9.26)	7(12.96)	13(24.07)	1(1.85)	4(7.41)	54

* Figures within the brackets indicate respective percentages.

Table 15
Languages Status of Elite*

	Mother Tongue				Othe Than Mother Tongue				Total No. of Languages Known			
	Oriya	Kui	Urdu	Telugu	Hindi	English	Telugu	Bengali	One	Two	Three	Four
Phulbani NAC	25 (80. 64)	4 (12.90)	1 (3.23)	1 (3.23]	20 (64.52)	14 (45.16)	1 (3.23)	2 (6.45)	8 (25.81)	7 (22.58)	13 (41.93)	3 (9.68)
G. Udayagiri NAC	11 (47.83)	12 (52.17)	... ...	... ...	12 (52.17)	10 (43.48)	1 (4.35)	... ...	6 (26.09)	6 (26.09)	5 (21.73)	6 (26.09)
Urban Phulbani District	36 (66.67)	16 (29.63)	1 (1.85)	1 (1.85)	32 (59.26)	24 (44.44)	2 (3.70)	2 (3.70)	14 (25.93)	13 (24.07)	18 (33.33)	9 (16.67)

* Figures within the brackets indicate respective percentages.

Hindus. Except one Muslim elite in Phulbani N.A.C. and one Christian elite in G.Udayagiri N.A.C. the rest 52 elite members are Hindus. Thus, together the elites are Hindus by 96.30 per cent.

As to occupation, the political elites of Phulbani N.A.C. are Businessmen by 25.81 per cent, cultivators by 12.90 per cent, contractors by 16.13 per cent, Advocates by 19.35 per cent, housewives by 22.58 per cent and others by 3.23 per cent. In G.Udayagiri N.A.C. they are businessmen by 26.09 per cent, cultivators by 17.39 per cent, Agricultural labourers by 8.69 per cent, Advocates by 4.35 per cent, Housewives by 26.09 per cent, Journalists by 4.35 per cent and others by 13.04 per cent.

Aggregately, the urban political elites ofPhulbani district are businessmen by 25.93 per cent, cultivators by 14.82 per cent, Agricultural labourers by 3.70 per cent, contractors by 9.26 per cent, Advocates by 12.96 per cent, Housewives by 24.07 per cent, Journalists by 1.85 per cent and others by 7.41 per cent. In the occupational structure the political elites of both the Notified Area Councils are predominantly businessmen and housewives. Together, they constitute just 50 per cent of the urban political elites of Phulbani district. However, the advocates are also prominent in Phulbani N.A.C. as elites.

100 per cent elites of both the Notified Area Councils - Phulbani and G.Udayagiri know Oriya whether it is their mother tongue or not. As to mother tongue status of elites in Phulbani N.A.C., 80.64 per cent of them speak Oriya, 12.90 per cent speak Kui, the local tribal dialect particularly of the kandhas of Phulbani, 3.23 per cent speak Urdu and the same per cent of elites speak Telugu there. Regarding knowledge of languages other than mother tongue, in Phulbani N.A.C., 64.52 per cent elites speak Hindi, 45.16 per cent speak English, 3.23 per cent speak Telugu, and 6.45 per cent speak Bengali. Regarding knowledge in maximum number of

languages, 25.81 per cent of the political elites of urban Phulbani district know one language, 22.58 per cent of them know two languages and 41.93 per cent and 9.68 per cent of them have knowledge in three and four languages respectively.

In G. Udayagiri N.A.C., 47.83 per cent ofthe political elites speak Oriya as their mother tongue and the rest 52.17 per cent speak Kui. Other than their mother tongue, 52.1 7 per cent of the political elites of the town know Hindi, 43.48 per cent of them know English and 4.35 per cent of them know Telugu. As to the maximum number of languages known by elites of the town, 26.09 per cent know one language and also the same percentages of them know two languages and four languages respectively. 21.73 per cent of them know three languages.

In a consolidated form 66.67 per cent of the urban political elites of Phulbani district speak Oriya as their mother tongue. The respective percentages of them who speak Kui, Urdu, and Telugu as their mother tongue are 29.63, 1.85 and 1.85 respectively. As to their knowledge in language(s) other than their mother tongue 59.26 per cent of urban political elites of the district know Hindi, 44.44 per cent of them know English, 3.70 per cent of them know Telugu and the same per cent of them know Bengali. Regarding the maximum number of languages known by them, 25.93 per cent of them know one language, 24.07 per cent, 33.33 per cent and 16.67percent of them know two, three and four languages respectively.

It is found that more than 50 per cent of the elites in G.Udayagiri N.A.C. know the local tribal dialect of the district (*kui*) which is known by only about 13 per cent of the elites of Phulbani N.A.C. In solving local problems and going closer to the local people, every elite should be expected to have knowledge in the local language/ dialect which is very rare in Phulbani N.A.C. This is not a good sign. However, a good trend in this regard still continues in G.Udayagiri N.A.C.

Table 16
Educational Status*

	Just Literate	*Primary level (up to standard V)*	*Middle Level (up to std. VII)*	*High school level (up to std. X)*	*HSC Pass*	*Intermediate or +2*	*Bachelors degree*	*Master's degree*
Phulbani NAC	...	8(25.81)	4(12.90)	3(9.68)	7(22.58)	...	8(25.81)	1(3.22)
G. Udayagiri NAC	2(8.70)	4(17.39)	2(8.70)	9(39.12)	4(17.39)	...	2(8.70)	...
Urban Phulbani District	2(3.71)	12(22.22)	6(11.11)	12(22.22)	11(20.37)	...	10(18.52)	1(1.85)

* Figures within the brackets indicate respective percentages.

Regarding educational qualifications of the political elites in Phulbani N.A.C., 25.81 per cent have primary level education, i.e., up to standard V, 12.90 per cent have middle level education, i.e., up to standard VII, 9.68 per cent have High School level education, i.e., up to standard X, 22.58 per cent have passed High School Certificate Examination or, in other words, are Matriculates, 25.81 per cent are Bachelor degree holders and 3.22 per cent are Master's Degree holders. Among the Bachelor degree holders 62.5 per cent are Law graduates.

Among the elites of G.Udayagiri N.A.C., 8.70 per cent are just literates, 17.39 per cent are educated up to standard V (Primary level), 8.70 per cent are educated up to standard VII (Middle level), 39.12 per cent are educated up to standard X (High School level), 17.39 per cent have passed High School Certificate Examination or, in other words, are Matriculates, 8.70 per cent are Bachelor's degree holders. Among the Bachelor's degree holders 50 per cent are law graduates. No post-graduate elite was found in the town.

In an aggregate form, 3.71 per cent of the urban political elites of Phulbani district are just literates, 22.22 per cent are educated up to standard V (Primary level) and the same per cent of the elites are educated upto standard X (High School level). 11.11 per cent of them are educated up to standard VII (Middle level), 20.37 per cent have passed High School Certificate Examination, or, in other words are Matriculates, 18.52 per cent of them are Bachelor's degree holders among whom 60 per cent are law graduates. Only 1.85 per cent have Master's degree qualification. No elite with Intermediate or +2 degree was found in either of the N.A.Cs. Numerically speaking, the elites having education up to standard X or having passed H.S.C. dominate the urban government in Phulbani district. Together, they constitute 42.59 per cent of the total elites. Also the elites educated up to Primary level and the graduates forming two extremes in educational status have the next numerical strength.

Regarding family size of the political elites of Phulbani N.A.C., 35.48 per cent have families with 1 to 5 members, 45.16 per cent have families with 6 to 10 members and 19.36 per cent have families with more than 10 members. In G. Udayagiri N.A.C. 21.74 per cent of the elites have families with 1 to 5 members, 56.52 per cent have families with 6 to 10 members and 21.74 per cent have families with more than 10 members.

Table 17
Family Size of the Elite*

	1 to 5 members	*6 to 10 members*	*Above 10 members*	*Total*
Phulbani NAC	11 (35.48)	14(45.16)	06(19.36)	31
G. Udayagiri NAC	5 (21.74)	13(56.52)	5(21.74)	23
Urban Phulbani District	16(29.63)	27(50.00)	11(20.37)	54

* The figures within the brackets indicate respective percentages.

In a consolidated form, in the urban Phulbani district 29.63 per cent of the political elites have families with 1 to 5 members, 50 per cent of them have families with 6 to 10 members and 20.37 per cent of them have families with more that 10 members. It is interesting to note that while 3.70 per cent of elites have a family with single member (self), only 5.56 per cent of them have families with more than 20 members reaching the highest point of 23 members of a family. It is observed that the elites generally come from middle size families.

Regarding Annual family income of the Political elites of Phulbani N.A.C, it is found that 12.90 per cent of the elites have an annual family income upto Rs. 15,000, 38.71 per cent have a family income between Rs. 16,000 to Rs. 30,000, 29.03 per cent of them belong to the Annual family income group of Rs. 31,000 to Rs. 70,000, 16.13 per cent of them have a family income between Rs 71,000 and Rs 1 lakh and 3.23 per cent of them earn an annual family income of above Rs 1 Lakh. In G. Uadayagiri N.A.C. 65.21 per cent of the political elites have an annual family income upto Rs 15,000, 4.35 per cent of them have

Table 18
Annual Family Income Range of the Elite*

	Upto Rs. 15,000	*Rs.16,000/- to Rs. 30,000*	*Rs.31,000/- to Rs. 70,000*	*Rs.71,000 to Rs, 100,000*	*Above Rs. 100,000*	*Total*
Phulbani N.A.C	4(12.90)	12(38.71)	9(29.03)	5(16.13)	1 (3.23)	31
G.Udayagiri N.A.C	15(6521)	1 (4.35)	5 (21.74)	1 (4 35)	1 (4.35)	23
Urban Phulbani District	19(35.19)	13(24.07)	14(25.93)	6(11 11)	2(3.70)	54

* Figures within the brackets indicate respective percentages.

Table 19
Status Symbols*

	Landed Property		*Buildiing*		*Motor Vehicle*		*Telephone*	
	Yes	*No*	*Yes*	*No*	*Yes*	*No*	*Yes*	*No*
Phulbani N.A.C	20 (64.52)	11 (35.48)	25 (80.65)	6 (19.35)	17 (54.84)	14 (45.16)	19 (61.29)	12 (38.71)
G.Udayagiri N.A.C	11 (47.83)	12 (52.17)	13 (56.52)	10 (43.48)	7 (30.43)	16 (69.57)	4 (17.39)	19 (82.61)
Urban Phulbani District	31 (57.41)	23 (42.59)	38 (70.37)	16 (29.63)	24 (44.44)	30 (55.56)	23 (42.59)	31 (57.41)

* Figures within the brackets indicate respective percentages.

a family income from Rs. 16,000 to Rs. 30,000, 21.74 per cent of them have an annul income from Rs. 31,000- to Rs. 70,000, 4.35 per cent of them earn a family income from Rs 71,000 to Rs. 1 lakh and the same per cent of them have an annual family income of above Rs. 1 lakh.

In aggregate 35.19 per cent of political elites of Phulbani district have an annual family income upto Rs. 15,000s, 24.07 per cent of them have a family income from Rs 16,000 to Rs30,000, 25.93 per cent of them have a family income from Rs. 31,000 to Rs. 70,000, 11.11 per cent of them earn a family income from Rs. 71,000 to Rs. 1 lakh and 3.70 per cent of them earn an annual family income above Rs. 1 lakh. It is interesting to note that 9.25 per cent of the total urban elites of the district, totally concentrated in G. Udayagiri N.A.C earn an annual family income of Rs. 5,000 or less and on the other hand 1.85 per cent of the said group concentrated only in Phulbani N.A.C earn an annual family income of Rs 3 lakh. It is pertinent here to observe that of their respective total elites, 38.71 per cent in Phulbani N.A.C, 30.43 per cent in G. Udayagiri N.A.C and together 35.19 per cent in the urban Phulbani district have at least one person among the rest members of the family in service. The study shows almost the diametrically opposite economic statuses of the elites of Phulbani N.A.C as compared to that of the elites of G. Udayagiri N.A.C. While political elites of Phulbani N.A.C generally hail from middle class and higher class families, their counterparts in G.Udayagiri N.A.C are drawn basically from poor and very poor economic background.

At the very first asking about annual family income, except a brave and self-convinced few, most of the elites tried to conceal the real income. The poor tried to be apparently more poor to avail more government benefits thinking at first that the report might reach the Government.The middle and higher income groups tried to conceal it apparently to avoid the attention of the Income Tax Department. However, after duly convinced, almost all of them gave the real picture of their income.

To corroborate the table on the Annual family income of the elites, given here is the table showing the status symbols of the elites. Four items such as landed property, building, motor vehicle and telephone were included as tokens of status symbol. Television was deliberately not included in it as it has become a common man's bare necessity now and is not expensive too. Thus, it no more counts as a status symbol today. Among the political elites of Phulbani N.A.C. 64.52 per cent have landed property and 35.48 per cent do not have it. While 80.65 per cent of them have a building, 19.35 per cent do not have the same. 54.84 per cent of them possess a motor vehicle while 45.16 per cent do not enjoy the opportunity. 61.29 per cent of them are having a personal telephone while 38.71 per cent of them do not have the scope.

Among the political elites of G.Udayagiri N.A.C 47.83 per cent have landed property and 52.1 7 per cent do not have the same. 56.52 per cent of them have a building while 43.48 per cent of them do not enjoy the opportunity. While only 30.43 per cent of them have a motor vehicle, the rest 69.57 per cent are deprived of the chance. Personal telephone is enjoyed by only 17.39 per cent of them, while the rest 82.61 per cent do not enjoy the opportunity.

In totality, 57.41 per cent of the urban political elites of Phulbani district do have landed property while 42.59 per cent of them do not have the same. 70.37 per cent of them do have a building while only 29.63 per cent of them are not having it. Only 44.44 per cent of them do have a motor vehicle and the rest 55.56 per cent are deprived of the opportunity. Personal telephone is enjoyed by only 42.59 per cent of the elites but not enjoyed by the rest 57.41 per cent of them. In all the four items taken here as counting status symbols the political elites of Phulbani N.A.C are far better than those of the G.Udayagiri N.A.C., again confirming the fact that the latter generally hail from poor economic background and are devoid of status symbols.

Table 20
Political Awareness

	Phulbani NAC				G. Udayagiri NAC			
	Right	Partially right	Wrong	Can't say	Right	Partially right	Wrong	Can't say
How many districts are there in Orissa ?	20	...	6	5	13	...	2	8
Which party is ruling at the Centre ?	14	6	4	7	12	1	1	9
Who was Mahatma Gandhi ?	26	...	1	4	15	...	3	5
Who was Jawaharlal Nehru ?	24	2	...	5	12	1	2	8
Who was Indira Gandhi ?	26	2	...	3	15	2	3	3
Who was B.R. Ambedkar ?	19	1	1	10	8	1	...	14
Who was Biju Patnaik ?	24	4	1	2	17	...	2	4
Who was Harekrishna Mahatab ?	19	1	3	8	9	...	2	12
Who was Mother Teresa ?	20	2	1	8	11	3	1	8
Who is Nandini Satpathy ?	24	...	1	6	14	...	1	8
Who is T N Sheshan?	19	3	...	9	11	...	...	12
Who is K.R. Karayanan ?	17	...	2	12	12	...	...	11
Who is the Chief Minister of Orissa ?	30	...	...	1	19	...	...	4
What is the name of your District Collector ?	20	3	1	7	6	2	1	14
What is the name of our Prime Minister ?	20	3	...	8	12	3	...	8
Why is 15th August famous ?	28	...	...	3	19	...	1	3
Can you name the three colours of our National flag ?	10	15	2	4	5	15	...	3
Can you name the election symbols of the following political parties : Cong.(I), JD, BJP, and CPI(M) ?	28	1	2	...	20	3	...	...
How can a vote be invalid ?	29	...	...	2	16	1	...	6

Contd...

Table 20 Contd...

Which day is the Republic Day of India ?	22	...	2	7	13	...	...	10
How many MLA seats are there in Orissa ?	20	...	2	9	8	...	4	11
What is the minimum age to become an N A C Councillor ?	9	...	19	3	...	...	17	6
Who is your MP ?	31	...	...	...	21	...	...	2
Who is your MLA ?	30	...	...	1	21	...	1	1
What is the maximum time that the police can detain a person ?	30	...	...	1	17	...	1	5
According to law how many living wives can a Hindu male have ?	30	...	...	1	21	...	...	2
AVERAGE (BY PERSONS)	22.65	1.65	1.85	4.85	13.35	1.23	1.61	6.81
PERCENTAGE (BY PERSONS)	73.06	5.32	5.97	15.65	58.04	5.35	7.00	29.61
AVERAGE (BY RESPONSES)	19	1.39	1.55	4.06	15.09	1.39	1.83	7.69
PERCENTAGE (BY RESPONSES)	73.08	5.35	5.96	15.61	58.04	5.34	7.04	29.58
URBAN PHULBANI DISTRICT								
AVERAGE (BY PERSONS)	36	2.88	3.46	11.66				
PERCENTAGE (BY PERSONS)	66.67	5.33	6.41	21.59				
AVERAGE (BY RESPONSES)	17.05	1.39	1.69	5.87				
PERCENTAGE (BY RESPONSES)	65.58	5.34	6.50	22.58				

Political Awareness

In order to assess the political awareness of the urban political elites of Phulbani district, two questions were included in the questionnaire. One of them contained 26 bits mostly in the form of *who's who* ? They were (a) How many districts are there in Orissa ? (b) Which Party is ruling at the centre ? (c) Who was Mahatma Gandhi ? (d) Who was Jawaharlal Nehru? (e) Who was Indira Gandhi ? (f) Who was B.R Ambedkar? (g) Who was Biju Patnaik? (h) Who was Harekrushna Mahatab? (i) Who was Mother Teresa? (k) Who is Nandini Satpathy? (k) Who is T.N.Sheshan ? (l) Who is K.R. Narayanan ? (m) Who is the Chief Minister of Orissa ? (n) What is the name of your district collector ? (o) What is the name of our Prime Minister ? (p) Why is 15th August famous? (g) Can you name the three colours of our national flag? (r) Can you name the election symbols of the following parties: Congress (I), Janata Dal, BJP and CPI (M) ? (s) How can a vote be invalid ? (t) Which day is the Republic Day of India ? (u) How many M.L.A. seats are there in Orissa ? (v) What is the minimum age to become an N.A.C councillor? (w) Who is your M.P.? (x) Who is your MLA ?(y) What is the maximum time that the police can detain a person without court order? and (z) According to law how many living wives can a Hindu male have?

The questions included prominent political personalities and office-bearers, both past and present from the state as well as national level, national days, national flag, membership, constitution, election symbols of political parties, voting, number of districts etc.

This survey on political awareness of the elites in Phulbani N.A.C revealed that on an average out of 31 members interviewed 22.65 persons or 73.06 per cent of elites gave the right answers while 1.65 persons or 5.32 per cent of the elites gave partially right answers, 1.85 persons or 5.97 per cent of the elites responded to the questions wrongly while 4.85 persons or 15.65 per cent of the elites expressed their ignorance. Presenting it otherwise in terms of answers or responses, each elite member of Phulbani N.A.C made on an average 19 or 73.08 per cent right responses out of the total questions of 26; made 1.39 or 5.35 per cent partially right responses; made 1.55 or 5.96 per cent wrong responses; expressed ignorance for 4.06 or 15.61 per cent answers.

In G. Udayagiri N.A.C, out of 23 elite members interviewed, on an average, 13.35 persons or 58.04 per cent of the elites made right responses on the 26 questions on political awareness; 1.23 persons or 5.35 per cent elites made partially right responses; 1.61 persons or 7.01 per cent elites made wrong answers, while 6.81 persons or 29.61 per cent of the elites expressed their ignorance. Responsewise each of the elite members interviewed there made, on an average, 15.09 or 58.04 per cent right responses out of the said 26 questions; made 1.39 or 5.34 per cent partially right answers; made 1.83 or 7.07 per cent wrong responses and expressed ignorance for 7.69 or 29.58 per cent answers.

In aggregate, out of the 54 urban political elites of Phulbani district interviewed, on an average, 36 or 66.67 per cent of them made right responses to the 26 queries on political awareness; 2.88 or 5.33 per cent of them made partially right responses; 3.46 or 6.41 per cent of them answered wrongly and 11.66 or 21.59 per cent of them expressed their ignorance. Responsewise each of the elite members interviewed made, on an average, 17.05 or 65.58 per cent right responses to those 26 queries; made 1.39 or 5.34 per cent partially right responses; made 1.69 or 6.50 per cent wrong responses and expressed ignorance for 5.87 or 22.58 per cent answers.

The study revealed that, on an average, the political elites of Phulbani N.A.C have far greater political awareness than their counterparts in G. Udayagiri N.A.C. It is also seen that the magnitude of ignorance, either by responses or by persons is nearly 30 per cent with the political elites of G.Udayagiri N.A.C which is almost double the same with their counterparts in Phulbani N.A.C. This is evidently due to the fact that the elites of Phulbani N.A.C generally hail from middle and higher classes while their counterparts in G.Udayagiri N.A.C are generally drawn from poor economic background. Besides, allied facilities for such awareness are better available in the district headquarters town of Phulbani than at G.Udayagiri which is only a tehsil headquarters.

In aggregate, the political awareness of the urban elites of Phulbani district which, either by persons or by responses, is just above 65 per cent can be termed as satisfactory but not comfortable. The percentage of ignorance is just above 21 in either ways. This should improve.

Individual questionwise, the study revealed that except on the query — who is your M.P. ? — which fetched 100% right responses from the political elites of Phulbani N. A.C. no other question was awarded with such credit there. No question elicited 100 per cent right responses from the political elites of G. Udayagiri N.A.C. However, on the questions — who is your MLA?, According to law how many living wives can a Hindu male have ? — the elites in both the N.A.Cs made more than 90 per cent right responses. The other questions which elicited more than 90 per cent right responses in Phulbani N.A.C are, who is the Chief Minister of Orissa ?, Why is 15th August famous?, How can a vote be invalid ?, What is the maximum time that the police can detain a person without court order ?, Similarly, the questions which elicited 80 per cent or more right answers from the elites of G. Udayagiri N.A.C. are—who is the chief minister of Orissa?, Why is 15th August famous?, Who is your M.P.? On the question, can you name the election symbols of the following political parties: Congress (I), Janata Dal, BJP and CPI(M)? — almost all answers from both the towns were either right or partially right except 2 wrong responses in Phulbani N.A.C. However, most of the answers were devoid of either any response or right response about the symbol of CPI(M), but this was not counted as wrong or partially right answer.

16.13 per cent of elites in Phulbani and 34.78 per cent of the elites in G. Udayagiri either do not know or wrongly know Mahatma Gandhi, the father of the nation, the apostle of non-violence and peace and the greatest leader of Indian national freedom movement. Among the Political elites, 9.68 per cent in Phulbani N.A.C. and 17.39 per cent in G. Udayagiri N.A.C either can't say or say wrongly why is 15th August famous. To mention, this is the Independence Day of India as on this day in 1947 India was declared free. 35.48 per cent of the elites in Phulbani and 43.48 per cent of the elites in G.Udayagiri do not know or wrongly know how many districts are there in Orissa. Among the elites 45.16 per cent in Phulbani and 47.83 per cent in G.Udayagiri either do not know or wrongly know the President of the Indian Republic. Among the elites, 35.48 per cent in Phulbani and 47.83 per cent in G. Udayagiri either do not know or partially know the name of the Prime Minister of the country; 29.03 per cent of the elites in Phulbani, 43.48 per cent of the elites of G.Udayagiri either do not know or know it wrongly that the Republic Day of India falls on 26th January. 35.48 per cent of elites in Phulbani and 65.23 per cent of elites in G. Udayagiri either do not know or know it wrongly how many MLA (Member of Legislative Assembly) seats are there in Orissa.

It is very serious to observe here that 70.97 per cent of elites in Phulbani and 100 per cent elites of G.Udayagiri either do not know or know it wrongly the minimum age to become an N.A.C councillor (elite) as they are or were. Similarly, only 67.74 per cent of elites in Phulbani and 78.26 per cent of elites in G.Udayagiri either can't say or say wrongly the three colours of our national flag.

On the closed-end question—How do you collect information and gather knowledge ? —eight choices were given. The choices were (a) from newspapers, (b) from books and magazines, (c) from radio, (d) from Television, (e) from family members, (f) from friends, relatives and neighbours, (g) from party leaders and party workers, (h) from all of the above sources. Among the political elites, 67.74 per cent in Phulbani N.A.C., 39.13 per cent in G.Udayagiri N.A.C. and 55.56 per cent in entire Urban Phulbani district collect information and gather knowledge from all the sources mentioned. 3.23 per cent in Phulbani N.A.C, 13.04 per cent in G.Udayagiri N.A.C. and 7.41 per cent in Urban Phulbani district acquire the same from newspapers only. 3.23 per cent of the elites of Phulbani N.A.C and 4.35 per cent of elites in G Udayagiri N.A.C acquire the same each from television and from party leaders and party workers. 13.04 per cent of the elites in G.Udayagiri N.A.C. acquire the same from friends, relatives and neighbours while in Phulbani NAC nobody comes under this category. 13.04 per cent in G.Udayagiri N.A.C. and 12.96 per cent in Urban Phulbani district collect information and gather knowledge from both newspapers and television. The rest collect information and gather knowledge from any two sources mentioned, but are insignificant by their percentage.

Political Involvement and Leadership Process

Table 21
Political Affiliation of the Elite*

	Congress (I)	*J.D.*	*BJP*	*Indepen dents*	*Total*
Phulbani N.A.C.	16 (51.61)	9(29.03)	2(6.45)	4(12.91)	31
G.Udayagiri N.A.C	12 (52.17)	7(30.44)	1(4.35)	3(13.04)	23
Urban Phulbani District	28(51.85)	16(29.63)	3(5.56)	7(12.96)	54

* Figures within the brackets indicate respective percentages.

On the open question—why did you contest for such post(s)? —90.32 per cent of the elites of Phulbani N.A.C, 95.65 per cent in G.Udayagiri N.A.C. and in aggregate 92.59 per cent in Urban Phulbani district responded that they contested for such post(s) for area development and to work for the people. In Phulbani, 3.23 per cent and 6.45 per cent of the elites contested the councillor's post for image building and for capturing the post of chairperson respectively, while 4.35 per cent of elites in G.Udayagiri N.A.C. did it to fight corruption.

By political affiliation 51.61 per cent of the elites in Phulbani N.A.C. and 52.17 per cent of the elites in G.Udayagiri N.A.C belong to Congress(I); 29.03 per cent in Phulbani N.A.C. and 30.44 per cent in G.Udayagiri N.A.C. belong to Janata Dal; 6.45 per cent in Phulbani N.A.C. and 4.35 per cent in G.Udayagiri N.A.C belong to Bharatiya Janata Party (B.J.P.) and 12.91 per cent in Phulbani N.A.C and 13.04 per cent in G.Udayagiri N.A.C. are independents. In a consolidated form among the Urban Political elites of Phulbani district 51.85 per cent belong to Congress(I), 29.63 per cent belong to Janata Dal, 5.56 per cent belong to Bharatiya Janata Party (BJP) and 12.96 per cent are independents. It is found that in Urban Politics of Phulbani district, Congress(I) has dominated the scene while B.J.P is rising as a new force. It was observed that majority of the independents were rebel candidates of different political parties which implies that the parties do not work democratically and on the prospective principles of electoral game.

On the closed question—in election(s) support to you was ?— the following choices were given as answers : (a) spontaneous and voluntary, (b) due to dominant caste factor, (c) due to powerful religious lobby, (d) by show of muscular force, (e) by monetary underhand deals and supply of liquor, (f) due to negative voting against the prospective candidate, (g) due to influence of tradition, and (h) mixed factors. Among the political elites 87.10 per cent in Phulbani N.A.C, 95.65 per cent in G.Udayagiri N.A.C and 90.74 per cent in Urban Phulbani district opined that in election(s) support to them was spontaneous and voluntary. Other responses were insignificant. Nobody in both the towns reasoned the factors as given in (b), (c), (d), (e) and (f) though, more or less, they played some roles in elections.

As to the closed question—why are you a leader (elite)?— the following alternative answers were given : because (a) I have desire to be so, (b) people want it, (c) Party wants it, (d) Religion/caste people compel, (e) of family tradition, (f) of no other engagement, (g) leadership is a type of business, (h) I want to serve people, and (i) can not say.

Among the elites, 25.81 per cent in Phulbani NAC, 26.09 per cent in G.Udayagiri NAC and together 25.93 per cent in Urban Phulbani district viewed that they are elites or leaders because people want it. Exactly the same percentages of the elites respectively are applicable to the answer that they are elites or leaders because they want to serve the people. 9.68 per cent of the elites in Phulbani NAC, 17.39 per cent of them in G.Udayagiri NAC an in total 12.96 per cent of them in Urban Phulbani district expressed that they are so because party wants it. In Phulbani NAC 16.13 per cent of the elites came to such status because of both self-desire and people's desire, while 13.04 per cent of elites in G.Udayagiri N.A.C say that they are leaders because both people and party want it. Others showing joint reasons are divided among themselves and are very insignificant.

On the closed question-How do you inform and influence people/voters?-the following alternative answers were given; (a) by face-to-face contact, (b) by general meetings, (c) through pamphlets/ handbills, (d) through agents/call boys and (c) no need to ask them. In responses, 67.74 per cent of elites in Phulbani N.A.C., 43.48 per cent of elites in G.Udayagiri N.A.C and together 54.41 per cent of Urban elites of Phulbani district are known to have face-to-face contact with their people or voters in informing and influencing them. For the same purpose, 22.58 per cent elites of Phulbani N.A.C., 52.17 per cent of elites in G.Udayagiri N.A.C, and together 35.19 per cent of the Urban elites of Phulbani district call general meetings. Percentages in other choices or joint choices are very insignificant.

As to the closed question-How do you influence the decision-making process?-the following alternative answers were given : (a) by logical and practicable arguments (b)by direction of party (c) by conciliation and consensus (d) acting as an agent of local MLA/MP, (e) by threatening, (f) by hitting the area, caste and religious sentiments and (g) as per desire of my voters.

The study revealed that 45.16 per cent of the elites in Phulbani NAC, 39.13 per cent of the elites in G.Udayagiri N.A.C. and together, 42.59 per cent of Urban elites in Phulbani district influence the decision-making process by logical and practicable arguments. 29.03 per cent of elites in Phulbani N.A.C, 39.13 per cent of the elites in G.Udayagiri N.A.C. and together 33.33 per cent of the Urban elites of Phulbani district influence the decision-making process by giving due respect to the desire of their voters. In Phulbani N.A.C,9.68 per cent of the elites use both logical and practicable arguments and their voters' desire to influence the decision-making process while the same percentage of elites there use both logical and practicable arguments and conciliation and consensus methods to do the same. However, in G.Udayagiri N.A.C.,17.39 per cent of the elites use the single method of conciliation and consensus to influence the people and their voters. None of the responses in both the towns, either singularly or jointly, was in favour of the methods as given in (d), (e), and (f) above.

As to the closed question-from where do you raise your election expenses?- the following choices as answers were given : (a) from the party (b) from own income, (c) from donations and (d) from other sources. 61.29 per cent of the elites in Phulbani N.A.C., 56.52 per cent of elites in G.Udayagiri N.A.C. and together, 59.26 per cent of Urban elites of Phulbani district raised their election expenses from their own income. The respective percentages of elites who raised such expenses from their own political parties are 9.68, 26.09 and 16.67. Likewise, the respective percentages of the elites who raised their election expenses from both their political party and own income are 22.58, 17.39 and 20.37. Only 6.45 per cent elites of Phulbani N.A.C. raised their election expenses from donations.

Political Ideals and Aspirations

In order to assess the political ideals and aspirations of the urban political elites in Phulbani district, 15 questions were asked. Out of these, first ten questions were closed ones asking for answers in the from of either 'yes' or 'no'.

Table 22
Political Ideals and Aspirations

Aspects	*Phulbani NAC* Yes	No	*G. Udayagiri NAC* Yes	No
Do you aspire for higher political posts such as MLA / MP?	18(58.06)	13(41.94)	7(30.43)	16(69.57)
Do you support political corruption ?	1(3.23)	30(96.77)	1(4.35)	22(95.65)
Do you support *bandhs*, riots, violence and destruction of public property?	......	31(100.00)	......	23(100.00)
Should dowry be banned?	29(93.55)	2(6.45)	23(100.00)	......
Should reservation for Scheduled Castes & Scheduled Tribes continue?	15(48.39)	16(51.61)	17(73.91)	6(26.09)
Should liquor be banned?	30(96.77)	1(3.23)	23(100.00)	......
Should voting be made compulsory?	20(64.52)	11(35.48)	17(73.91)	6(26.09)
Should election be state-funded?	26(83.87)	5(16.13)	18(78.26)	5(21.74)
Are elections in India free and fair?	5(16.13)	26(83.87)	5(21.74)	18(78.26)
Do you violate code of conduct during elections?	2(6.45)	29(93.55)	1(4.35)	22(95.65)
Do you like to oppose for opposition sake?	2(6.45)	29(93.55)	1(4.35)	22(95.65)

* The figures within the brackets indicate respective percentages.

Among the elites 58.06 per cent is Phulbani N.A.C, 30.43 per cent in G. Udayagiri NAC and together, 46.30 per cent of urban elites of Phulbani district aspire for higher elective posts such as M.L.A and M.P. The respective percentages of the elites who do not aspire this are 41.94, 69.57 and 53.70. As many as 96.77 per cent of the elites in Phulbani N.A.C, 95.65 per cent of the elites in G.Udayagiri N.A.C and together, 96.30 per cent of the urban elites of Phulbani district do not support political corruption. 100 per cent of the elites in both the Notified Area Councils do not support bandhs, riots, violence and destruction of public property. 93.55 per cent of the elites in Phulbani N.A.C, 100 per cent of elites in G.Udayagiri NAC and together 96.30 per cent of the urban elites of Phulbani district desire that dowry should be banned. On these two aspects which are considered as great social crimes, the elites show the highest degree of concern and thus, show a positive and constructive attitude towards society and the nation. To buttress this concern, 96.77 per cent of the urban elites of Phulbani NAC, 100 per cent elites in G. Udayagiri NAC and together 98.15 per cent of the urban elites of Phulbani district desire that liquor should be banned.

Among the elites,48.39 per cent in Phulbani NAC, 73.91 in per cent in G. Udayagiri NAC and together 59.26 per cent in urban Phulbani district do aspire for continuance of reservation for Scheduled Castes and Scheduled Tribes and the rest oppose it. Unfortunately, under the study 59.26 per cent of the elites belong to scheduled castes, scheduled tribes and the other backward classes, together, who avail the opportunity of reservation in services and political posts. The percentage of total urban elites of Phulbani district who support continuance of such reservation is exactly the same, i.e., 59.26.

It was observed that no elite not coming under the purview of this privilege did support it. Thus, the privilege is being treated by the beneficiaries as a protective shield of economic security and a ladder to social status. Race, not merit, determines the fate of a progressive nation. Theocracy guides a secular state committed to protect human dignity. Claim for backwardness is gradually increasing trying to perpetuate the prevailing *staus quo* to drag the nation to the second rates. This is undemocratic and revolting. The sooner it evaporates; the better the nation would be. 64.52 per cent of the elites in Phulbani N.A.C, 73.91 per cent of the elites in G. Udayagiri N.A.C and together, 68.52 per cent of urban elites of Phulbani district do support compulsory voting in elections while the respective percentages of the elites who do no support it are 35.48, 26.9 and 31.48. On the question --- should election be state funded ? -- 83.87 per cent in Phulbani N.A.C, 78.26 per cent in G.Udayagiri N.A.C and together, 81.48 per cent in urban Phulbani district support it and the respective percentages of the elites who oppose it are 16.13, 21.74 and 18.52. To support or to oppose the move--- Are elections in India free and fare ?---the respective percentages are just the reverse of those in the previous question, i.e., should elections be state funded ? — 93.55 per cent of the elites in Phulbani N.A.C and 95.65 per cent of the elites in G.Udayagiri N.A.C and together 94.44 per cent of the urban elites of Phulbani district do not violate code of conduct during elections and the respective percentages of the elites who do violate the same are 6.45, 4.35 and 55.56. The respective percentages of responses for 'No' and 'Yes' on this question remain the same for 'No' and 'Yes' responses to the question---Do you like to oppose for opposition sake ? In toto, the urban political elites of Phulbani district, by their political ideals and aspirations, show a greater degree of social and national concern besides having a positive and constructive approach for development, except in a few aspects such as reservation.

Table 23

Choice for Best Political Party*

	Congress(I)	*BJP*	*Janta Dal*	*No Party*	*Total*
Phulbani NAC	8(25.81)	4(12.90)	-	19(61.29)	31
G. Udayagiri NAC	5(21.74)	2(8.70)	-	16(69.56)	23
Urban Phulbani District	13(24.07)	6(11.11)	-	35(64.82)	54

* The figures within the brackets indicate respective percentages.

As to the open-end-question ---in your opinion which political party is the best and why ?— 25.81 per cent of elites in Phulbani NAC, 21.74 per cent of the elites in G. Udayagiri N.A.C and together, 24.07 per cent urban elites of Phulbani district choose Congress (I) as the best political party. In other words, 25.81 per cent of elites of Phulbani N.A.C, 30.43 per cent of elites in G.Udayagiri N.A.C. and together, 27.78 per cent urban elites of Phulbani district who belong to Congress(I) do not consider their own party as the best. None of the Janata Dal elites who constitute 29.63 per cent of the total elites under the study considers his/her own party as the best. No other elite also does it either, leading the party's percentage in this regard to zero. 12.90 per cent elites in Phulbani NAC, 8.70 per cent elites in G. Udayagiri N.A.C and together 11.11 per cent of the elites in urban Phulbani district choose Bharatiya Janata Party (BJP) as the best party. These percentages are higher than the percentages of B.J.P elites in the respective places. 61.29 per cent of elites in Phulbani N.A.C, 69.56 per cent of elites in G.Udayagiri NAC and together 64.82 per cent of urban elites of Phulbani district consider 'No' party is the best. Thus, the study reveals that the Janata Dal has lost its image altogether while Congress (I)'s image has dwindled down severely. B.J.P as a new force is rising gradually. But all parties fail to fulfill the aspirations of the people and the nation. Thus, a high degree of discontentment is shown by the 'best party' crown to no political party.

Among those who treated Congress(I) as the best party reasoned that it is a complete party which provides stable Government, as the original party brought independence to the country, besides it is a secular party and has concern for the poor and the depressed. Those who termed BJP as the best party adduced reasons such as value-based politics, no conflict and anti-corruption drive.

As to the open question — In your opinion, who at present is the most suitable person for the post of Prime Minister of India ?—-35.48 per cent of the elites in Phulbani NAC, 30.43 per cent of the elites in G.Udayagiri N.A.C and together 33.33 per cent of the urban elites of Phulbani district in their response opted for the B.J.P leader Atal Bihari Vajpayee. Interestingly enough, in opting for him 25.81 per cent of the elites in Phulbani N.A.C, 21.74 per cent of the elites in G.Udayagiri N.A.C and together 24.07 per cent of the urban elites of the Phulbani district made such option across their own party lines and party discipline. This shows the high image and capability of the person. Besides, the elites here have shown a high degree of impartiality, objectivity and done so on the call of their conscience.

32.26 per cent of the elites in Phulbani NAC, 34.78 per cent of the elites in G.Udayagiri N.A.C, and together 33.33 per cent of the urban elites of Phulbani district expressed their inability to find out a suitable person. Only in G.Udayagiri N.A.C 13.04 per cent of the elites found no one suitable for the post. The percentages of elites who found other persons suitable for the post were insignificant. Such persons include T.N. Sheshan, Sonia Gandhi, Priyanka Gandhi, Madhav Rao Scindhia, Rajesh Pilot, Jyoti Basu, P.A.Sangma, H.D.Devegowda etc.

Regarding the open question ---How can you give justice to one of your voters who has been harassed by the police unjustly? — 45.16 per cent of the elites in Phulbani N.A.C, 73.91 per cent of the elites in G.Udayagiri N.A.C and together 57.41 per cent of the urban elites of

Phulbani district like to have a dialogue with the police first and to ascertain whether the person has actually committed a crime. 32.26 per cent of the elites in Phulbani N.A.C, 4.35 per cent of elites in G. Udayagiri NAC and together 20.37 per cent of the urban elites in Phulbani district want to take recourse to law. 9.68 per cent of the elites of Phulbani NAC, 21.74 per cent the elites in G. Udayagiri NAC and together 14.81 per cent of the urban elites of Phulbani district can not say what to do under such circumstances. The rest are confused.

About the open question-- How do you serve the people when not elected ? — as many as 93.55 per cent of the elites in Phulbani N.A.C, 65.22 per cent in G. Udayagiri NAC and together 81.48 per cent of the urban political elites of Phulbani district are committed to serve the people any way even when not elected. To majority of them, serving the people was a part of their activities even prior to their entrance to political posts and they shall continue this even when they are not in office. Only 6.45 per cent of the elites in Phulbani NAC, 37.78 per cent in G.Udayagiri N.A.C and together 18.52 per cent of the urban political elites of Phulbani district can not say for certain as to how they can serve the people even when not elected.

Approach to Development

Table 24

Should Octroi Tax be abolished ?*

	Yes	*No*	*Cant' say*	*Total*
Phulbani NAC	9(29.03)	19(61.29)	3(9.68)	31
G. Udayagiri NAC	3(13.04)	16(69.57)	4(17.39)	23
Urban Phulbani District	12(22.22)	35(64.82)	7(12.96)	54

* The figures within the brackets indicate respective percentages.

To assess their approach to development, the elites were asked 9 questions. The first one in the form of a closed question to be answered in either 'Yes' or 'No' or 'can't say' was— should octroi tax be abolished ? It may be mentioned here that under Orissa Municipal Act, 1950 the urban bodies including the Notified Area Councils after getting due permission from the state Government can impose octroi taxes on the commodities entering into the concerned town area for consumption there. Naturally the town-dwellers are taxed by it extra.

On this question 29.03 per cent of elites in Phulbani NAC, 23.04 per cent of the elites in G Udayagiri N.A.C and together 22.22 per cent of the urban elites of Phulbani district responded strongly in favour of abolition of octroi taxes. 100 per cent of those who had such opinion reasoned that people are overtaxed and a lion's share of revenue collected out of such taxes do not reach the N.A.C., but manipulated by the staff at the collection source. 61.29 per cent of elites in Phulbani NAC, 69.57 per cent of elites in G. Udayagiri N.A.C and together 64.82 per cent of the urban elites of Phulbani district desire its retention for revenue of the N.A.C., but would like its abolition only if state Government agreed to pay grant-in-aid to the tune of Octroi collections. But, 9.68 per cent of the elites in Phulbani NAC, 17.39 per cent of the elites in G. Udayagiri N.A.C. and together 12.96 per cent of the urban elites of Phulbani district could not make up their mind whether it should be abolished or not.

Table 25.
Establishment of NAC is Helpful or Harmful ? *

	Helpful	*Harmful*	*Cant'say*	*Total*
Phulbani NAC	28(90.32)	... ...	3(9. 68)	31
G. Udayagiri NAC	4(17.39)	17(73 .91)	2(8.70)	23
Urban Phulbani District	32(59.26)	17(31.48)	5(9.26)	54

* The figures within the brackets indicate respective percentages.

On the closed question — (whether) establishment of your Notified Area Council (NAC) is helpful or harmful ?—the elites of the two towns expressed opposite views. 90.32 per cent of the elites in Phulbani N.A.C, 17.39 per cent elites in G.Udayagiri NAC and together 59.26 per cent of the urban elites of Phulbani district consider that establishment of their N.A.C is helpful for various development works. But interestingly enough, while, no one in Phulbani N.A.C said that the establishment of his/her N.A.C is harmful, 73.91 per cent of the elites in G.Udayagiri N.A.C (urban Phulbani district 31.48 per cent) consider it so and desire its abolition because the subsidised rice, other essential commodities, specially subsidised or free loans available to the rural poors in the periphery are not available to the large number of poor people in the N.A.C. simply because they are urban-dwellers. On the other hand they are taxed heavier than the rural people are but without any reciprocal benefits, even basic minimum facilities. This shows that G. Udayagiri NAC needs special attention and support. However, 9.68 per cent of the elites in Phulbani N.A.C, 8.70 per cent of the elites in G.Udayagiri N.A.C and together 9.26 per cent of the urban elites of Phulbani district can not say whether establishment of their N.A.C is helpful or harmful.

Table 26

Are NAC taxes Reciprocal to the Benefits rendered to the People?*

	Yes	*No*	*Can't say*	*Total*
Phulbani NAC	16(51.61)	14(45.16)	1(3.23)	31
G. Udayagiri NAC	4(17.39)	15(65.22)	4(17.39)	23
Urban Phulbani District	20(37.04)	29(53.70)	5(9.26)	54

* The figures *within* the brackets indicate respective percentages.

For the closed question - Are the N.A.C taxes reciprocal to the benefits rendered to the people ? — three alternative answers such as 'Yes', 'No' and 'Can't say' were given. 51.61 per cent of the elites in Phulbani NAC, 17.39 per cent of the elites in G. Udayagiri N.A.C. and together 37.04 per cent of the urban elites of Phulbani district nodded 'yes' as their reply. 45.16 per cent of the elites in Phulbani N.A.C, 65.22 per cent of the elites in G. Udayagiri N.A.C and together 53.70 per cent of the urban

Table 27

Are these facilities in your NAC adequate and satisfactory?*

	Phulbani NAC			G. Udayagiri NAC		
	Yes	*No*	*Can't Say*	*Yes*	*No*	*Cant'say*
Lighting	13(41.94)	18(58.06)	...	7(30.43)	16(69.57)	...
Water supply	8(25.81)	23(74.19)		10(43.48)	13(56.52)	...
Roads and parks	14(45. 16)	17(54.84)	...	4(17.39)	19(82.61)	...
Medical facilities	12(38.71)	19(61.29)	...	3(13.04)	20(86.96)	...
Education and Library	14(45.16)	17(54.84)	...	10(43.48)	13(56.52)	...
Sewerage & sanitation	7(22.58)	24(77.42)	...	4(17.39)	19(82 61)	...
Cultural activities and Entertainment	5(16.13)	26(83.87)	...	...	23(100.00)	...
AVERAGE (by	10.43	20.57	...	5.43	17.57	...
persons)	(33.65)	(66.35)	...	(23.61)	(76.39)	...
AVERAGE (by	2.35	4.65	...	1.65	5.35	...
responses)	(33.57)	(66.43)	...	(23.57)	(76.43)	...
URBAN PHULBANI DISTRICT						
AVERAGE (by	15.86	38.14				
persons)	(29.37)	(70.63)				
AVERAGE (by	2	5				
responses)	(28.57)	(71.43)				

* The figures within the brackets indicate respective percentages.

elites of Phulbani district responded that the N.A.C. taxes are not reciprocal to the benefits rendered to the people. However, 3.23 per cent of the elites in Phulbani NAC, 17.39 per cent of the elites in G.Udayagiri N.A.C and together 9.26 per cent of the urban elites of Phulbani district could not say whether the taxes are reciprocal or not.

To assess the extent of availability of primary civic amenities such as (a) lighting, (b) water supply, (c) roads and parks, (d) medical facilities, (e) Education and library, (f) sewerage and sanitation, (g) cultural activities and entertainment in the urban areas, the elites were asked a closed question-- Are these facilities in your N.A.C adequate and satisfactory ?— with 'Yes', 'No' and 'can't say' as three alternative answers. But all the elite members answered straight either in 'Yes' or in 'No' and nobody in both the towns was found to be confused to be grouped under the answer 'can't say'.

On an average, 66.35 per cent of the elites in Phulbani N.A.C,76.39 per cent of the elites in G. Udayagiri N.A.C and together 70.63 per cent of the urban elites of Phulbani district feel that these seven primary civic amenities in their Notified Area Councils are not adequate and satisfactory. The corresponding percentages of the elites of these areas who feel that these facilities are adequate and satisfactory are 33.65, 23.61 and 29.37. In terms of responses, on an average, for every person the percentage of availability of these facilities taken together is 33.57 in Phulbani N.A.C, 23.57 in G. Udayagiri N.A.C and 28.57 in urban Phulbani district. For non-availability of these facilities; the corresponding percentages are 66.43, 76.43 and 71.43. In both the towns, except in education and library facilities, the provisions in all other six fields are abysmally low and far from being satisfactory. Further, except in water supply the facilities in all other fields are lower in degree in G. Udayagiri N.A.C than those available in Phulbani N.A.C. 45.16 per cent of elites in Phulbani N.A.C, 43.48 per cent of elites G. Udayagiri NAC and together 44.44 per cent of the urban elites of Phulbani district say that, facilities in education are adequate and satisfactory and the corresponding percentages of elites of these areas who do not agree with this are 54.84, 56.52 and 55.56.

In cultural activities and entertainment both the towns are extremely poor. 83.87 per cent of elites in Phulbani N.A.C, 100 per cent of elites in G. Udayagiri N.A.C and together 90.74 per cent of the urban elites of Phulbani district opine that this facility is not available in the town. According to the survey, in Phulbani N.A.C the inadequacy and dissatisfaction of lighting is 58.06 per cent, water supply 74.19 per cent, roads and parks 54.84 per cent, medical facilities 61.29 per cent, and sewerage and sanitation 77.42 per cent. The corresponding percentages of inadequacy and dissatisfaction of these facilities in G.Udayagiri N.A.C are 69.57, 56.52, 82.61, 86.96 and 82.61.

The study reveals clearly that G.Udayagiri is an N.A.C only by name but not with minimum civic amenities while in Phulbani N.A.C these are manageably poor. The urban status to these towns has not improved the quality of life that the status generally connotes.

Table- 28

Are you Satisfied with the Government Programmes for Tribal Development in Your Area?*

	Yes	*No*	*Can't say*	*Total*
Phulbani NAC	7(22.58)	22(70.97)	2(6.45)	31
G. Udayagiri NAC	1(4.35)	20(86.96)	2(8 .69)	23
Urban Phulbani District	8(14.81)	42(77.78)	4(7.41)	54

* The figures within the brackets indicate respective percentages.

On the closed question — Are you satisfied with the government programmes for tribal development in your area ? — three alternative answers such as 'Yes', 'No' and 'can't say' were given. 22.58 per cent of the elites in Phulbani N.A.C, 4.35 per cent of the elites in G.Udayagiri N.A.C and together 14.81 per cent of the urban elites of Phulbani district responded that they are satisfied with the government programmes for tribal development in their area. Among the elites who are not satisfied with this include 70.97 per cent in Phulbani N.A.C, 86.96 per cent in G Udayagiri N.A.C. and 77.78 per cent in urban Phulbani district. 100 per cent of the elites who expressed such dissatisfaction attributed to their answer the reason of misappropriation of the relevant funds by the big-ups, the officials and the Non-Government Organisations (N.G.Os) and thus, strongly feel that the benefits do not percolate to the real beneficiaries. However, 6.45 per cent of the elites in Phulbani N.A.C., 8.69 per cent of the elites in G. Udayagiri N.A.C and together 7.41 per cent of the urban elites of Phulbani district can not say whether they are satisfied or unsatisfied with this.

Table 29

Status of Women*

	Satisfactory /good	*bad/ miserable*	*Can't say*	*Total*
Phulbani NAC	6(19.35)	24(77.42)	1(3.23)	31
G. Udayagiri NAC	8(34.78)	12(52.18)	3(13.04)	23
Urban Phulbani District	14(25.92)	36(66.67)	4(7.41)	54

* The figures within the brackets indicate respective percentages.

As to the open question - What is the status of women in your area ? — the responses given by the elites were grouped under three heads such as (a) satisfactory / good, (b) bad/miserable and (c) can't say. 19.35 per cent of the elites in Phulbani N.A.C, 34.78 per cent of the elites in G. Udayagiri N.A.C and together 25.92 per cent urban elites of Phulbani district express that the status of women in their area is good or satisfactory. But 77.42 per cent of the elites in Phulbani N.A.C, 52.18 per cent of the elites in G. Udayagiri N.A.C and together 66.67 per cent of urban elites in Phulbani district consider the status of women in their area as bad or miserable. However, 3.32 per cent of elites in Phuibani NAC, 13.04 per cent of the elites in G.Udayagiri NAC and together 7.41 per cent of urban elites of Phulbani district can't say exactly what is the status of women in their area.

Table- 30

Suggestions to Curb Exploitation of and Atrocities on Women and Tribals*

	Education, awareness & organisation	*Strong legal action*	*Vague /confused/ can't say*	*Total*
Phulbani NAC	12(38.71)	8(25.81)	11(35.48)	31
G. Udayagiri NAC	6(26.09)	3(13.04)	14(60.87)	23
Urban Phulbani District	18(33.33)	11(20.37)	25(46.30)	54

* The figures within the brackets indicate respective percentages.

As to the open question — what do you suggest to curb exploitation of and atrocities on women and tribals?—the responses given by the elites were grouped under three headings such as (a) Education, awareness and organisation, (b) strong legal action (c) vague, confused or can't say. 38.71 per cent of the elites in Phulbani N.A.C., 26.09 per cent of the elites in G. Udayagiri N.A.C and together 33.33 per cent of the urban elites of Phulbani district suggest that by better and wider education, awareness and organisation of the people including women organisation, the exploitation of and atrocities on women and tribals can be curbed. But to achieve this goal, 25.81 per cent of elites in Phulbani N.A.C, 13.04 per cent of elites in G. Udayagiri N.A.C and together 20.37per cent of urban elites of Phulbani district suggest strong legal action on the defaulters. But unfortunately among the elites 35.48 per cent in Phulbani N.A.C, 60.87 per cent in G. Udayagiri N.A.C and in aggregate 46.30 per cent in urban Phulbani district either give vague suggestions or are confused and can't say anything.

Table 31

Should Deforestation and Shifting Cultivation be Banned?*

	Yes	*No*	*Can't say*	*Total*
Phulbani NAC	27(87.10)	3(9.68)	1(3.22)	31
G. Udayagiri NAC	19(82.61)	...	4(17.39)	23
Urban Phulbani District.	46(85.18)	3(5.56)	5(9.26)	54

* The figures within the brackets indicate respective percentages.

On the closed question - should deforestation and shifting cultivation be banned ? Three alternative answers such as 'Yes', 'No' and 'can't say' were given 87.10 per cent of the elites in Phulbani N.A.C., 82.61 per cent of the elites in G.Udayagiri N.A.C. and together 85.18 per cent of the urban elites of Phulbani district are convinced that deforestation and shifting cultivation should be banned because they know it fully well that these things are responsible for ecological imbalance and environmental hazards in various forms. Only 9.68 per cent of the elites of Phulbani N.A.C do not support banning of deforestation and shifting cultivation as tribals basically depend on these two things. It may be mentioned here that Phulbani district is traditionally known to be a land of shifting cultivation which is done by deforestation. However, 3.22 per cent of the elites in Phulbani N.A.C, 17.39 per cent of the elites in G.Udayagiri N.A.C and together, 9.26 per cent of the urban elites of Phulbani district can't say for certain whether deforestation and shifting cultivation should be banned or not.

Table 32

Forest and Agricultural Products of the Tribals should be : *

	Purchased by the Govt.	*Allowed to face open market*	*Left to the middleman*	*Marketed through cooperatives*	*Total*
Phulbani NAC	7(22.58)	5(16.13)	...	19(61.29)	31
G. Udayagiri NAC	8(34.78)	4(17.39)	...	11(47.83)	23
Urban Phulbani District	15(27.78)	9(16.67)	...	30(55.55)	54

*The figures within the brackets indicate respective percentages.

For a just and better deal to the forest and agricultural products of the tribals what should be done was a closed question with four answer choices such as (a) purchased by the Government (b) allowed to face open market (c) left to the middlemen (d) marketed through cooperatives. 61.29 per cent of elites in Phulbani N.A.C, 47.83 per cent of elites in G. Udayagiri N.A.C and together 55.55 per cent of the urban elites of Phulbani district favour marketing of the said products through cooperatives. 22.58 per cent of the elites in Phulbani N.A.C, 34.78 per cent of the elites in G.Udayagiri N.A.C and together 27.78 per cent of the urban elites of Phulbani district want that the products should be purchased by the Government. But 16.13 per cent of the elites in Phulbani N.A.C., 17.39 per cent of the elites in G. Udayagiri N.A.C and together 16.67 per cent of the urban elites of Phulbani district want that the products should be allowed to face open market while no one in both the towns want to leave the products to the middlemen

Table 33

Fields of Tribal Development*

	In Education only	*In Education and Agriculture only*	*In Edu. Agri., Ser., Economy only*	*In no field*	*Total*
Phulbani NAC	9(29.03)	4(12.90)	5(16.13)	13(41.94)	31
G. Udayagiri NAC	7(30.44)	3(13.04)	4(17.39)	9(39.13)	23
Urban Phulbani District	16(29.63)	7(12.96)	9(16.67)	22(40.74)	54

* The figures within the brackets indicate respective percentages.

As to the open question — After 50 years of Indian independence what are the fields the tribals in your area (a) have developed ? (b) are lagging behind ? — the responses given by the elites were grouped under four heads such as (a) in education only, (b) in education and agriculture only, (c) in education, services and economy only and (d) in no field 29.03 per cent of the elites in Phulbani N.A.C., 30.44 per cent of the elites in G. Udayagiri N.A.C. and together 29.63 per cent of the urban elites of Phulbani district feel that the tribals in their area have developed only in the field of education after fifty years of Indian independence. The corresponding percentages of the elites who feel that the tribals in their area have developed in education and agriculture only are 12.90, 13.04 and 12.96. Those elites who feel that the tribals in their area have developed in the fields of education, agriculture, services and economy only, constitute 16.13 per cent, 17.39 per cent and 16.67 per cent of the total elites in Phulbani N.A.C., G. Udayagiri N.A.C. and urban Phulbani district respectively. 41.94 per cent of the elites in Phulbani N.A.C. 39.13 per cent of the urban elites of Phulbani district strongly feel that elites in G. Udayagiri N.A.C. and together 40.74 per cent of the tribals in their area have developed in 'no field' after fifty years of national independence.

References

1. Gazetter of India - Orissa - Boudh - Khondhmals, Department of Revenue, Govt. of Orissa, Bhubaneswar, 1983, pp. 381-382.
2. *Ibid.*
3. *India Today,* April 30, 1983, New Delhi, p. 110.
4. P.K. Patnaik, ; *Onlooker,* May 15, 1982, Bombay, pp 40-41.
5. *Ibid.*

Hindus. Except one Muslim elite in Phulbani N.A.C. and one Christian elite in G. Udayagiri N.A.C. the rest 52 elite members are Hindus. Thus, together the elites are Hindus by 96.30 per cent.

As to occupation, the political elites of Phulbani N.A.C. are Businessmen by 25.81 per cent, cultivators by 12.90 per cent, contractors by 16.13 per cent, Advocates by 19.35 per cent, Housewives by 22.58 per cent and others by 3.23 per cent. In G. Udayagiri N.A.C. they are businessmen by 26.09 per cent, cultivators by 17.39 per cent, Agricultural labourers by 8.69 per cent, Advocates by 4.35 per cent, Housewives by 26.09 per cent, Journalists by 4.35 per cent and others by 13.04 per cent.

Aggregately, the urban political elites ofPhulbani district are businessmen by 25.93 per cent, cultivators by 14.82 per cent, Agricultural labourers by 3.70 per cent, contractors by 9.26 per cent, Advocates by 12.96 per cent, Housewives by 24.07 per cent, Journalists by 1.85 per cent and others by 7.41 per cent. In the occupational structure the political elites of both the Notified Area Councils are predominantly businessmen and housewives. Together, they constitute just 50 per cent of the urban political elites of Phulbani district. However, the advocates are also prominent in Phulbani N.A.C. as elites.

100 per cent elites of both the Notified Area Councils - Phulbani and G. Udayagiri know Oriya whether it is their mother tongue or not. As to mother tongue status of elites in Phulbani N.A.C., 80.64 per cent of them speak Oriya, 12.90 per cent speak Kui, the local tribal dialect particularly of the Kandhas of Phulbani, 3.23 per cent speak Urdu and the same per cent of elites speak Telugu there. Regarding knowledge of languages other than mother tongue, in Phulbani N.A.C., 64.52 per cent elites speak Hindi, 45.16 per cent speak English, 3.23 per cent speak Telugu, and 6.45 per cent speak Bengali. Regarding knowledge in maximum number of

5
Conclusion : Findings and Forecasts

The hypothesis that the urban political elite in Tribal India as sampled out from Phulbani district is traditionally patriarchal and is mostly composed of native tribals has been proved to be false by the primary data under study. As many as 85.19 per cent of the elite being under the age group of 21-50 and in a different way 51.86 per cent of the elite belonging to the age group of 21-40 shows a very different picture that the youngsters have dominated the scene contrary to the age-old belief that in the tribal societies eldest males in the community took to the elite role. Further, it is revealed by the fact that as many as 29.63 per cent of the elite are women as against the traditional practice of fair sex not allowed to play that role. While the present level of women's participation against the odd situation is encouraging, the new statutory provisions hold the promise of further improvement.

The tribal areas were believed to be secluded and the tribal communities were treated as isolated. There was no question of outsiders living with them or interfering in their problems. But the study reveals that 38.89 per cent or as nearly as two-fifths of the elite are non-natives. Thus, it shows a serious change in the picture and falsifies the hypothesis. Besides, only 20.37 per cent or nearly one-fifth of the elite being tribals shows a grave concern that the tribals themselves are like foreigners in the management of their own homeland. Not only that, the study reveals that the key posts like the chairpersons and vice-chairpersons in the urban bodies of tribal areas are very often occupied by the non-tribals and the non-natives.

The hypothesis that the urban political elite in tribal India as sampled out from Phulbani district primarily consisted of cultivators and labourers who generally hail from large-size families with small income and without any status symbol has been proved to be partially true and partially false. Among the elite, the businessmen and housewives, in almost equal proportions and together constituting exactly fifty per cent of the total elite, steal the show, while the advocates have the third contributory role. The role of the cultivators and labourers who together constitute less than twenty per cent of the elite play a very insignificant role. Above 70 per cent of the elite members have large size families with 6 to 10 members or above and as many as 20.37 per cent of them have very large size families having membership of above 10.

As nearly as 60 per cent of the elite have an annual family income of rupees 30,000 (thirty thousand) or less and significantly, above 35 per cent of the elite have an annual family income of rupees 15,000 (fifteen thousand) or less. Thus, the majority of the elite members have a large size family with low family income and it has been proved to be true. Contrary to this dismal picture, quite a large number of elite, members own status symbols 70.37 per cent of them have building, 57.41 per cent of them own landed property, 44.44 per cent of them occupy motor vehicles and 42.59 per cent of them enjoy own telephone.

Thus, in the respect of status symbols, the hypothesis has been proved to be false.

The hypothesis that the elite under study is moderately educated with knowledge in the local and the state languages and not knowing other languages has also been proved to be partially true and partially false. Interestingly enough, 70.37 per cent of the elite members do not know the prevailing local tribal dialect and one-third of them do not know the state language. However, it is encouraging to note that 59.26 per cent of the elite know Hindi, the national language and 44.44 per cent of them know English. One-third members of the elite have knowledge in three languages or more. The presence of a variety of people in elite role knowing various other languages such as Telugu, Bengali, Urdu, etc. shows the growth of a pluralistic nature of society with cultural synthesis which is a positive sign of liberal democratic society and harmonious coexistence in the secluded tribal pockets. In this respect the hypothesis has been proved to be wrong. But in the respect of educational status, the hypothesis has been proved to be true. Above three-fourths or 75.92 per cent of the elite members have an educational qualification ranging between primary level (up to standard V) and High School Certificate pass.

The hypothesis that the elite under study do have political awareness of very low order has been proved to be false. The percentage of awareness both in persons as well as by responses having crossed 70 (both right and partially right) is definitely satisfactory, though not very comfortable. But it is certainly not low. About the political awareness of the said elite, queries on 26 items were made which included questions about political heavyweights, statesmen, constitutional dignitaries and public figures of India and Orissa, both past and present, common political and legal knowledge.

The hypothesis that the elite under study is traditional, backward and less advanced in its political involvement and leadership process has been proved to be partially true but mostly false. It is true that more than 50 per cent of the elite members have a traditional political affiliation with the Indian National Congress. More than 90 per cent of the elite members contest elections only to serve the people and to do some developmental works for them and not because their parties want so. In more than 90 per cent cases, the support to the elite in elections is voluntary and spontaneous and not due to the influence of caste, religion, money or liquor. It is true that as many as 54.41 per cent of the elite members use 'the informal face-to-face contact device to inform and influence the people and the voters, it has not been clearly proved or disproved as to any single device adopted in influencing the decision-making process. However, as many as 42.59 per cent of the elite influencing the decision-making process by logical and practical arguments is an encouraging symbol of forward movement. It is grossly false that the elite members raise their election expenses from their respective political parties as 59.26 per cent of them meet such expenses from their own funds.

The hypothesis that the elite under study has traditional, poor and low political ideals and aspirations has been proved to be false. 53.70 per cent of the elite members aspire for higher political posts such as an MLA or an MP; 96.30 per cent of them do not support corruption and dowry, 100 per cent of them do not support *bandhs*, riots, violence and destruction of public property; 98.15 per cent of them want liquor to be banned; 68.52 per cent of them want compulsory voting at elections; 81.48 per cent of them desire state-funding of elections and feel that elections in India are not free and fair; 94.44 per cent of them do neither violate any code of conduct during elections nor do like to oppose for the sake of opposition. Thus, the elite possesses political ideals and aspirations of high order. The exception is that 59.26 per cent of them, the figure being equal with the percentage of the Scheduled Caste and Scheduled Tribe elite members as the exclusive beneficiaries, want that reservation in political posts and services should continue.

As many as 64.82 per cent of the elite members do

not find any political party to be the best even though most of them belong to one political party or the other. However, only one-third of the elite, even some across their own party lines, choose the BJP leader Atal Behari Vajpayee as the most suitable person for the post of Prime Minister. In order to give justice to a voter who may be harassed unjustly by the police, as many as 57.41 per cent of the elite would follow the democratic method of first having a dialogue with the police in order to ascertain whether the person has committed a crime or not. 81.48 per cent of the elite would still like to serve the people even if they are not elected.

The hypothesis that the elite is not conscious, reasonable and progressive in its approach to development has been proved to be false. 64.82 per cent of them do not want abolition of Octroi tax; 59.26 per cent of them feel that establishment of NAC or Urban body is helpful. But 53.70 per cent of them feel that the Urban (NAC) taxes are not reciprocal to the benefits rendered. On the availability of the Urban (NAC) facilities like lighting, water supply, Roads and Perks, Medical aid, Education, Library, Sewerage, Sanitation, Cultural activities and entertainment, on an average, more than 70 per cent of the elite feel that these (NAC) facilities are not adequate and satisfactory. 77.78 per cent of them are not satisfied with Government programmes for tribal development in their area. 66.67 per cent of them feel that the status of women in their area is bad and even miserable. But 46.30 per cent of them are either confused or can not say anything or would give vague answers as to how exploitation of and atrocities on women and tribals can be curbed. However, one-third of them suggest education, awareness and organisation as a remedy for it. Only 20.37 per cent of them want strong legal action on the offenders. 85.18 per cent of the elite want that deforestation and shifting cultivation should be banned. 55.55 per cent of the elite suggest that the forest and agricultural products of the tribals should be marketed through cooperatives. As many as 40.74 per cent of them feel that tribals have not developed in any field. However, a very minor percentage of them feel that tribals have developed only in the fields of education and agriculture.

The hypothesis that the elite under study is, in broad outlines and in its composite perspective, poor in background, traditional in nature, backward and non-progressive in its orientation has been proved to be partially true but mostly false. They are poor but not rigidly so. Though they continue to be traditional in certain respects, they seem to be progressive in many other ways. Thus, they can not be called purely traditional in outlook. In orientation and approach they are forward and progressive as against the hypothesis.

Contribution to Knowledge

The study has unravelled many novel and serious issues of leadership in the tribal societies as against the general belief on the basis of which the hypotheses have been framed. The planners and the policy-makers in the field of social engineering and economic planning would have to pay due attention to such problems and issues. It is a positive sign that both, i.e. the youth and women have come forward to take a leading role in nation-building. It is pertinent to note here that the housewives have come out from the four walls of their household drudgery to take part in political decision-making in the tribal areas. These two vital sections of the human resources should be properly utilised towards progress of the nation. The non-natives and the outsiders have vitiated the secluded tribal pockets socially and culturally, exploited them economically and neglected them politically. The percentage of flow from the state fund towards tribal sub-plan for the last 20 years from the beginning of 6th plan in 1980 is gradually on the decrease, which shows the lack of government interest towards tribal development. It has to be taken seriously and due corrective measures be taken to protect them and their surroundings.

However, one point of satisfaction, as seen from a different angle, is that they are gradually mingling with the national mainstream in many fields. To some extent, they are developed in the educational, cultural, social, political and économic fields and have availed amenities of modern civilization. Economic and commercial activities have replaced the traditional agrarian and labour activities in a sizable manner leading to a progressive monetary transaction replacing barter. The continuity of tradition has been provided by large size families with poverty still reigning though status symbols have changed to certain extent. The educational front has to be given special emphasis. The good sign is that the elite has become, to a considerable extent, politically aware with a good deal of political involvement and leadership process and above all, on the orders of a high political ideals and aspirations. The society which the elite represents depicts high political morals which can be judged from its approach to selection of the best political party and the most suitable person for the post of Prime Minister. By tolerating opposition and not opposing only for the sake of opposition and also having faith in the legal and constitutional provisions of the land, the society shows that it has become democratised.

The urban societies in the tribal pockets of India have not been provided with adequate amenities particularly due to lack of adequate funds including government grants. Tribal society is still being exploited by the government officials, political big bosses and the non-government organisations. The tribal leadership has been conservative in preserving the protective shield of special privileges of backwardness to grab political posts and services through reservation. No doubt it has benefited them, but it should not be a long term provision to stamp them as permanent backwards.

In spite of the sporadic flashes of lightning hopes they generate, the Urban Political Elite in tribal India as sampled out from Phulbani district, show as a whole, some backward trends. However, under the dark clouds of backwardness, they promise a silver lining of a lustrous future, if proper and adequate funds and opportunities are provided to them. In this respect, the development of their area and the people they represent is a must; and it is a must on priority basis. Political development and change have come to them but not adequately and proportionately. This has to be done, let all sources and ways be open for it.

Appendix

Questionnaire

A. Socio-Economic Information :

1. Name of the Urban Body (Notified Area Council) : Phulbani/G. Udayagiri
2. Name of the Elite Member : ____________
3.
(a) Sex : Male / Female
(b) Marital Status : Married / Unmarried
(c) Age in completed Years : __ Years
(d) Place of Birth: ________
(e) Length of residence : ________
(f) Caste : SC/ST/OBC/General
(g) By Religion : Hindu/Muslim/Christian
(h) Occupation : ________
(i) Mother tongue : ________
(j) Other languages known : ____________
4. Educational Status :
(a) Just literate
(b) Can sign only
(c) Can read and write
(d) Primary level (Upto standard-V)
(e) Middle school level (Upto standard-VII)
(f) High school level (upto standard-X)
(g) H.S.C Pass
(h) Intermediate/+2
(i) Bachelor's Degree
(j) Master's Degree
(k) Any technical Degree (Please mention) : ____________
5. No. of family members : ________
6. No. of other member(s) of the family with : (a) Political posts (Please mention) ________
(b) Service (Please mention)
7. Annual Income of the family : Rs. ____________
8.
(a) Do you have landed property?: YES/NO
(b) Do you have a building? : YES/NO
(c) Do you have a motor vehicle ? : YES/NO
(d) Do you have a telephone ? : YES/NO

B. Political Awareness :

9.

(a) How many districts are there in Orissa ?
_______________/can't say

(b) Which party is ruling at the centre?
_______________/can't say

(c) Who was Mahatma Gandhi ?
_______________/can't say

(d) Who was Jawaharlal Nehru ?
_______________/can't say

(e) Who was Indira Gandhi ?
_______________/can't say

(f) Who was B.R. Ambedkar ?
_______________/can't say

(g) Who was Biju Patnaik ?
_______________/can't say

(h) Who was Harekrushna Mahatab?
_______________/can't say

(i) Who was Mother Teresa?
_______________/can't say

(j) Who is Nandini Satapathy ?
_______________/can't say

(k) Who is T.N. Sheshan ?
_______________/can't say

(l) Who is K.R. Narayanan?
_______________/can't say

(m) Who is the Chief Minister of Orissa?
_______________/can't say

(n) What is the name of your district collector ?
_______________/can't say

(o) What is the name of our Prime Minister?
_______________/can't say

(p) Why is 15th August famous?
_______________/can't say

(q) Can you name the three colours of our national flag ?
_______________/can't say

(r) Can you mention the election symbols of the following political parties? (i) Congress (I) (ii) Janata Dal (iii) B.J.P. (iv) CP.I.(M)
______________________/can't say

(s) How can a vote be invalid ?
______________________/can't say

(t) Which day is the Republic Day of India ?
______________________/can't say

(u) How many M.L.A. seats are there in Orissa ?
______________________/can't say

(v) What is the minimum age to become an NAC Councillor?
______________________/can't say

(w) Who is your M.P.?
______________________/can't say

(x) Who is your M.L.A. ?
______________________/can't say

(y) What is the maximum time that the police can detain a person without court order?
______________________/can't say

(z) According to law how many living wives can a Hindu male have? ______________________/can't say

10. How do you collect information and gather knowledge ?

(a) From Newspapers
(b) From books and Magazines
(c) From Radio
(d) From Television
(e) From family members
(f) From friends, relatives & neighbours
(g) From party leaders & party workers
(h) All of the above

C. Political Involvement and Leadership Process :

11. When did you contest for these posts and how many times won ?

	Contested (Please mention years)	Won (Please mention years)
(a) Councillor	______	______
(b) Chairperson	______	______
(c) Vice-Chairperson	______	______
(d) Any other political post (please mention the post).	______	______

12. Are you a reserved candidate but won from an unreserved ward/constituency ? (a) YES/NO (b) If yes, please mention year(s) ____________

13. Reason(s) for your (a) victory ____________ (b) defeat ____________

14. Why did you contest for such post(s)?

____

15. Your political affiliation is to : Congress (I)/Janta Dal/BJP/CPI/CPI (M)/Jharkhand/Independent.

16. In election(s) support to you was :

(a) Spontaneous and voluntary
(b) Due to dominant caste factor
(c) Due to powerful religious lobby
(d) By show of muscular force
(e) By monetary underhand deals and supply of liquor
(f) Negative voting against the prospective candidate
(g) Due to influence of tradition
(h) Mixed factors

17. Why are you a leader ?
Because :—

(a) I have desire to be so
(b) People want it
(c) Party wants it
(d) Religion/caste people compel
(e) Of family tradition
(f) of no other engagement
(g) Leadership is a type of business
(h) I want to serve people
(i) Cannot say

18. How do you inform and influence people/voters ?
Religion/caste people compel

(a) By face-to-face contact
(b) By general meetings
(c) Through pamphlets/handbills
(d) Through agents/call boys
(e) No need to ask them

19. How do you influence the decision-making process ?

(a) By logical and practicable arguments
(b) By direction of party
(e) By threatening
(f) By hitting the area, caste and religious sentiments.

(c) By conciliation and consensus
(d) Acting as an agent of local MLA/MP
(g) As per desire of my vot ers

20. From where do you raise your election expenses ?
(a) From the party (b) From own income
(c) From donations (d) From other sources

D. Political Ideals and Aspirations ?

21. Do you aspire for higher elective posts such as MLA/MP? YES/NO
22. Do you support political corruption ? YES/NO
23. Do you support *bandhs*, riots, violence & destruction of public property? YES/NO
24. Should dowry be banned ? YES/NO
25. Should reservation for SC & ST continue ? YES/NO
26. Should liquor be banned ? YES/NO
27. Should voting be made compulsory ? YES/NO
28. Should election be state-funded ? YES/NO
29. Are elections in India free & fair? YES/NO
30. Do you violate code of conduct during elections? YES / NO
31. Do you like to oppose for opposition sake ? YES / NO
32. In your opinion which political party is the best & why ?

    ____

33. In your opinion who, at present, is the most suitable person for the post of Prime Minister of India?

    ____

34. How can you give justice to one of your voters who has been harassed by the police unjustly ?

    ____

    ____

35. How do you serve the people when not elected ?

    ____

    ____

E. Approach to Development :

36. (a) Should octroi tax be abolished ? YES/NO/Cant' Say
    (b) If 'yes' then why ? ______________________

37. (a) Establishment of your NAC is :
helpful / harmful / can't say
(b) Please give reasons for your answer

____

38. Are the NAC taxes reciprocal to the benefits rendered to the people ?

YES/NO/Can't say

39. Are these facilities in your NAC adequate and satisfactory ?
(a) Lighting : YES/NO/Can't say
(b) Water supply : YES/NO/Can't say
(c) Roads & Parks : YES/NO/Cant' Say
(d) Medical facilities : YES/NO/Can't say
(e) Education & Library : YES/NO/Can't say
(f) Sewerage & Sanitation : YES/NO/Can't say
(g) Cultural activities and entertainment :
YES/NO/Can't Say

40. (a) Are you satisfied with the Government programmes for tribal development in your area ?
YES/NO/ Can't say
(b) If not please give reasons :

____

41. (a) What is the status of women in your area ?

____

(b) What do you suggest to curb exploitation of and atrocities on women and tribals ?

____

42. (a) Should deforestation and shifting cultivation be banned ?
YES / NO / Can't say
(b) If 'Yes' then please give reasons

____

43. Forest & Agricultural products of the tribals should be
(a) Purchased by the Government (c) Left to the middlemen.
(b) Allowed to face open market (d) Marketed through co-operatives.

44. After 50 years of Indian Independence, what are the fields the tribals in your area

(a) have developed ?

____

(b) are lagging behind ?

____

Bibliography

Almond, G. & G.B. Powell (Jr.), *Comparative Politics : A developmental Approach,* Oxford & IBH Publishing Co., New Delhi, 1972.

Anderson, N., *The Urban Community,* Routledge & Kegan Paul Lid., London, 1960.

Armstrong, J. A, *The European Administrative Elite,* princeton, 1973.

Aron, R, *Democracy and Totalitarianism,* Weidenfeld and Nicolson, London, 1968.

Avasthi, A., *Municipal Administration in India,* Lakshmi Narain Agarwal, Agra, 1972.

Avasthi, A. and A.P, Avasthi, *Indian Administration,* Lakshmi Narain Agarwal, Agra, 1996.

Bailey, F.G., *Politics and Social change: Orissa in 1959,* University of California Press, London, 1963.

Barker, E., *Principles of Social and Political Theory,* Oxford University Press, Calcutta, 1983.

Basham, A.L., *The Wonder that was India,* Rupa & Co., Calcutta, 1992.

Berhers, J.M., *Urban Social Structure,* Free Press, New York, 1962.

Bhogle, S.K., *Local Government and Administration in India,* Parimal Prakashan, Aurangabad, 1977.

Blondel, J., *Comparative Government - A Render* (ed.), MacMillan, London, 1985.

Bottomore, T.B., *Elites and Society,* Penguin, Middlesex, 1966.

Chakravarty, M. & D. Mukherjee, *Indian Tribes,* Saraswat, Calcutta, 1971.

Chauhan, B.R., *Towns in the Tribal Setting,* National Publishing House, Delhi, 1970.

Chopra, P.N., *Gazetteer of India (Vol. IV) - Administration and Public Welfare* (ed.), Ministry of Education and Social Welfare, Govt. of India, New Delhi, 1978.

Collins, L. and D. Lapierre, *Freedom at Midnight,* Tarang Paperbacks, New Delhi, 1990.

Czudnowski, M.N., *Political Elites and Social Change* (ed.), Dekalb, Illi., 1983.

Dahl, R.A., *Modern Political Analysis,* Prentice Hall of India, New Delhi, 1963.

Das, P., *Emerging Pattern of leadership in Tribal India,* Manak Publications Pvt. Ltd., Delhi, 1994.

Davis, K., *Human Society,* Surjeet Publications, Delhi, 1981.

District Statistical Handbook - Kandhmal, Directorate of Economics & Statistics, Govt. of Orissa, Bhubaneswar, 1993.

Dube, S.C, *Tribal Heritage of India* (ed.), Vol. I, Vikas, Delhi, 1977.

Easton, D., *The Political System,* New York, 1953.

Elwin, V., *A new deal for tribal India* (ed.), Ministry of Home Affairs, New Delhi, 1962.

Tribal Myths of Orissa, Oxford University Press, London, 1954.

Encyclopaedia Britanica, Vol.18, Chicago, 1981.

Eulan, H. and M. Czudnowski, *Elite Recruitment in Democratic Politics* (ed.), New York, 1979.

Galbraith, J.K., *The Affluent Society,* Pelican books, Middlesex, 1984.

Gallion, A.B. and S. Eisner, *The Urban Pattern,* Affiliated East West Press Pvt Ltd., New Delhi, 1969.

Garner, J.W., *Political Science and Government,* World Press, Calcutta, 1951.

Ghurye, G.S., *The Scheduled Tribes,* Popular Prakashan, Bombay, 1963.

Hunter, F., *Community Power Structure,* Newyork, 1963.

Imperial Gazetteer of India, Vol. IV, Oxford, Clarendon Press, 1909.

Jena, B.B. and J.K. Baral, *Government and Politics in Orissa* (ed.), Print House (India), Lucknow, 1988.

Joad, C.E.M., *Introduction to Modern Political Theory,* Oxford University Press, Delhi, 1976.

Karve, I., *Kinship organisation in India,* The Deccan College Post-graduate and Research Institute, Poona, 1953.

Kennedy, P., *Preparing for the twenty-first Century,* Indus, New Delhi, 1994.

Kothari, R., *Politics in India,* Orient Longman, New Delhi, 1986.

Kuper, A. & J. Kuper, *The Social Sciences Encyclopaedia* (ed.), Routledge & Kegan Paul, London, 1985.

Lal, S.C., *Orissa Municipal Manual,* The Law, Cuttack, 1995.

Lal, S.K., *The Urban Elite,* Thomson Press (India) Ltd., Publications Division, New Delhi, 1974.

Laski, H.J., *A Grammar of Politics,* S. Chand & Company Ltd., New Delhi, 1984.

Lasswell, H.D., *Politics: Who Gets What, When, How?* Collected in the political writings of H.D. Lasswell, Free press, Illions, 1951.

Leach, E., *Elites in South Asia* (ed.), Cambrige, London 1970.

Lewis, M., *Urban Prospect,* Warburg, 1968.

Lipset, W.M., *Political Man,* Heinemann, London, 1960.

Maclver, R.M., *The Modern State,* Oxford, London, 1966.

Maclver, R.M. and C.H. Page, *Society - An introductory Analysis,* MacMillan, Madras, 1990.

Macpherson, C.B., *Democratic Theory,* Oxford, 1973.

Maheshwari, S.R., *Comparative Government and Politics,* Lakshmi Narain Agarwal, Agra, 1994.

Local Government in India, Lakshmi Narain Agarwal, Agra, 1992-93.

Mannheim, K., *Freedom, Power and Democratic Planning,* OUP, New York, 1950.

Marvick, D., *Political Decision - Makers,* Amerind Publications, New Delhi, 1972.

Marx, K. and F. Engels, *Manifesto of the Communist Party,* Progress Publishers, Moscow, 1977.

Merkel, P.H., *Political Continuity and change,* New york, 1972.

Morris-Jones, W.H., *The Government and Politics of India,* B.I. Publications, New Delhi, 1979.

Mosca, G., *The Ruling Class,* McGraw-Hill, New York, 1939.

Myrdal, G., *Asian Drama - An Inquiry into the Poverty of Nations,* Vols. I, II & III, Pelican Books, Middlesex, 1968.

Nayak, G.C. (self), *Indian Political Tradition,* 2nd Edn, Kalyani Publishers, New Delhi, 1995.

Nehru, J.L., *Glimpses of World History,* Oxford University Press, J.L., Nehru Memorial Fund, New Delhi, 1989.

Nigam, S.R., *Local Government,* S. Chand & Company, New Delhi, 1987.

Odegard, P.H., *Political Power and Social Change,* Oxford, Calcutta, 1969.

Palkhivala, N.A., *We, the Nation - the lost decades,* UBS

Publishers Distributors Ltd., New Delhi, 1994.

Palmer, N.D., *Indian Political System,* Houghton Mifflin, Boston, 1971.

Pareto, V., *The Mind and Society* (third volume), Jonathan Cape, London, 1935.

Patnaik, N. & P.S. Daspatnaik, *The Kondh of Orissa,* Tribal and Harijan Research-cum-training Institute, Bhubaneswar, 1982.

Putman, R.D., *The comparative study of Political Elites,* Englewood Cliffs, Newjersy, 1976.

Radhakrishnan, S., *Towards a New World,* Orient Paperbacks, Delhi, 1980.

Rao, V.V. & N. Hazarika, *Local Self - Government in India,* S. Chand & Company, New Delhi, 1986.

Ray, B.C., *Tribals of Orissa - The Changing Socio-Economic Profile* (ed.), Gian Publishing House, New Delhi, 1989.

Rout, B.C., *Orissa Administration* (ed.), Panchasheela, Bhubaneswar, 1991.

Russel, B., *The Conquest of Happiness,* Allen & Unwin, London, 1930.

Sabine, G.H. & T.L. Thorson, *A History of Political Theory,* Oxford & IBH, New Delhi, 1973.

Sahay, B.N., *Dynamics of Leadership,* Bookhive, New Delhi, 1968.

Seligman, R.A. & A. Johnson, *Encyclopaedia of the Social Sciences* (ed.), Vol.IX-X, MacMillan, New York, 1953.

Senapati, N., *Gazetteer of India -Orissa- Boudh-Khondmals* (ed.), Department of Revenue, Government of Orissa, Bhubaneswar, 1983.

Senapati, R.N., *Tribes of Orissa* (ed.), Harijan and Tribal Welfare Department, Government of Orissa, Bhubaneswar, 1990.

Sharan, P., *Comparative Government and Politics,* Meenakshi Prakashan, Meerut, 1981.

Sharma, B.K., *The Constitution of India,* Ministry of Law, Justice and Company Affairs, New Delhi, 1991.

Sharma, M.P., *Local Self-Government in India,* M.M. Publishers, New Delhi, 1978.

Singh, B., *The Saora Highlander - Leadership and Development,* Somaiya Publications, Bombay, 1984.

Singh, S.K., *Tribal Situation in India* (ed.), Vol. 13, Indian

Institute of Advanced Study, Simla, 1972.

Sovani, N.V., *Urbanisation and Urban India,* Asia Publishing House, Bombay, 1965.

Statistical Outline of Orissa, Directorate of Economics & Statistics, Government of Orissa, Bhubaneswar, 1995.

Thakur, R.N. and M.K. Gaur, *Elites - Paradigm and change in Transnational Perspective* (ed.), Indian Institute of Public Administration, New Delhi, 1988.

The Constitution of India, Ministry of Law, Justice and Company Affairs, New Delhi, 1991.

Thoenes, P., *The Elites in the Welfare State,* Glencoe, lllions, 1966.

Vidyarthi, L.P., *Leadership in India* (ed.), Asia Publishing House, Bombay, 1967.

Vidyarthi, L.P. & B.K. Rai, *The Tribal Culture of India,* Concept Publishing Company, New Delhi, 1985.

Vir, D., *Political Efficacy in Urban India - A Sociological Exploration,* Classical Publishing Company, New Delhi, 1989.

ARTICLES

Ahmed, F., Damsels in Distress, *India Today*, New Delhi, April 30, 1983.

Bailey, F.G., Leadership, *The Social Sciences Encyclopaedia*, A. Kuper and J. Kuper(ed.), Routledge & Kegan Paul, London, 1985.

Behura, N.K., Tribe development-A critical Review, *Adibasi* (Special Issue), Vol. XXXII, No. 4, Bhubaneswar,1992.

Tribal Societies in Orissa, *Tribes of Orissa*, Tribal & Harijan Welfare Department of Orissa, Bhubaneswar, 1990.

Bhowmick, P.K., Nature of Exploitation in the Tribal Situation-An Overview, *Adibasi*, Vol. XXIV, Nos. 3&4, Bhubaneswar, 1984-85.

Chandra, P. R., Tribal Economy, *Adibasi*, Vol. XII, Nos. 1—4, Bhubaneswar, 1 970-71.

Das, N.,The Tribal Situation in Orissa, *Tribal Situation in India* (ed.), Vol.13, K. S. Singh, Indian Institute of Advanced Sludy, Shimla, 1972.

Marvick, D., Elites, *The Social Sciences Encyclopaedia*, op.cit.

Mathur, K.S., Tribe in India : A problem of identification and Integration, *Tribal situation in India*, op.cit.

Mishra, B., Problems of Tribal Economy in Orissa, *Adibasi* (special issue). Vol. XXXII, No. 4,Bhubaneswar,1992.

Mohanty, K.K., B. Choudhury & S.C., Biswal Pattern of Land Holding among Major Tribes of the Tribal Sub-plan Area in Orissa (Based on Universal Bench-Mark Survey, 1978-80), *Adibasi*, Vol. XXXIII, No. 2, Bhubaneswar, 1993.

Mohapatra, K., Leadership—A Sociological Analysis, *Adibasi*, No. 2, Bhubaneswar, 1963.

Narain, I., Democratic Decentralisation the Idea, the Image and the Reality , *Indian Journal of Public Administration*, Vol. IX, No. 1, New Delhi.

Nayak, R.K., Tribals : An Exploitation- Conflict- Syndrome, *Government and Politics in Orissa* (ed.), B.B. Jena and J.K. Baral, Print House (India), Lucknow, 1988.

Patnaik, L.K., Urban Government and Politics in Orissa, *Government and Politics in Orissa* (ed.), *op. cit.*

Patnaik, P.K., The Town of Deserted Wives, *Onlooker*, Bombay,

May 15, 1982.

Rout, B.C., Democracy in the 21st Century, *The Orissa Political Science Journal*, Vol. IX, Bhubaneswar, 1990-91.

Sanganna, T., Significance of Adibasis, *Adibasi*, No. 1, Bhubaneswar, 1963-64.

The New Dimension and Approach of Tribal Welfare, *Adibasi*, No.2, Bhubaneswar, 1963.

Satpathy, G.N., Orissa Tribes and Their Homeland, *Tribes of Orissa*, op.cit.

Singh, B., Tribal development in the Fifth plan - some Political and Administrative Aspects, *Adibasi*, Vol.XIV, No.4, Bhubaneswar, 1972-73.

Vidyarthi, L.P., An Appraisal of the Leadership Pattern , *Tribal Situation in India* (ed), op.cit.

NEWSPAPERS

The Anupam Bharat, Berhampur.
The Dharitri, Bhubaneswar.
The Indian Express, Bhubaneswar.
The Samaj, Cuttack.
The Times of India, New Delhi.

INDEX